Developing Primary
Mathematics Teaching

Developing Primary Mathematics Teaching

Reflecting on Practice with the Knowledge Quartet

Tim Rowland, Fay Turner, Anne Thwaites and Peter Huckstep

SAGE

Los Angeles • London • New Delhi • Singapore • Washington DC

First published 2009

SAGE Publications Ltd
1 Oliver's Yard
55 City Road
London EC1Y 1SP

SAGE Publications Inc.
2455 Teller Road
Thousand Oaks, California 91320

SAGE Publications India Pvt Ltd
B 1/I 1 Mohan Cooperative Industrial Area
Mathura Road
New Delhi 110 044

SAGE Publications Asia-Pacific Pte Ltd
33 Pekin Street #02-01
Far East Square
Singapore 048763

Library of Congress Control Number: 2008937822

British Library Cataloguing in Publication data

A catalogue record for this book is available from the British Library

ISBN 978-1-4129-4847-0
ISBN 978-1-4129-4848-7 (pbk)

Typeset by C&M Digitals (P) Ltd., Chennai, India
Printed in India at Replika Press Pvt Ltd
Printed on paper from sustainable resources

Contents

The companion website (www.sagepub.co.uk/rowland) has extracts from the videotapes of some of the lessons described in this book.

List of figures

List of tables

Index of teachers and lessons

Name	Career stage	Year group	Chapter (part of lesson)	Mathematical content of lesson or extract	Focus dimension/s of Knowledge Quartet	Video clip (approx. time)
Amy	NQT	Reception	Chapter 7 Lesson on counting	Counting principles	Foundation	
			Chapter 8 Short extract	Counting in tens	Connection Transformation	
Caroline	PGCE	Year 2	Chapter 5 Introduction to main activity	Fractions	Connection	
			Chapter 6 Short description of main part of the lesson	Fractions of shapes		
			Chapter 5 Introductory activity	Money	Connection	
Chantal	PGCE	Year 1	Chapter 6 Beginning of lesson	Counting odd/even	Contingency	
Chloë	PGCE	Year 1/2	Chapter 3 Extract from main teaching section	Addition and subtraction of near 10 and 20	Transformation – representation	

Name	Career stage	Year group	Chapter (part of lesson)	Mathematical content of lesson or extract	Focus dimension/s of Knowledge Quartet	Video clip (approx. time)
Colin	PGCE	Reception	Chapter 4 Short extract	Number bonds to 10	Transformation – examples	
			Chapter 5 Introductory activity	Money – counting	Connection	
Ellie	PGCE	Year 2	Chapter 8 Short extract	Missing numbers – empty box	Connection Transformation	
James	NQT	Year 4	Chapter 8 Short extract	Fractions	Transformation Connection Contingency	Clip 11 (5 minutes)
Jason	PGCE	Year 3	Chapter 5 Short extract from main teaching section	Fractions	Connection	
			Chapter 6 Short extract from main teaching section	Counting the value of coins	Contingency	
John	NQT	Year 4	Chapter 8 Short extract	Telling the time	Transformation Connection	
Joyce	ECT	Year 3	Chapter 8 Short extract	Division	Transformation Foundation	Clip 10 (7 minutes)
Kate	ET	Year 6	Chapter 4 Description of lesson	'Jailer problem' investigation	Transformation – examples	
Kate	PGCE	Year 1	Chapter 8 Short extract	Doubling	All	Clip 9 (7 minutes)

(Continued)

Name	Career stage	Year group	Chapter (part of lesson)	Mathematical content of lesson or extract	Focus dimension/s of Knowledge Quartet	Video clip (approx. time)
Kim	NQT	Year 1/2	Chapter 8 Short extract	Capacity	Transformation Connection Contingency	
Kirsty	PGCE	Year 6	Chapter 4 Short extract, introduction	Coordinates	Transformation – examples	Clip 4 (4.5 minutes)
Laura	PGCE	Year 5	Chapter 4 Brief overview of the lesson	Multiplication facts Grid and column layouts	Transformation – examples	Clip 3 (18 minutes)
			Chapter 5 Extract from main teaching section	Grid and column methods for multiplication	Connection	Clip 5 (5.5 minutes)
			Chapter 6 Short extract	Symmetry	Contingency	
			Chapter 6 Short extract from plenary	Grid/column multiplication	Contingency	Clip 6 (5 minutes)
Linda	NQT	Reception	Chapter 3 Short description of main part of lesson	Adding 10	Transformation – representation	
Lindsay	PGCE	Year 4	Chapter 8 Short extract	Positive and negative numbers	All	
Lisa	PGCE	Year 1	Chapter 8 Short extract	Place value	Foundation Transformation	
Lucy	ECT	Year 1	Chapter 8 Short extract	Multiplication	Foundation Transformation	
Melanie	Student teacher	Year 5	Chapter 7 Short extract	Division	Foundation	

Name	Career stage	Year group	Chapter (part of lesson)	Mathematical content of lesson or extract	Focus dimension/s of Knowledge Quartet	Video clip (approx. time)
Naomi	PGCE	Year 1	Chapter 1 Synopsis of whole lesson	Number bonds to 10 Subtraction as difference		Clip 1 (18.5 minutes)
			Chapter 4 Short extracts from introduction	Subtraction	Transformation – examples	Clip 2 (2.5 minutes)
			Chapter 6 Short extracts from plenary	Subtraction as difference	Contingency	Clip 7 (5 minutes)
			Chapter 7 Extract from main teaching section	Subtraction as difference	Foundation	Clip 8 (9.5 minutes)
Natalie	PGCE	Year 6	Chapter 8 Short extract	Probability	Foundation Contingency Connection	
Sally	PGCE	Reception	Chapter 8 Short extract	Addition and subtraction to 10 on number line	Transformation Foundation	
Sonia	PGCE	Year 4	Chapter 4 Short extract	Translations/Reflections	Transformation – examples	
			Chapter 7 Short extract		Foundation	

Acknowledgements

We acknowledge with thanks and gratitude the assistance of the many people who have contributed to the development and production of this book. In particular we thank Jane Warwick for her contribution to the research which is at the heart of the book, David Thwaites for expert help with video editing, and Jamie Turner for his imaginative work on the cover photographs. The book would never have come into being without the collaboration of the many teacher-participants whose lessons are featured in it. Their willingness to offer their practice for others to reflect on, warts and all, demonstrates their commitment to the improvement of mathematics teaching – their own, and that of the readers of this book.

Introduction

This book differs, in some significant ways, from other books on primary mathematics teaching. A short explanation of who the book was written for, what it is intended to do, and how best to use it, may therefore be helpful.

The book is for primary mathematics teachers and those who support their professional development in schools, local authorities and universities. It will be especially useful to student teachers (sometimes called 'trainees' in England) and early-career teachers, for whom the information in the book is likely to be novel. But the heart of this book is not so much information, as a *process* of structured reflection whereby teachers – at any stage of their career – can take control of the development of their expertise in teaching mathematics. The reflective process is the outcome of five years of research at the University of Cambridge. It is built on a framework which enables teachers and teacher educators to engage critically with actual lessons and teaching episodes – their own, or others' – with the aim of learning from teaching-in-action. We call our framework *The Knowledge Quartet*: because it is in four parts, and because it is a way of building up professional knowledge for mathematics teaching. A full explanation is given in Chapter 2.

Theory and practice are interwoven throughout the book. In each chapter you will find:

- justification for the focus of the chapter;

- some exposition related to the topic, or some illuminating aspect of it;

- tasks – things for you to think about and discuss, where possible, with colleagues;

- descriptions of actual lessons, or episodes from lessons, for you to consider, discuss and analyse. Some of these episodes can be viewed as video clips on the book's companion website;

- our own reflections and analytical comments on these lessons and episodes.

The final chapter is devoted to accounts, tasks and analyses relating to a wide range of classroom scenarios, all taken from actual lessons taught by beginning or early-career teachers.

Each chapter can be read on its own, but you will gain most from the book if you read Chapters 1 and 2 first. Chapter 2, in particular, explains the *Knowledge Quartet*, the framework for reflection which features throughout Chapters 3 to 8.

Of course, the book can be read at home, or on the bus or the train. It is also recommended as a stimulus for group work and plenary discussion in teacher education settings and in continuing professional development. The *Knowledge Quartet* framework is also ideally suited for use in the improvement of teaching through lesson observation, both within initial teacher education and ongoing teaching development. In these various settings, the observer could be a mentor, tutor, colleague, subject coordinator or school manager of some kind. We would add, however, that we wrote this book so that teachers at different career stages might be encouraged and supported, and not as a means for them to be judged. The key to this positive, critical support is to allow time – if only 15 minutes – for post-lesson review and discussion, shared by teacher and observer, and structured by the *Knowledge Quartet*.

We hope that readers will find the book enjoyable, useful and informative: we welcome any feedback on the content, and on the ways that the book is being used.

Tim Rowland, Fay Turner, Anne Thwaites, Peter Huckstep.
Cambridge, 2008

1

Inside Naomi's Classroom

> **In this chapter you will read about:**
>
> - **the focus of the book on teachers' knowledge;**
> - **the distinction between mathematical content knowledge and generic knowledge;**
> - **how teachers can develop knowledge for mathematics teaching;**
> - **a particular lesson on subtraction taught by a student teacher.**

This book is about some of the things that teachers know, that help them to teach mathematics well. There will be some 'theory', but most of the book is rooted firmly in real classrooms, with some teachers and pupils who helped to make the book possible. In fact, we shall visit one of these classrooms very soon.

Teachers are very serious about their work, and constantly want to get better at what they do. This improvement comes about through a variety of influences. You might want to pause a moment to think what these influences include, and list a few of them.

One obvious possibility is 'experience'. We hope to get better at doing something simply by *doing* it. So we might imagine that our teaching of, say, mental addition strategies would be better in our second year of teaching than it was in the first, and so on. This may well be the case, although it is worth asking *why* it should, or what would help to make it more likely that it would. At the very least, you would need to be able to recall what you learned from your last experience of teaching mental addition strategies – what seemed to work well, and what did not. Fortunately, we learn a lot from things that do not go well, because we want to avoid them happening again. The key to all this is what is usually called 'reflection' on practice. Teachers' open-mindedness and their desire to do a good job lead them to look for reasons for their actions in the classroom, and to analyse the educational consequences of those actions. Donald Schön's term 'reflective practitioner' (Schön, 1983) is often used to conjure up the notion of teachers as professionals who learn from their own actions – and those of others. Schön distinguished between two kinds of reflection. The first, reflection *on* action, refers to thinking back on our actions after the event. Most of this book is about that kind of reflection, and we promote the idea that it is most fruitful to reflect on action with a supportive colleague who observed you teaching mathematics. The second kind of reflection is what Schön called reflection *in* action, being a kind of monitoring and self-regulation of our actions even as we perform them. This is also something that we think about in this book, especially in Chapter 6. Because reflection *in* action is especially difficult, a supportive observer can also be helpful in drawing attention to opportunities or issues that the teacher may have missed, often because their attention was on something more urgent.

We should also point out, from the outset, that in observing and commenting on someone else teaching, the supportive observer stands to learn as much as, or more than, the one being observed. This book is witness to this claim. We could not have written it, and we would not have learned much of what we have to say in the book, without the benefit of a great deal of supportive observation of other teachers teaching mathematics. If we take any credit, it would be for our own efforts at reflection on other teachers' actions in the past, and on and in our own teaching more recently.

In this spirit, then, this book offers you the opportunity to 'observe' other teachers and to reflect on what they do. Your observation may be fairly direct, because some lesson excerpts can be watched as video clips. Others will be 'observed' as you read succinct accounts of them and read some verbatim transcript selections. The advantage of the transcripts is that you can easily revisit and dissect them if you wish. With few exceptions, these teachers whom you will observe are relatively inexperienced, and their lessons are not offered as models for you to copy. You can read about why we videotaped these lessons in Chapter 2. Sometimes you will think that a teacher could, or should, have done something differently. As we have already said, you will learn something merely by thinking, and especially by making, that reflection explicit in discussion, or in a written note of some kind. Paradoxically, you would learn very little from commenting that 'it went well'.

In the UK, many graduate student teachers (sometimes called 'trainees') follow a one-year, full-time course leading to a Postgraduate Certificate in Education (PGCE) in a university education department. About half the year is spent teaching in a school under the guidance of a school-based mentor. All primary trainees are trained to be generalist teachers of the whole primary curriculum. The mathematics lessons featured in this book were filmed while the teachers were in their PGCE year or in the early stages of their teaching career. The index of teachers and lessons on pp. x–xiii summarises where each teacher's lesson occurs in the book along with the career stage of the teacher, an indication of the mathematical content, the part of the lesson and, where appropriate, the video clip number on the companion website.

In this chapter, you will observe a lesson on subtraction. The pupils, boys and girls, are in Year 1 (age 5–6 years). The teacher is Naomi, who was, at the time, a PGCE student in the third and final term of her course. For most of that term, she was on a teaching placement in a primary school. Naomi chose to specialise in early years education in her PGCE. In most of the UK, it is usual to study only three or four subjects at school between 16 and 18. At school, Naomi had specialised in mathematics, English, French and psychology. Relatively few primary PGCE students have undertaken such advanced study in mathematics. Following school, Naomi's undergraduate degree study had been in philosophy.

In this book, we will sometimes ask you to read a description of a lesson, or part of a lesson. Sometimes we will give verbatim transcripts of short lesson episodes. In the case of the lesson featured in this chapter, you can also view a video clip (Clip 1) on the companion website if you wish.

Naomi's lesson

Naomi's classroom is bright and spacious, with a large, open, carpeted area. We can see around 20 young children in the class: there might be a few more off-camera. There is also a teaching assistant positioned among the children. The learning objectives stated in Naomi's lesson plan are: 'To understand subtraction as "difference". For more able pupils, to find small differences by counting on. Vocabulary – *difference, how many more than, take away.*' Naomi notes in her plan that they have learnt *how many more than*.

Naomi settles the class in a rectangular formation around the edge of the carpet in front of her, then the lesson begins with a seven-minute oral and mental starter designed to practise number bonds to 10. A 'number bond hat' is passed from child to child until Naomi claps her hands. The child wearing the hat is then given a number between 0 and 10, and expected to state how many more are needed to make 10. Naomi chooses the numbers in turn: her sequence of starting numbers is 8, 5, 7, 4, 10, 8, 2, 1, 7, 3. When she chooses 8 the second time, it is Bill's turn. Bill rapidly answers 'two'. Next it is Owen's turn:

Naomi: Owen. Two.

[12-second pause while Owen counts his fingers]

Naomi: I've got two. How many more to make ten?

Owen: [six seconds later] Eight.

Naomi: Good boy. [addressing the next child] One.

Child: [after 7 seconds of fluent finger counting] Nine.

Naomi: Good. Owen, what did you notice ... what did you say makes ten?

Owen: Um ... four ...

Naomi: You said two add eight. Bill, what did you say? I gave you eight.

Bill: [inaudible]

Naomi: eight and two, two and eight, it's the same thing.

Later, Naomi gives two numbers to the child with the number bond hat. The child must add them and say how many more are then needed to make 10.

The introduction to the main activity lasts nearly 20 minutes. Naomi wants to introduce them to the idea of subtraction as difference, and the language that goes with it. To start with, she sets up various difference problems, in the context of frogs in two ponds. Magnetic 'frogs' are lined up on a board, in

4 frogs

2 frogs

Note: the arrows and dotted line have been added for clarity.

Figure 1.1   Naomi's representation of the frogs

two neat rows. In the first problem, Naomi says that her pond has four frogs, and her neighbour's pond has two, as shown in Figure 1.1.

Naomi: I went to my garden this weekend, and I've got a really nice pond in my garden, and when I looked I saw that I had … [Naomi tries to stick some 'frogs' on the board] … I don't think they're sticking. Let me get some Blu-tack. It's supposed to be magnetic, but it doesn't seem to be sticking. Right. I had four frogs, so I was really pleased about that, but then my neighbour came over. She's got some frogs as well, but she's only got two. How many more frogs have I got? Martin?

Martin: Two.

Naomi: Two. So what's the difference between my pond and her pond in the number of frogs? Jeffrey.

Jeffrey: Um, um when he had a frog you only had two frogs.

Naomi: What's the difference in number? […] this is my pond here, this line – that's what's in my pond, but this is what's in my neighbour's pond, Mr Brown's pond, he's got two. [Gender of neighbour has changed!] But I've got four, so, Martin said I've got two more than him. But we can say that another way. We can say the difference is two frogs. There's two. You can take these two and count on three, four, and I've got two extra.

           Right, let's see who wants to be my helper.

A couple of minutes later, Naomi says:

Naomi: Morag's been sitting beautifully, oh no, Morag's been reading a poetry book. […] That should be on my desk, thank you. Put your hand up please, you know the rule. Yes Hugh?

Hugh: You could both have three, if you give one to your neighbour.

Naomi: I could, that's a very good point, Hugh. I'm not going to do that today though. I'm just going to talk about the difference. Morag, if you had a pond, how many frogs would you like in it?

Pairs of children are invited forward to choose numbers of frogs (e.g. 5, 4) and to place them on the board. The differences are then explained and discussed.

Before long, Naomi asks how these differences could be written as a 'take away sum'. With assistance, a girl, Zara, writes $5 - 4 = 1$. Later, Naomi shows how the difference between two numbers can be found by counting on from the smaller.

The children are then assigned their group tasks. The usual class practice is to group the children by 'ability' for mathematics. The actual numbers used in the difference problems are the same for each group, but the activity is differentiated by resource. One group (called the Whales), supported by a teaching assistant, has been given a worksheet on which drawings of cars, apples and the like are lined up on the page, as Naomi had done earlier with the frogs. Two further groups (Dolphins and Octopuses) have difference problems set in 'real life' scenarios, such as 'I have 8 sweets and you have 10 sweets'. These two groups are directed to use multilink plastic cubes to solve them, lining them up and pairing them, as Naomi had done with the 'frogs' in her demonstration. The remaining two groups have a similar problem sheet, but are directed to use the counting-on method to find the differences. Naomi works with individuals.

In the event, the children in the Dolphin and Octopus groups experience some difficulty working with the multilink. This is partly because 'lining up' requires some manual dexterity, and also because the children find more interesting (for them) things to do with the interlocking cubes. Naomi comes over to help the Dolphins. She emphasises putting eight cubes in a row, then ten. 'Then you can *see* what the difference is.' She demonstrates again, but none of the children seems to be copying her. Jared can be seen moving the multilink cubes around the table, apparently aimlessly. Another child says 'I don't know what to do'. Naomi moves away to give her attention to the Octopuses. In her absence from the table, one boy sets about building a tower with the cubes. Later, Naomi returns to the Dolphins, and tries once again to clarify the multilink method. She asks: 'What's the difference between seven and twelve?' Without looking up, the boy who is making the tower replies 'Don't ask me, I'm too busy building'. Naomi responds by saying 'Goodness me, let's put these away. I'll show you a different way to do it.' She collects up the multilink cubes into a tray, and takes the Dolphins and Octopuses back to the carpet, where she shows them the counting-up strategy for the difference between 8 and 10. 'You start with the lower number … you start with the smallest number. Count on – show me your fist – nine, ten.' She then works through the fist three worksheet questions, doing them for the children, by counting up.

Finally, Naomi calls the class together on the carpet for an eight-minute plenary, in which she uses two large foam 1–6 dice to generate two numbers, asking the children for the difference each time. Their answers indicate that there is some confusion among the children about the meaning of 'difference'.

Naomi:	Right, I'm going to roll the dice, and I want you to find the difference between the two numbers. Five and three. Now starting with the smaller number can you count up to see what the difference is. […] I can show it with the frogs as well. Jeffrey, can you have a go at working it out? The difference between three and five.
Jeffrey:	Seven.
Naomi:	No, we're starting with three …
Jeffrey:	Eight.
Naomi:	and counting up to five. What's the difference? It's like a take away sum. Stuart.
Stuart:	Two.
Naomi:	Excellent. Can you tell us how you worked it out? Come to the front. Owen stand up. Sit in your rows please. Right, Stuart just worked out the difference between three and five and said it was two. How did you work it out? Stuart.
Stuart:	I held out three fingers and five and then there's two left.
Naomi:	Ah, OK. That *does* work because you've got five fingers on your hands so if you've got five here and three you've got two left to make five. But I know an even *better* way to work it out. Does anybody know another way to work it out? Ayesha. No. Who knows another way to work it out? Leo.
Leo:	Count in your head …
Naomi:	Yeah, how did you count? What did you count in your head?
Leo:	I thought of three …
Naomi:	Jeffrey stand up, Hugh stand up!
Leo:	Then I added two. But I still had two left.
Naomi:	Right, started with, started with three, did you say, and then you counted on two, till you got five. Right, let's see what we get next.

Who can do this one for me? Three and six. Three and six. What's the difference between three and six? Jim.

The plenary continues in this way, and finishes with:

Naomi: What is the difference between four and six? So hold the number four in your head and count on. Four, five, six. What's the difference? Jared?

Jared: Uh, can't remember.

Naomi: The difference between four and six. Jeffrey?

Jeffrey: Two.

Naomi: Good boy. Right, the difference between two and four? What's the difference? So start with the smaller number, two and count up till you get to four. What's the difference?

The one-hour videotape tape ran out here, just before the conclusion of the lesson.

Reflecting on Naomi's lesson

You should now have a good sense of what Naomi was trying to achieve in her lesson, how she intended to go about it, and how things turned out. You might feel that you 'know' Naomi a little, or someone like her. You might recognise some of the children in her class, in that they remind you of children that you have taught or seen in other classes.

At this point we would like you to do some thinking about Naomi's lesson. You can do this on your own. Better still, discuss it with a friend, colleague, another student or small group of students, according to your circumstances at the moment. Have ready a piece of paper to write on, a whiteboard, or a flipchart – whatever suits those circumstances. Think and talk about anything that came to your attention as you read the account of the lesson, and/or watched the video clips. Later in the book, we will ask you to focus on specific aspects of this and other lessons. For the moment, we leave it to you to make the choice. You might imagine that you are Naomi's friend, or her mentor, and that she is expecting you to offer her some comments on the lesson.

Once you have begun to think and talk about particular aspects of the lesson, make a note of what they are – write a brief statement of what it is that you are thinking about, and what people are saying.

Magnetic frogs. Like fridge magnets. Have
Seen something like this used before —
magnetic numbers on a 1–100 square, but
they kept falling off! Seems that Naomi
had the same problem. Issue of resources
that won't distract from intended purpose
because they don't work. Naomi resorted
to blu-tack. She could have checked the
magnets before the lesson.

Figure 1.2   A note about Naomi's lesson

For example, you might write something such as the notes in Figure 1.2. This is not meant to be a particularly good example of the notes that you might write. It isn't particularly bad, either. It's just an example of the kind of thing that you might discuss and how you could record it briefly.

You could spend a long time thinking about Naomi's lesson, but we suggest about 20–30 minutes.

Now group the issues that you've chosen to focus on into a small number of categories. The issues in each category will have something in common. What that 'something' is is entirely up to you. There are no right and wrong categories. Give a short name to each category. Don't spend too long on this. If you are in a class situation, and several pairs or groups are also doing this exercise, it will be valuable and interesting to compare the categories that different pairs or groups come up with.

Then make a note of anything that your reflections and discussion have particularly highlighted for you. Perhaps something you might not have noticed on your own. Perhaps something you think is a key issue for this topic, or for teaching generally. Perhaps something to keep in mind when you prepare a lesson, or when you teach a class, in the future. This could be at various possible levels – preparing or teaching any lesson, or a mathematics lesson, or a Year 1 lesson, or a lesson on subtraction, or ...

Naomi's lesson – our reflections

We want to offer some ideas of our own about Naomi's lesson. We emphasise now, and will repeat again and again in the book, that these are not in any sense 'the answers' to our earlier questions! Some of the issues or questions that we raise might be matters that you considered earlier in your own reflections and discussions. Others might not have occurred to you, or might seem to you to be rather unimportant. We might even agree with you on this last point, but we are trying hard to be open to a wide range of possibilities. Finally, you will almost certainly have considered issues that we do not raise here, and that may well be because they haven't come to our notice. If they had, the book might be different in some particulars. In this sense, we repeat, the following suggestions are not the only answers to our questions.

So here is a list of a dozen things that came to our attention.

1   Was Naomi's teaching brisk, did it have good pace?

2   What is meant by 'subtraction as difference'? What other kinds of subtraction are there?

3   Was it a good idea to use the number bond hat in the oral and mental starter?

4   Does Naomi use the 'frogs' in a way that helps the children to understand the 'difference' notion of subtraction?

5   Is there a lesson plan for this topic on the internet?

6   Does Naomi use mathematical vocabulary in a helpful way? Are the children learning to use it?

7   Should Naomi have given more attention to the Whales when they were working with the teaching assistant?

8   How does Naomi deal with the ideas put forward by the children (e.g. Hugh's idea about having three frogs each)?

9   Did Naomi spend too much time on the oral and mental starter?

10   Why did Naomi chose that particular sequence of numbers (8, 5, 7...) in the oral and mental starter?

11   Which suppliers can you get magnetic animals (and other fridge magnets) from?

12   Were the differentiated group activities well chosen? What principles, beliefs or theories about learning might have underpinned them?

These are all relevant to Naomi's teaching, and to her development as a teacher. Because Naomi was on a PGCE school-based placement, she would get regular feedback on her teaching, in written notes and discussions, from her class teacher – her mentor – and other experienced teachers, as well as from her university tutor. All of the issues raised in the questions above could usefully be considered in a review discussion of the lesson. We deliberately listed one or two – like issue 11 above – that were intended to be less important. But 'importance' involves value judgement: issue 11 is not at all frivolous if you are due to teach this topic later in the term and you want to use that equipment!

The fact that all of the 12 issues in our list *could* usefully be considered in a review discussion does not mean that all of them *should* be discussed with Naomi after the lesson. It is quite useful to be selective, so that you can focus on and think deeply about just a few things in detail. The same would be true of Naomi in the post-lesson review discussion. An attempt to think about too many different things, in a limited time, can lead to information overload. It might be *possible* to advise Naomi about ten things that she should do differently another time, but she would then be likely to be overwhelmed (and perhaps depressed!) by the effort to keep it all in mind. If, on this occasion, you choose not to reflect on Naomi's handling of the children's comments (issue 8) it will not be the end of the world. The same would be true for Naomi's lesson review. However, we do want to draw out here one possible outcome when you grouped your issues into categories in the earlier task.

Issues for reflection and discussion: a key distinction

If we were to put the 12 issues that we listed above into categories, as we asked you to do, we would start with two. One category singles out those issues that are *content-specific*. By that, we mean that they are specific to the subject being taught – mathematics in this case. The other is those that are not content-specific, sometimes called *generic* issues, that would be pertinent whatever subject was being taught. We appreciate that one of the characteristics of the primary school curriculum is that subject boundaries are sometimes blurred, often deliberately so. Nevertheless, we are likely to agree that Naomi is primarily teaching mathematics in this lesson, although she is also teaching literacy, personal and social education, and so on. Generic issues include, for example, those to do with the management of behaviour in the lesson, general aspects of the management of learning (such as ability grouping), general assessment frameworks, and so on.

Again, we appreciate that these categories are all fuzzy at the edges. For example, we would say that number 1 in our list, 'Was Naomi's teaching brisk, did it have good pace?', is an example of a *generic* issue – pacing the teaching well, so that children are stimulated and on-task. It would be an issue in the teaching of any subject. However, we also recognise that getting the balance, between lively interaction *and* giving children time to think and to articulate their thoughts, is particularly delicate in mathematics teaching (Sangster, 2007). Nevertheless, we stand by our *content-specific* versus *generic* distinction for the time being. We would claim, and think that few would dispute, that number 2, 'What is meant by "subtraction as difference"? What other kinds of subtraction are there?', is very clearly a *content-specific* issue. Subtraction is a mathematical operation and a mathematical concept. The question would make no sense at all in the context of a history lesson.

Research has shown (Strong and Baron, 2004) that the vast majority of mentors' comments on lessons that they observe are generic in nature. Very little is said about the actual content being taught. That is one reason why we have written this book. In order to develop mathematics teaching, it is necessary to think about the subject-matter being taught, as well as the more generic issues. The research therefore suggests that ways of thinking about and discussing the content of lessons are needed. Our own research into classroom mathematics teaching led us to develop such a way. It is based on a framework of categories for thinking about teaching – the *Knowledge Quartet*. You will read about this framework, and how it came about, in Chapter 2.

The odd-numbered questions 1, 3, 5, ..., 11 above are intended to be examples of generic issues that relate to the lesson being observed, whereas the even-numbered 2, 4, 6, ..., 12 are intended to be content-specific. We are more confident about the second category (the even ones) than the first. We recognise, for example, that an online unit plan (question 5) is highly relevant to the teaching of this particular mathematical content. What the content of such an off-the-shelf plan would not reveal, however, is anything about Naomi's own knowledge about subtraction and how to teach it. This *knowledge base* is a key factor in what this book is about, as will become apparent in the next chapter.

Teacher knowledge

The theme of *teacher knowledge* will be apparent throughout this book, and we begin to develop it in Chapter 2.

One would expect teachers to be knowledgeable about their work. One of the most important ways in which teaching is improved and developed is by developing *knowledge* about teaching and learning. This book is about ways of building up your knowledge about mathematics and mathematics teaching. It is structured around *reflection on classroom situations*, and in this way we are trying to complement, not to duplicate, what other primary mathematics books for teachers already do very well. We mention some of them at the end of this chapter.

As we have already said, Naomi needs knowledge about subtraction *and* how to teach subtraction. These are two different kinds of knowledge, although sometimes it is difficult to separate teachers' own 'learner knowledge' – what they needed to pass school exams – from the 'teacher knowledge' that they need to help someone else to learn. One aspect of this, which we revisit in Chapter 2, is the distinction between the *common content knowledge* of educated citizens on the one hand, and teachers' *specialised content knowledge* on the other. Naomi's everyday 'learner knowledge' about subtraction can, to a very large extent, be taken for granted. We do not doubt that she is able to perform whole number subtraction faultlessly. However, as we shall explain in Chapter 7, Naomi's fundamental conceptual understanding of the nature of subtraction as an operation may well be partial. This is no criticism of Naomi: the 'specialised' professional knowledge that she may not be aware of is not explicitly assessed in mathematics exams.

The way that people talk about teachers' 'teacher knowledge' (sometimes called pedagogical knowledge) conveys something of their beliefs about how people learn. Some people talk about skilful teachers being able to 'pass on' or 'put across' what they know. This is an enviable talent, but to describe it in this way conveys the notion of knowledge as a kind of commodity to be passed on to, or shared with, others. Teaching would then be associated with very careful explanations of what the teacher knows as part of their own learner knowledge. The expectation would be that the learner then acquires a kind of copy of what the teacher knows. It means that the mathematical behaviours of learners would mimic those of their teachers – most obviously, they would perform calculations in more or less identical ways. This amounts to looking at teaching as a process of *transmission*, and is in keeping with *behaviourist* theories of learning, which have their roots in the psychology of Thorndike (1922) and, more recently, Skinner (1974).

Over the last thirty or forty years, it has become more usual for teachers (though not necessarily for the public at large) to think about learning in a way that attributes greater autonomy to the *learner*, who is seen to play a more *active* part in learning than merely accepting what the teacher 'passes on' or 'hands down' to them. Children are viewed as not only receiving knowledge, but also actually *constructing* it for themselves. The role of the teacher is then reconceived from mere 'telling' (although there is always a place for that) to providing and initiating tasks and activities for the children, and to skilful management of group and class discussion to make sense of these tasks. What we are calling 'teacher knowledge' therefore does include knowing about how to explain things in helpful ways, but it also includes how to design tasks for learning, how to stimulate reflection, and to orchestrate discussion.

Teachers' knowledge resources

Every teacher has a wealth of learner knowledge *and* teacher knowledge, which they bring to their work as a teacher. Within a school context, this knowledge resource is both *individual* – what each teacher knows – and *collective* – what is accessible by reference to colleagues.

Both are important. Individual teachers draw on their own resources, and on their colleagues, at different times. In a group planning session, collective knowledge is paramount. In dealing with a child's spontaneous question in the classroom, individual knowledge is likely to be the first resort. This book aims to build up your individual knowledge base, encouraging you to draw on collective knowledge resources whenever possible.

When you reflect on the lesson excerpts presented in this book, or watch the online video clips, or when you reflect on your own teaching, questions and dilemmas will surface that make demands on your professional mathematics knowledge base. In many instances, you will be aware that some aspect of mathematics knowledge (either learner or teacher knowledge) has been significant in a particular episode – either because it was used to good effect, or because it seemed to be overlooked by the teacher in that episode. In other cases, you will not be aware in the same way, or to the same extent. As one beginning teacher recently said to us, 'You don't know what you don't know'. For example, in Chapter 7 an account will be given of a teacher teaching counting to young children. Of course, she knows how to count herself! But it is also evident (from her actions and from a discussion after the lesson) that she knows, and she knows that she knows, some important theoretical principles that underpin the teaching and learning of counting. As it happens, she learned them in a lecture on her PGCE course, but she might have read about them in a number of books (e.g. Maclellan, 1997), or a colleague might have brought them to her attention. The fact that she knew these principles enhanced her teaching. But if she had not known them, she wouldn't 'know what she didn't know'. For that reason, we will offer a few comments of our own on the lesson excerpts in this book. Joint reflection with a colleague or mentor is also valuable because the 'team' can pool their knowledge in discussion – a case of the collective knowledge that we described earlier. We also sometimes point out where other authors have explained some of what there is to be known about the teaching and learning of the relevant mathematics.

Summary

In this chapter, we argued that teachers can develop their mathematics teaching by focused reflection on their own classroom practice and that of others. Rather than thinking about some rather generalised notion of how you teach, most benefit is to be gained by reflection on *actual episodes* from lessons you or

(Continued)

(Continued)

others have taught. We gave a first illustration of how this can work with a visit to a lesson taught by a student teacher, Naomi, and we asked you to identify issues from her lesson for further consideration.

We made a key distinction between *content-specific* issues – specific to the subject being taught – and *generic* issues that would be pertinent whatever subject was being taught. We emphasised that this book will focus on issues *specific to the mathematics being taught* in Naomi's lesson, in your own lessons and those of your colleagues, and in many lessons to come later in the book. We also emphasised that our focus, and the ambition of the book, is to build up the knowledge that underpins effective mathematics teaching. The book is structured around a framework for analysing and reflecting on mathematics teaching. The framework is called the *Knowledge Quartet*. In the next chapter you will find out what the Knowledge Quartet is, and how it came about. This will be essential reading in order for you to understand and benefit from the rest of the book.

Further reading

We conclude this chapter with a selection of the kinds of books that you may find useful as a companion to this one. Their content, structure and style differs, but there should be at least one that you find approachable and helpful.

Julia Anghileri (2006) *Teaching Number Sense,* 2nd edn. London: Continuum.

Julia Anghileri (2008) *Developing Number Sense*, London: Continuum.

> Julia Anghileri is a leading researcher and writer in the field of children's arithmetic, and her authoritative and very readable books draw extensively on research in the UK, the Netherlands and the USA. The first of these focuses on the primary years, up to about age 10, the second straddles primary and middle years (ages about 9–13).

Derek Haylock (2006) *Mathematics Explained for Primary Teachers*, 3rd edn. London: Sage.

> Derek Haylock has a talent for lucid explanation, and the book offers a very clear and supportive introduction to primary mathematics pedagogy. Tens of thousands of student teachers have used and found reassurance in this book over the years. The most recent editions are more explicit in their reference to research findings.

Jennifer Suggate, Andrew Davis and Maria Goulding (2006) *Mathematical Knowledge for Primary Teachers*. London: David Fulton.

This very accessible text is also ideal for trainee and serving teachers who lack confidence in their own knowledge of mathematics. The emphasis throughout is on understanding and making connections between topics.

Ian Thompson (ed.) (1997) *Teaching and Learning Early Number.* Buckingham: Open University Press.

This is not just for early years teachers. Understanding how children learn number concepts and operations has been radically affected by recent research in the Netherlands, the USA and the UK. This book is a very readable summary of that research, with implications for classroom practice.

Ian Thompson (ed.) (1999) *Issues in Teaching Numeracy in Primary Schools.* Buckingham: Open University Press.

Ian Thompson (ed.) (2003) *Enhancing Primary Mathematics.* Maidenhead: Open University Press.

These two books are compiled as readers in primary mathematics education, with contributions from a number of individuals who have influenced policy in the UK.

Louise O'Sullivan, Andrew Harris, Margaret Sangster, Jon Wild, Gina Donaldson and Gill Bottle (2005) *Reflective Reader: Primary Mathematics.* Exeter: Learning Matters.

This slim, approachable book sets out to introduce 'challenging and topical theory' in primary mathematics education to beginning teachers. This firmly relates to what we call 'foundation knowledge' (see Chapters 2 and 7), and is very much in keeping with the emphasis on reflection in this book.

Linda Dickson, Margaret Brown and Olwen Gibson (1984) *Children Learning Mathematics.* Eastbourne: Holt Education.

Marilyn Nickson (2000) *Teaching and Learning Mathematics: A Teacher's Guide to Recent Research.* London: Cassell.

The first of these is a classic and unrivalled popular guide to research findings in mathematics education. You may still find reasonably priced, used copies online. Marilyn Nickson's book is perhaps a little less user-friendly than Dickson et al., but her research update has an international flavour, and has been well received.

2

Knowledge for Teaching Mathematics: Introducing the Knowledge Quartet Framework

> **In this chapter you will read about:**
>
> - different types of knowledge needed for teaching mathematics;
> - the importance of teachers' mathematical content knowledge;
> - a framework for helping teachers to focus on and develop their mathematical content knowledge.

What kinds of things do teachers need to know in order to teach primary mathematics well?

In Chapter 1 we started to focus your attention on what teachers need to know in order to teach primary mathematics. We suggested that this knowledge might be held individually by the teacher or accessible to them through reference to colleagues. We asked you to identify issues from Naomi's lesson, and suggested that such issues might be grouped under the headings of *content-specific* and *generic*. The issues you identified in Naomi's teaching can be seen as indications of her knowledge for teaching. For example, her use of the magnetic frogs to show the 'difference' notion of subtraction told us something about her knowledge of subtraction. The generic issues that you identified indicate something about Naomi's generic knowledge for teaching, while content-specific issues indicate something about her mathematics content knowledge for teaching. As well as content-specific or generic knowledge, we also introduced the notion of pedagogical knowledge and what this might mean. In this chapter we go on to examine in greater detail the types of knowledge needed by teachers for teaching primary mathematics. We will then explain how a framework for identifying content-specific aspects of this knowledge was developed for use when observing and reflecting on mathematics teaching.

Make a list of some of the things you think a primary school teacher needs to know in order to teach mathematics. You can do this on your own, but ideally you should work with a friend, colleague or group of teachers or student teachers, depending on your circumstances.

Are all of the things you have in your list specific to teaching mathematics or are some of them applicable to other curriculum areas? Focus only on those things that are specific to mathematics teaching. These can be further divided into different types of content-specific knowledge. There are different ways that you could group your ideas; we suggest one way here, but you may find different categories are more suitable for your own list.

You may have some ideas in your list that are to do with:

- knowledge of calculation strategies, e.g. knowing how to do long division, or multiplication using the grid method;

- understanding of concepts, e.g. knowing the three types of averages or the difference between ratio and proportion;

- knowing how to use resources, e.g. hundred grids, place-value cards or ICT resources;

- knowledge of the prescribed curriculum, e.g. in England and Wales, the Mathematics Programmes of Study in the National Curriculum and the Primary Strategy.

Consider how the things in your list fit under these (or other) categories. You may wish to think of some more examples in order to clarify the meaning of each category. If you have ideas that do not fit under any of the headings, what additional headings do you need to introduce?

This exercise was not intended to result in an exhaustive list of all the mathematics content knowledge you need to teach primary mathematics. However, it should begin to give you an idea of the different *kinds* of mathematical content knowledge that are important. Some of the ideas in your list may be the kinds of things you would expect people who are not teachers to know, particularly those in the first two categories. You would not, however, expect people who are not teachers to know about appropriate resources for teaching mathematics, or to know what is in official curriculum guidance. It is clear, then, that the types of mathematical content knowledge teachers need include some of what we would expect other people to know; however, teachers also need 'professional' knowledge that others are not expected to have. Deborah Ball and her colleagues (Ball et al., 2005) use the term *common* content knowledge to refer to what we might expect non-teachers to know. The knowledge which only teachers are expected to have is termed *specialised* content knowledge.

All professions (e.g. lawyers, architects and bakers) have knowledge bases that are specific to their realm of operation, and teaching is no exception. In the 1980s, Lee Shulman, a former president of the American Education Research Association, gave a seminal account of the knowledge bases needed by teachers (Shulman, 1986). He identified seven categories of teacher knowledge. Four of these are generic in nature:

- general pedagogical knowledge;

- knowledge of learners;

- knowledge of context;

- knowledge of the purposes of teaching and learning.

The other three relate to content-specific knowledge, and it is these that we are most interested in here:

- subject-matter knowledge;

- pedagogical content knowledge;

- curriculum knowledge.

In the case of mathematics, *subject-matter knowledge* is concerned with both *substantive* and *syntactic* knowledge. Substantive knowledge refers to the facts, concepts and processes of mathematics and the links between them – such as knowing the properties of an isosceles triangle, understanding what is meant by a fraction, knowing how to multiply by 10, and knowing that division undoes multiplication. Syntactic knowledge refers to knowing how mathematical truths are established: that is, with the means of inquiry in mathematics. Syntactic knowledge concerns the *process* of doing mathematics rather than the product of such activity. It includes knowing how to *prove* an idea through deductive reasoning – for example, being able to demonstrate why the sum of two odd numbers must always be an even number. Another aspect of syntactic knowledge is knowing how to *disprove* a conjecture – for example, being able to use *counterexamples* to disprove the conjecture that the area of a rectangle necessarily increases as the perimeter increases.

In mathematics, *pedagogical content knowledge* refers to how teachers transform their own knowledge into a form that makes it accessible to learners. This includes knowledge of how to use resources and representations or analogies for teaching mathematical ideas. Pedagogical content knowledge is also concerned with the way in which teachers break down ideas and explain concepts to learners.

Curriculum knowledge refers to knowing what it is that children are expected to learn and knowledge of related resources, such as textbooks and published plans that can be used in teaching.

The four categories that we used in the exercise earlier in this chapter, to group ideas about teacher knowledge, can be seen in relation to Shulman's three categories of content knowledge. The first two of these (knowledge of calculation strategies and understanding of concepts) would come under *subject-matter knowledge*, the third (knowing how to use resources) under *pedagogical content knowledge,* and the fourth (knowledge of the prescribed curriculum) under *curriculum knowledge.*

> Consider your own knowledge for teaching mathematics in relation to Shulman's three categories of content-specific knowledge. Think of the two aspects of subject-matter knowledge, substantive and syntactic knowledge, separately, and rate your own confidence level in each of the four aspects of subject knowledge.

If you are a mathematics graduate, you might be expected to rate highly on subject-matter knowledge, but perhaps not so highly on pedagogical content knowledge or curriculum knowledge. If you have worked for a while in primary school classrooms – as say, a teaching assistant – you might rate yourself highly in relation to curriculum knowledge and possibly pedagogical content knowledge, but less highly for subject-matter knowledge. How important is it that, as a teacher of primary mathematics, you have a good knowledge base in *all* these areas? We turn now to consider the evidence.

The importance of mathematical content knowledge for teaching

A number of research studies have shown different aspects of teacher knowledge to be important for primary school mathematics teaching. If we simply look at the level of formal qualifications in mathematics held by teachers, then no direct relationship is found between teacher knowledge and effective teaching (Eisenberg, 1977; Begle, 1979; Askew et al., 1997). In a survey of the empirical research, Begle (1979) concluded that the widely held belief that effectiveness as a teacher is directly related to knowledge of the subject was false. You have probably known people who really 'know their subject' but who were not good at helping others to learn. We have shown above that subject-matter knowledge is not the whole picture; however, that is not to say that it is not important. Clearly, you cannot teach what you do not know. As Deborah Ball (1988: 13) so succinctly wrote, 'It is obvious that knowledge of mathematics is basic to being able to help someone else learn it'. Fennema et al. (1989) found that teachers taught areas of elementary mathematics about which they were knowledgeable more effectively than areas in which they were not. In her important comparative study of US and Chinese teachers, Liping Ma (1999) demonstrated that it was important for teachers to have a deep knowledge of the mathematics *at the level they were teaching* rather than having knowledge of advanced mathematics. She called this 'profound understanding of fundamental mathematics', and showed that Chinese teachers' more profound knowledge of elementary school mathematics equipped them to teach more effectively than their US colleagues with less profound knowledge. In the UK, Rowland et al. (2001) found that the mathematics teaching of student teachers who scored higher on an audit of their mathematics content knowledge was generally assessed as better than that of their contemporaries with lower scores. Hill et al. (2005) found that pupils of teachers with stronger mathematical knowledge for teaching made greater progress than pupils whose teachers had relatively weaker knowledge.

All these studies, which found teachers' mathematical content knowledge to be linked to the effectiveness of teaching, went beyond looking at formal qualifications. Ma's study considered the teachers' ability to give a rationale for familiar calculation algorithms, as well as their awareness of the structures of the mathematics to be taught. The audit in Rowland et al.'s study assessed the student teachers' *current* knowledge of mathematics relevant to primary school teaching, rather than the kind of mathematics assessed in earlier formal examinations. Hill et al. measured teacher knowledge using a multiple-choice questionnaire containing items that posed questions related to situations involving the teaching of mathematics. These items tested both *common* and *specialised* content knowledge.

Other researchers have found that it is not only the depth of knowledge about elementary mathematics that is important, but also the connectedness of that knowledge. In the UK a team of researchers from King's College London (Askew et al., 1997) found that the pupils of teachers with what they called a 'connectionist orientation' made the most progress in their mathematics learning. These 'connectionist teachers' had a coherent set of beliefs, and believed that pupils should have a 'rich network of connections between different mathematical ideas' (p. 1).

Both the substantive and syntactic aspects of subject-matter knowledge are important for primary school teachers. It may not be important to understand advanced mathematics to teach primary mathematics effectively, but it is important to have a profound and connected understanding of primary school mathematics.

Making a case for the importance of pedagogical content knowledge for teaching mathematics would seem to be straightforward. In simple terms, this equates directly to knowing how to teach mathematics. Knowing what resources to use to teach a particular idea or process, and being able to explain in a way that children will understand, is an essential component of mathematics teaching. But how can we tell if a teacher *has* this kind of knowledge? We have suggested above that we cannot simply rely on levels of formal qualifications to see if teachers have sufficient subject-matter knowledge for teaching primary mathematics. It would seem even less likely that the level of a teacher's pedagogical content knowledge might be assessed through such qualifications. Deborah Ball and her colleagues working in the USA have produced a multiple-choice questionnaire which, they claim, assesses teachers' subject knowledge for teaching

(Ball et al., 2005). Items in Ball et al.'s questionnaire test both common and specialised knowledge for teaching mathematics by asking questions about specific teaching scenarios. If you were to take such a test, it might give some indication of your pedagogical content knowledge. However, although your responses would give a measure of your theoretical pedagogical content knowledge, they might not necessarily reflect how you would act in practice. In order to make such assessments someone would need to actually observe you teaching.

A number of experts have suggested that teacher knowledge that is necessary for teaching may only be seen through observations of teaching. Hegarty (2000) suggested that the different aspects of a teacher's knowledge base are brought together in any teaching moment, and can only be viewed in that moment. It is difficult to imagine a situation in which a teacher is able to make good use of resources and give clear explanations if they do not have secure knowledge of the content. Both the subject-matter knowledge and the pedagogical content knowledge aspects of their knowledge, as well as knowledge of the curriculum, must interact to enable them to teach effectively. It is in the dynamic situation of teaching that subject-matter knowledge, pedagogical content knowledge and curriculum knowledge are brought together. The effectiveness of this teaching will depend on factors from all three categories of knowledge, and on the relationships between them.

In her study of four early years teachers, Carole Aubrey (1997a, 1997b) demonstrated how the interaction of teachers' subject-matter knowledge, pedagogical content knowledge and knowledge of learners affected their teaching. Though Shulman (1986) included 'knowledge of learners' as a separate category of *generic* teacher knowledge, Deborah Ball et al. (2005) saw such knowledge as an aspect of specialised *content* knowledge. Aubrey's use of 'knowledge of learners' follows Ball et al. in focusing on knowledge of children as *learners of mathematics*. Aubrey found that a teacher who had strong subject-matter knowledge was able to relate her knowledge to that of her pupils. This teacher presented new ideas systematically and made useful links between different ways of representing the mathematics. Aubrey was able to see the different elements of the content knowledge of this teacher, as they came together in the teaching situation.

We have argued for the importance of having good mathematical content knowledge – both subject-matter knowledge and pedagogical content knowledge. Curriculum knowledge is another aspect of knowledge self-evidently necessary for teaching.

Earlier we asked you to rate your own knowledge in relation to Shulman's three categories of content knowledge for teaching. You will find it useful to consider how you might go about developing your own knowledge in terms of each of these categories of teacher knowledge. We offer some starters in Table 2.1 to which you should add your own, based on personal knowledge.

Tables 2.1 Some suggestions for improving your knowledge for teaching mathematics

Knowledge base	Examples of activities to develop your own knowledge
Subject-matter knowledge	Read one or more of the books on mathematics content knowledge for primary school teachers suggested at the end of Chapter 1. Revise relevant aspects of school mathematics.
Pedagogical content knowledge	Look at resources for teaching primary mathematics, in your placement schools, and consider how you might use them. Read books on mathematics pedagogy such as those suggested at the end of Chapter 1.
Curriculum knowledge	Read government documents and/or those developed by your placement school that give guidance on the content of mathematics teaching. Look critically at published lesson/activity plans for mathematics teaching.

How can your mathematical content knowledge be identified and developed?

You may have found rating your own mathematical content knowledge quite difficult. How do you know whether you have the depth and connectedness of subject-matter knowledge necessary for effective mathematics teaching? Assessing your pedagogical content knowledge is even more problematic. How can you judge whether you will give clear explanations and use the most appropriate resources without knowing the context? We have suggested above that mathematical content knowledge for teaching will be most clearly seen in the action of teaching. We also suggested that this knowledge is a complex combination of different types of knowledge that interact with each other to inform teaching. So, how might we identify different aspects of teacher knowledge that have an impact on teaching from observations of that teaching? This was a question that interested the authors. We recognised the importance of the different aspects of teachers' mathematics content knowledge, and wanted to help beginning teachers to develop this knowledge.

In initial teacher education courses, student teachers are helped to develop their teaching through *feedback* on their teaching from tutors and class teacher-mentors. Another important way in which beginning teachers develop their teaching is through critical *reflection* on their own teaching. If feedback and reflection are to be helpful in developing mathematical content knowledge, then such knowledge needs first to be identified in acts of teaching. Our aim then was to help tutors, mentors and beginning teachers identify where mathematical content knowledge could be seen in a lesson to influence teaching. Tutors and mentors would then be able to give constructive feedback on how this might be developed. Teachers reflecting on their own lessons would gain understanding of how their own content knowledge affected their teaching and think about how to improve it. We turn now to an account of how we developed our framework for observation of mathematics lessons with a focus on content knowledge. We call this framework the *Knowledge Quartet*.

Development of the Knowledge Quartet

We began our research by investigating how different kinds of primary mathematics teachers' content-related knowledge 'played out' in the classroom, that is, how this knowledge was made evident. For our study, we worked with 12 student teachers – Naomi was one of them – towards the end of their one-year postgraduate initial teacher training course. They were chosen to represent a range of differences in PGCE students as a whole. For example, Naomi was well qualified in mathematics (she had studied it at A level and done well in the exam) and was confident about doing mathematics herself. This made her typical of some PGCE students, but not of the majority of primary trainees who gave up mathematics at 16 (for some mature students, many years ago), some of whom were quite anxious about their own competence to do mathematics. In the same spirit of representation, six of the trainees were specialising in the Foundation Stage and Key Stage 1 (age 3–8), and the other six in Key Stage 2 (age 7–11).

We observed and videotaped two mathematics lessons taught by each of these trainees – 24 lessons in total. The participating students were asked to provide a copy of their planning for the observed lesson. As soon as possible after the lesson (usually the same day) the person who had observed and videotaped the lesson wrote what we called a *descriptive synopsis* of the lesson. This was a brief account of what happened in the lesson, so that someone reading the synopsis would be able to contextualise discussion of events within the lesson. Such a synopsis was similar to the account of Naomi's lesson that we gave in Chapter 1, but without the transcribed passages at that stage. These descriptive synopses were usually written from memory and classroom notes, with occasional reference to the videotape if necessary. The writer of each synopsis also flagged up, at that stage, anything in the lesson that immediately struck them as being potentially significant for our subsequent scrutiny of the lesson.

The approach that we then took to analysing and making sense of the videotaped lessons is known as *grounded theory* (Glaser and Strauss, 1967). It is worthwhile our saying something about this approach, because the reliability and usefulness of our approach to developing teaching depend on it. In one approach (sometimes called 'theory-driven') to the analysis of data, the researcher brings a ready-made theory, or theories, about the kind of situation being investigated and applies them to the data. Here, 'theory' does not mean a wild guess of some sort, but a well-established system of notions (such as 'conservation' in child development) that serve to explain observed behaviours and other phenomena. The polar opposite to this approach – grounded theory research – does not bring existing theory to make sense of the data, but aims to use the data for the purpose of generating or 'discovering' a theory or theories. This is not the place to elaborate in detail on how this is achieved, but it always involves the researcher in deep and detailed engagement with the data, trying, as far as possible, not to be blinkered by preconceived ideas. Approaches to grounded theory research always involve *coding* and *categorising* the data in some way, as you did when you discussed and reflected on Naomi's lesson in Chapter 1.

In our grounded theory approach to the videotapes of the lessons, we watched the tapes of all the lessons, usually in twos and threes, sometimes as a whole team. As we watched, we identified aspects of the trainees' actions in the classroom that seemed to be significant in the limited sense that they seemed to be informed by the trainee's mathematical subject knowledge or mathematical pedagogical knowledge. In this way, we homed in on particular moments or episodes in the tapes. Each such moment or episode was assigned a preliminary code such as 'concentration on procedures', 'choice of examples', 'making connections between procedures' or 'responding to children's ideas'. We just invented these codes as we went along, although some would be repeated as we saw what looked like the same kind of phenomenon in different episodes within the same, or another, lesson.

Eventually, by a process of negotiation within the team, we merged different codes that seemed to be describing the same thing, and we abandoned some codes which turned out to occur only a few times over all the 24 lessons. That left us with 18 codes. Next, we revisited each lesson in turn and, after further intensive study of the tapes, elaborated each *descriptive synopsis* into what we called an *analytical account* of the lesson. In these accounts, we associated one or more of the 18 codes with each of the significant moments and episodes, with appropriate justification and analysis concerning the role of the trainee's content knowledge in the identified passages, and links to relevant literature.

The emergence of the Knowledge Quartet

Our 18 codes gave us a way of looking at and talking about primary mathematics teaching in practice, with a focus on the teacher and their mathematical knowledge for teaching. This was useful to the extent that we had a set of concepts and an associated vocabulary sufficient to identify and describe various ways in which mathematics content knowledge plays out in primary mathematics teaching. At the same time, 18 codes is really too many for practical use, for ourselves and probably for others. It would be very difficult to observe or reflect on a lesson, holding in mind 18 different ways in which content knowledge might be 'played out'. Therefore we began to think how we could group the codes into a smaller set of 'big ideas' for mathematics teaching. Eventually, we made a large paper label for each of the codes, spread these labels out on the floor, and began to separate them into sets. Each suggestion for putting two or more codes together had to be backed up with a reason of some sort. For example, someone put 'choice of examples' and 'choice of representation' together, saying that these were both ways that teachers use to explain an idea when they are teaching it. In fact, they said, these two codes are characteristic examples of the ways that teachers 'transform' their subject knowledge, as Lee Shulman (1986) put it, in order to help others to learn it. Eventually we ended up with four 'big idea' categories, which we later

Table 2.2 The codes of the Knowledge Quartet

Foundation	Adheres to textbook
	Awareness of purpose
	Concentration on procedures
	Identifying errors
	Overt subject knowledge
	Theoretical underpinning
	Use of terminology
Transformation	Choice of examples
	Choice of representation
	Demonstration
Connection	Anticipation of complexity
	Decisions about sequencing
	Making connections between procedures
	Making connections between concepts
	Recognition of conceptual appropriateness
Contingency	Deviation from agenda
	Responding to children's ideas
	Use of opportunities

called the *Knowledge Quartet*. Each of the four categories is a unit or dimension of the Knowledge Quartet. In time, we also came to talk about the four 'members' of the quartet. We continued to debate the elements of each dimension in the following days and weeks, until they were settled, at least until further research suggests that we need to make amendments.

We named the four dimensions *foundation, transformation, connection* and *contingency*. Table 2.2 shows all the codes associated with each of the four dimensions.

We shall now give a first explanation of the distinctive nature of each of the four dimensions of the Knowledge Quartet. We will explore each dimension in the following chapters, giving illustrations of teaching in which aspects of that dimension were seen as key determinants of practice.

Foundation

The first member of the Knowledge Quartet refers to a teacher's theoretical background and beliefs. By 'theoretical', we mean the kind of knowledge acquired at school, or in teacher education, sometimes before it is put to use in the classroom. It differs from the other three units in the sense that it is about knowledge possessed, irrespective of whether it is being put to purposeful use.

The other three dimensions of the Knowledge Quartet all rest on this one: being able to make conceptual connections in your teaching, for example, is largely determined by relevant foundation knowledge. We take the view that the possession of such knowledge has the potential to inform pedagogical choices and strategies in a fundamental way. By 'fundamental' we mean a rational, reasoned approach to making decisions about teaching based on something other than imitation or habit. The three key components of this theoretical background are:

- knowledge and understanding of mathematics itself;

- knowledge of mathematics pedagogy;

- beliefs about mathematics, including beliefs about why and how mathematics is learnt.

Not surprisingly, what teachers believe affects their classroom practice as much as what they know (Thom, 1973; Thompson, 1992).

Transformation

The remaining three categories, unlike the first, refer to ways and contexts in which knowledge is brought to bear on the preparation and conduct of teaching. They focus on knowledge-in-action as *demonstrated* both in planning to teach and in the act of teaching itself.

Transformation, the second member of the quartet, gets to the core of what it means to *teach* a subject. As Lee Shulman (1987: 15) observed, the pedagogical content knowledge base for teaching is distinguished by 'the capacity of a teacher to *transform* the content knowledge he or she possesses into forms that are pedagogically powerful' (emphasis added). This characterisation has been echoed in the writing of Deborah Ball (1988), for example, who distinguished between knowing some mathematics 'for yourself' and knowing in order to be able to help someone else learn it. In order to present ideas to learners, the teacher must find ways of representing what they themselves already know. These representations, which we discuss in detail in Chapter 3, take the form of analogies, illustrations, examples, explanations and demonstrations. To take a simple example, even the positive whole numbers are abstractions, but several representations of them exist. These include sets of objects, base-10 blocks, place-value cards, number lines and grids, each emphasising a different facet of the idea of whole number. Teachers' choice and use of examples, which we discuss in detail in Chapter 4, has emerged from our research as a key aspect of transformation knowledge. This includes the use of examples to assist concept formation, to demonstrate procedures, and the selection of exercise examples for student activity.

Connection

The next category, which we call *connection*, concerns the coherence of the planning or teaching across an episode, lesson or series of lessons. Mathematics is notable for its coherence as a body of knowledge and as a field of inquiry, and the cement that holds it together is reason. The work of Askew et al. (1997) was referred to earlier in our discussion of what constitutes mathematical content knowledge for teachers. In their study of six teachers found to be highly effective, all but one gave evidence of a 'connectionist' orientation. Ball (1990b) also strenuously argued for the importance of connected knowledge for teaching.

In addition to the connectedness of mathematical content in the mind of the teacher and his/her teaching in the classroom, this dimension includes the *sequencing* of topics of instruction within and between lessons, including the ordering of tasks and exercises. To a significant extent, the ability to sequence teaching effectively involves making choices based on knowledge of structural connections within mathematics itself, and an awareness of the relative cognitive demands of different topics and tasks.

Contingency

No matter how thoroughly a lesson is planned, things arise that were not planned for or anticipated. Our final category concerns the teacher's response to these unplanned, unexpected classroom events. In some cases it is difficult to see how they could have been planned for, although that is a matter for debate. It can be argued that greater knowledge will lead to fewer surprises when teaching, since such knowledge enables the teacher to anticipate and plan for a greater number of pupil responses. In commonplace language this dimension of the Knowledge Quartet is about the ability to 'think on one's feet': it is about *contingent action*. Two key components of this category that arise from the data are the readiness to *respond to children's ideas* and a consequent preparedness, and when appropriate, to *deviate from an agenda* set out when the lesson was prepared. Shulman wrote that most teaching begins from some form of 'text' – a textbook, a syllabus, ultimately a sequence of planned, intended actions to be carried out by the teacher and/or the children within a lesson or unit of some kind. Whilst the stimulus – the teacher's intended actions – can be planned, the children's responses cannot.

Brown and Wragg (1993) wrote that 'responding' moves are the linchpins of a lesson, important in its sequencing and structuring, and observed that such interventions are some of the most difficult tactics for novice teachers to master. The quality of such responses is undoubtedly determined, at least in part, by the teacher's subject-matter knowledge. For example, Alan Bishop often retold an anecdote about a class of 9- and 10-year-olds who were asked to give a fraction between ½ and ¾. One girl answered ⅔, 'because 2 is between the 1 and the 3, and on the bottom the 3 lies between the 2 and the 4'. Bishop asked his readers how they might respond to the pupil. Although this was a correct answer, the child's reasoning was incorrect and would lead to wrong answers to different problems. The way in which a teacher is able to respond to this situation would depend on the knowledge resources available to them, including knowing how to explore the generalisation inherent in the pupil's justification (*syntactic knowledge*). We return to look in more detail at the mathematical knowledge involved in this anecdote in Chapter 6.

Links to Lee Shulman's seven categories of knowledge for teaching

The four dimensions that have arisen from our study of teaching in practice, as explained above, can be related to the seven categories of teacher knowledge proposed by Shulman. The *foundation* dimension encompasses the subject-matter knowledge category, as well as the knowledge of purpose category which relates to the Knowledge Quartet notion of teachers' beliefs about mathematics. *Transformation* was a term used by Shulman in describing what he meant by pedagogical content knowledge, and these two ways of categorising subject knowledge are closely related. The *connection* dimension is not so straightforwardly linked to any single category. The connectedness of a teacher's own mathematical knowledge is an aspect of their subject-matter knowledge, as is their understanding of the conceptual appropriateness of what is being taught. Being able to make connections for learners, however, would be part of their pedagogical content knowledge. *Contingency* would seem to involve all seven of Shulman's categories. Being able to make appropriate decisions – 'thinking on one's feet' – may require any combination of subject-matter knowledge, pedagogical and pedagogical content knowledge, knowledge of the curriculum, of learners, of the context and of purpose.

It is not surprising that the ways in which teachers' mathematical content knowledge were seen to play out in their teaching can be related to Shulman's seven categories of knowledge needed for teaching. What is significant about the Knowledge Quartet dimensions is that they emerged from observations and analysis of *mathematics* lessons. This is important when we go back to consider the purpose of the research that led to the identification of the Knowledge Quartet. We discussed earlier how difficult it is to disentangle different aspects of teacher knowledge when observing teaching, because of the way they interrelate to produce the teaching outcome. In the Knowledge Quartet research we set out to identify how tutors, class teacher-mentors and beginning teachers might observe and reflect on mathematics lessons in a way that helped them identify aspects of content knowledge that affected their teaching. The 18 codes that constitute the Knowledge Quartet were derived from instances where content knowledge was actually observed in the act of teaching, and which seemed to have an impact on that teaching. It should therefore be possible to turn this around and look for these types of instances when observing or reflecting on teaching. The Danish educator, Jeppe Skott (2006) observed that 'theories' that are bought to bear on the task of *improving* teaching increasingly derive from studies *of* teaching. Skott coined the term 'theoretical loop' to describe this relationship between theory and practice in teacher education. The development of the Knowledge Quartet is a clear example of this theoretical loop.

Using the Knowledge Quartet framework as a tool for observation and discussion of mathematics content knowledge observed in teaching

The next step was for us to develop the Knowledge Quartet in a way that would enable initial teacher education tutors, class teacher-mentors and beginning teachers who had not been involved in the research to use it in their own observations and reflections. In other words, we wanted to produce a *framework* for identification and discussion of mathematics content knowledge observed in teaching. In order to help tutors and mentors working with student teachers on our postgraduate primary and middle school courses, we produced some guidelines for the observation of mathematics lessons and introduced these to tutors and class teacher-mentors. They consist of a brief explanation of each of the dimensions of the Knowledge Quartet. Each explanation was followed by a list of questions that might be asked about a particular, observed lesson. These are not intended to be an exhaustive list of questions, but rather as examples to focus the thinking of the observer. The guidelines are reproduced in Table 2.3.

One of us has used the Knowledge Quartet framework as the basis for a longitudinal study of the development of mathematics teaching in a group of beginning teachers (Turner, 2007). In this study, the participants were introduced to the Knowledge Quartet framework in their training year and given intensive feedback on their mathematics teaching using that framework. In the first year of their teaching, they continued to be given feedback on observed lessons using the framework, as well as being required to use the framework to write reflections on their mathematics teaching. In the third year of the study the support of the 'tutor' was withdrawn, and they were left to use the framework independently to reflect on videotaped lessons and their other mathematics teaching. The fourth and final year of the project made use of interviews and group discussions to investigate how use of the framework might have helped develop the mathematics teaching of the participants. This study found that reflecting on their mathematics teaching using the Knowledge Quartet framework does help to focus attention on mathematical content knowledge and promotes development in mathematics teaching. The following comments are from teachers involved in the project:

> I found ... it does make you more reflective and it makes me, from the transformation section ... think of examples I am going to use or the images really carefully. (Amy at the end of her first year of teaching)

> Sometimes when I am doing things in lessons I think in terms of one of the headings. I think 'Oh this is something to do with contingency', or if I have made a small mistake or something I think 'Oh maybe I should have thought of that', it is like foundation or something, I do think about it as I am doing things. (Kate at the end of her second year of teaching)

Table 2.3 Guidelines for observing, supporting and assessing trainee teachers teaching mathematics

Members of the mathematics education team at the University of Cambridge, Faculty of Education, have been involved in research observing trainee teachers teaching mathematics. The focus of these observations has been concerned with the way in which content knowledge impacts upon the effectiveness of teaching. The definition of content knowledge is taken here to include pedagogical as well as subject-matter knowledge.

This research identified four main aspects of teaching that may be useful when observing, supporting and assessing trainee teachers teaching mathematics: *foundation, transformation, connection* and *contingency*. For each of these aspects of mathematics teaching some questions you might ask when reflecting on a trainee teacher's development are suggested below.

FOUNDATION

This category concerns subject knowledge per se as well as beliefs about mathematics and mathematical pedagogy which the trainee teacher brings to the teaching situation. Evidence for this may be found in both planning and teaching.

Does the trainee teacher:

- have a clear and coherent belief about the purposes of mathematics education and why his/her pupils are compelled to learn it;
- use appropriate teaching strategies to promote the required mathematical understanding in pupils;
- demonstrate knowledge of factors which have been shown to be significant in the teaching of mathematics, e.g. refer to writings of mathematics educators;
- concentrate on developing understanding rather than excessively on procedures (the latter would suggest an 'instrumental understanding' of mathematics in the trainee teacher);
- make use of his/her own resources and teaching strategies rather than adhering to textbook or National Numeracy Strategy unit plans;
- show, in his/her planning, knowledge of common errors and misconceptions and take steps to avoid them;
- show care in writing mathematical expressions correctly, e.g. use the = sign correctly;
- show a good understanding of the processes involved in +, −, × and ÷;
- demonstrate a knowledge of quick mental methods;
- use mathematical language correctly;
- demonstrate an accurate understanding of mathematical ideas or concepts, e.g. knows that 'adding zero' is not helpful when multiplying by 10 and an awareness that squares and rectangles do not form two disjoint sets?

(continued)

Table 2.3   (Continued)

TRANSFORMATION

This category deals with how well trainee teachers are able to transform what they know in ways that make this knowledge accessible and appropriate to children. Evidence for this may be found in both planning and teaching.

Does the trainee teacher:

- use equipment (e.g. base-10 apparatus) correctly to explain processes in number where appropriate;
- select appropriate forms of representation e.g. the use of a number line when teaching subtraction by 'counting back' or a place-value chart and arrow cards when teaching about values of digits;
- chose appropriate examples when demonstrating or eliciting an idea? 23 x 6 would be a good example for developing written multiplication whereas 19 x 4 would be a poor example as mental calculation would be more appropriate;
- give clear explanations of ideas or concepts, possibly making use of analogy;
- demonstrate clearly and accurately how to carry out procedures;
- make use of interactive teaching techniques to develop and assess understanding;
- use questioning effectively to assess and develop children's knowledge and understanding?

CONNECTION

This category is concerned with the decisions about sequencing and connectivity made by the trainee teacher so that the lesson hangs together and relates to the context of previous lessons and the pupils' knowledge. Such decisions will typically follow from a trainee teacher's ability to anticipate what is complex and what is conceptually appropriate for an individual or group of pupils. This will be evidenced in their planning and teaching of individual lessons as well as in their planning of sequences of lessons.

Does the trainee teacher:

- make links to previous lessons;
- make links between the mental and oral starter and the main part of the lesson;
- make appropriate conceptual connections within the subject matter e.g. between fractions of shapes and fractions of numbers;
- recognise the conceptual appropriateness of mathematical ideas for the children they are teaching;
- ask questions to ellicit children's understanding of connections between mathematical ideas;
- appear to be aware of the different levels of difficulty in a topic;

Table 2.3   (Continued)

- anticipate the complexity of an idea and break it down into steps that can be understood by the children;
- introduce ideas and strategies in an appropriately progressive order;
- make assessments of children's understanding and amend their lessons accordingly?

CONTINGENCY

This category may be summed up as the ability to 'think on one's feet'. This category is concerned with responding to the unexpected more than to the ability to make predictions at the planning stage.

Does the trainee teacher:

- respond appropriately to children's comments, questions and answers;
- cope adequately with questions from all children in the group;
- deal appropriately with children's responses to activities;
- respond appropriately when children give incorrect answers to questions or make incorrect statements during the course of a discussion;
- deviate from their agenda when appropriate;
- make ongoing assessments of children's understanding during the lesson and amend their teaching accordingly?

> I think the most important effect is having the four headings makes me more aware of what I am planning and teaching, and why. You find yourself questioning and justifying your decisions and choices. I am sure it makes you more purposeful in your choices, more precise. (Jane in her second year of teaching)

We have argued that teachers' mathematical content knowledge has an impact on the effectiveness of their teaching. We have also argued that this content knowledge may best be seen in the practice of teaching. We have introduced you to the Knowledge Quartet framework as a tool to facilitate observation and reflection on teachers' content knowledge demonstrated in their mathematics teaching. Now you are ready to try using the Knowledge Quartet framework to reflect on some mathematics teaching.

> Select a small part of a lesson that you have taught or have observed. This should be a part that you think may be significant in terms of mathematics content knowledge. It would be useful to discuss this with someone else, possibly your
>
> *(Continued)*

(Continued)

class teacher-mentor or a student teacher peer. Are any of the questions in the guidelines (or ones similar to them) relevant to the part of the lesson you have selected? Under which dimension, or dimensions, of the Knowledge Quartet would this aspect of your content knowledge come? For example, you may look at the beginning of a lesson where the children are asked some calculation questions. You could ask whether these questions were appropriate examples for the calculation strategies you wanted the children to use. In this case, the content knowledge would come under the *transformation* dimension of the Knowledge Quartet.

Summary

In this chapter we have considered the different kinds of knowledge that teachers need, but other educated people do not, in order to be able to teach primary school mathematics. We referred to Lee Shulman's seven categories of teacher knowledge, and focused in particular on two that are specifically related to mathematics content knowledge – *subject-matter knowledge* and *pedagogical content knowledge*. Having explained what is meant by these two categories of knowledge, we discussed why having these types of knowledge is important for teachers of primary school mathematics. You were asked to consider your own mathematics knowledge in relation to Shulman's categories and to think about ways that you might develop the different aspects of this knowledge.

We reviewed some of the literature that has demonstrated the importance of teachers' content knowledge, concluding that such knowledge may be identified most effectively through observation and analysis of actual teaching. We went on to explain how we developed the Knowledge Quartet as a way of categorising teachers' content knowledge observed in their teaching. The four dimensions of the Knowledge Quartet, *foundation, transformation, connection* and *contingency*, were outlined and linked to Shulman's categories of teacher knowledge. A way of using the Knowledge Quartet framework as a tool for reflecting on mathematics teaching with a focus on content knowledge was then explained. A suggestion was made indicating how you might begin to use this to reflect on your own mathematics teaching.

The Knowledge Quartet in the chapters to come

In the remainder of this book we will look in more detail at how content knowledge affects teaching, using examples of instances that we have observed ourselves, and using the Knowledge Quartet framework to illustrate this. In Chapters 3 and 4 we look closely at two aspects of the *transformation* dimension: in Chapter 3 the importance of using appropriate representations is explored and in Chapter 4 the choice of examples is analysed. Chapter 5 discusses connectedness in mathematics teaching and looks at ways in which instances that would be coded under the *connection* dimension seem to impact on teaching. Similarly, Chapter 6 explores what is meant by *contingency* and gives examples of instances where we have seen contingent action based on teacher knowledge. We have left the *foundation* dimension until last because then it is clear why it underpins the other three dimensions. In Chapter 7 we consider four aspects of foundation subject knowledge that are needed by primary school teachers but are generally poorly understood. As in the other chapters, aspects of content knowledge are considered in relation to examples from beginning teachers' lessons in which this knowledge was seen to be a key feature of the teaching. In the final chapter, we offer 12 'real' mathematics teaching episodes. These cover a range of pupil age groups and mathematical topics. Questions are posed after each episode to help you think about the way in which the teacher's content knowledge had an impact on their teaching. These examples are intended to help you focus on mathematics content knowledge when reflecting on your own lessons and to develop your own mathematics content knowledge in relation to the context of the teaching. Ultimately, you will use what you have learned in this book to help you focus on the mathematics content knowledge in your own teaching, and in this way you will develop your professional knowledge and practice.

Further reading

Lee Shulman (1986) 'Those who understand: knowledge growth in teaching', *Educational Researcher* 15(2): 4–14.

> In this seminal work, you can read about Lee Shulman's knowledge bases for teaching in more detail. You can also read about the different forms in which Shulman proposed these knowledge bases might be enacted. This paper will add to your understanding of what knowledge is generally important for teaching as well as that specific to the teaching of mathematics.

Liping Ma (1999) *Knowing and Teaching Elementary Mathematics: Teachers' Understanding of Fundamental Mathematics in China and the United States.* Mahwah, NJ: Lawrence Erlbaum.

This much-quoted book arose from Ma's doctoral study comparing the knowledge for teaching mathematics of primary school teachers in China and the USA. In this book she spells out several ways in which the Chinese teachers' knowledge was more profound than that of their American peers. She suggests that profound knowledge facilitates more effective teaching and indicates how this level of knowledge was developed in the Chinese teachers.

Carole Aubrey (1997) *Mathematics Teaching in the Early Years: An Investigation of Teachers' Subject Knowledge.* London: Falmer.

This book provides a good background to ways of thinking about the subject knowledge needed for teaching mathematics. It considers different approaches to investigating such subject knowledge, including through observation of teaching. Aubrey is particularly concerned with teachers' knowledge of children's understandings of mathematics and how such knowledge can facilitate teaching and learning. In this book Aubrey reports on her own work investigating how teachers' subject knowledge interacts with children's responses in mathematics classrooms.

Tim Rowland, Peter Huckstep and Anne Thwaites (2005) 'Elementary teachers' mathematics subject knowledge: the Knowledge Quartet and the case of Naomi'. *Journal of Mathematics Teacher Education* 8(3) pp. 255–281.

This research paper gives a more detailed account of the research for the *Knowledge Quartet* than we have been able to in this chapter, and a more extended conceptualisation of the four dimensions of the *Quartet* itself.

3

Transformation: Using and Understanding Representations in Mathematical Teaching

> **In this chapter you will read about:**
>
> - different types of representations that may be used in mathematics teaching;
> - the role of representations in the learning of mathematics;
> - ways of using representations in mathematics teaching;
> - how teachers sometimes choose unhelpful representations, and why;
> - considerations to guide your choice of mathematical representations.

In Chapters 1 and 2 we started to think about the different types of knowledge needed to teach primary school mathematics and how these might be played out in teaching. In Chapter 2 you were introduced to the Knowledge Quartet as a framework for reflecting on teaching in a way that focuses on mathematical content knowledge. In the next five chapters we will discuss different aspects of teachers' mathematics content knowledge that we have found to be particularly important when teaching primary school mathematics. We will illustrate each of these with lessons viewed through the lens of the Knowledge Quartet. We begin in this chapter by looking at *representation*, one aspect of mathematics pedagogical content knowledge from the *transformation* dimension of the quartet.

From the early years of primary school, mathematics becomes an abstract subject in which an understanding of symbols and their manipulation is a central feature. Physical and pictorial representations are widely used in order to support the teaching and learning of mathematics, acting as intermediaries between the concrete and the abstract. Jerome Bruner (1974) saw representations as important mediators in developing abstract understandings. Such mediators are often referred to as 'scaffolds' which support learning and which may be withdrawn once ideas are internalised. Bruner proposed a theory of learning development in which being able to hold a representation, or picture, in the mind freed the learner of the restraints of their physical world, enabling them to perform abstract operations. Bruner suggested three hierarchical but complementary modes of representation. The most practical of these he termed *enactive*, in which learning takes place through physical action. At the next level, *iconic* representation enables the learner to make use of 'pictorial' images in understanding the world, whilst at the highest level *symbolic* representations allow mental manipulation.

Before going on to discuss the use of representations by beginning teachers, it is worth considering what types of things might be used as representations in primary mathematics teaching. Classrooms from Reception to Year 6 in the UK are usually very busy and visually exciting places. Inside them there is a huge variety of objects stored on surfaces and in drawers, trays and cupboards, as well as interesting and informative teacher- or pupil-constructed displays on almost every horizontal or vertical surface. More transitory visual images may be drawn by the teacher on a whiteboard (or possibly blackboard) or displayed on an interactive whiteboard for use in a particular lesson. All these objects, displays and images are 'resources', which make the classrooms aesthetically pleasing and welcoming, but this is not their primary role. Many (if not most) resources found in primary classrooms are there to support children's learning. Resources may be used in different ways, one of which might be as a representation to bridge the gap between the physical world and the abstract world of mathematics. Resources may be used to aid learning in an enactive, iconic or symbolic way. In Table 3.1 there is a list of some resources for mathematics teaching that you may find in primary classrooms.

> What other mathematics resources have you seen in primary classrooms? Add further resources to each of the three categories in the table. Chose one or two resources from each category and think of all the different ways that you might use them in your mathematics teaching. Which of these would be enactive, iconic or symbolic representations? If possible, discuss this with a friend or colleague.

Table 3.1   Resources for mathematics teaching

Everyday objects	Objects designed for mathematics teaching	Pictures or diagrams
Conkers, dolls, coins, weighing scales, calculators, clocks, rulers, bottles, jugs, squares, cereal boxes, calendars, ...	Base-10 apparatus, multilink cubes, plastic 2-dimensional and 3-dimensional	Bar charts, number lines, pictures of purses containing different coins, hundred
	shapes, plastic shapes divided into fractional parts, ...	...

You will probably not have found it very easy to decide whether the resources you chose would be used in an enactive, iconic or symbolic way. Everyday objects certainly lend themselves to physical manipulation and are likely to be used in an enactive way – for example, balancing conkers and coins on a pan balance. However, the conkers can also be used to build a column graph representing the pets owned by children in the class or to represent other objects in a subtraction calculation. If used in these ways they would act as iconic representations. Objects such as base-10 materials, specifically designed for teaching mathematics, though clearly iconic representations in themselves, are also manipulated to represent operations such as addition or subtraction in an enactive fashion. The representational role of objects in the third column is more clear-cut. Pictures and diagrams are by definition iconic representations. However, even here there is some overlap. Although a number line may be an iconic representation of part of the number system, the numbers on it are symbols and jumps may be physically enacted along it. When working with resources in your mathematics teaching you will be using them in enactive, iconic and symbolic ways and also in combinations of all three of these modes of representation. We have come to realise that the way in which such representations are used is very important in primary mathematics teaching.

In our research we found that beginning teachers' use of representations regularly surfaced as a focus for discussion. One such lesson was that taught by Linda to a Reception (age 4–5) class during her final teaching placement.

Linda used a large hundred grid, laid on the floor with the children sitting around it. She had clearly thought about engaging the children in her lesson and had made use of a tortoise on a stick to represent movements of one, and a kangaroo on a stick to show jumps of ten. At the beginning of her lesson, she had moved the tortoise to various numbers on the hundred grid and demonstrated the addition of small numbers to these, by moving the tortoise one square at a time while counting out the number to be added.

In the main part of the lesson, Linda told the children that to add ten the kangaroo jumps one square down. She demonstrated this by placing the kangaroo on several numbers and 'jumping' it to the number directly below. She told the children that to add ten the kangaroo only has to jump one square and emphasised the direction of this jump as *down*.

What do you think might be problematic about Linda's use of the kangaroo's jumps to demonstrate adding ten?

Our reflections on Linda's lesson

This activity used an iconic representation of our number system – the hundred grid – and enacted jumps around the grid using tortoise and kangaroo jumps. We would suggest that the activity may have been problematic on two counts. Firstly, it suggested that the distance travelled by a jump of one was the same as that travelled by a jump of ten, albeit in a different direction. The focus on direction was also problematic as the children were sitting facing the hundred grid from different directions so that the jump did not appear 'down' to all of them. At no time did Linda either demonstrate, or get the children to explore, what happens when the tortoise makes ten individual jumps along the hundred grid. This may have helped the children to understand why moving down one square has the effect of adding ten. Rather, it was demonstrated to them almost like a magic trick using a kangaroo and a hundred grid.

Iconic representations commonly found in English classrooms

At the end of the last century, for the first time teachers in England were given detailed guidance from central government (DfEE, 1999) both on what mathematics should be taught, and also on pedagogy – how mathematics should be taught. This guidance suggested a number of resources that should be used in the teaching of primary mathematics. Many of these are the sort of iconic representations discussed above. The guidance stated that children should each have sets of digit cards from 0 to 10, which may be used in games and activities such as 'pairs', or to show the answer to questions in whole-class work. Children were also expected to have access to place-value or arrow cards in order to learn and demonstrate the way numbers are written. This apparatus exemplifies the *quantity value* of digits within numbers – that is, 234 is made up of '200', '30' and '4' (see Figure 3.1).

Base-10 apparatus and the spike abacus are mentioned in the 1999 curriculum guidance in relation to teaching place value. However, this recommendation comes with the caution that they should be used alongside digit cards to avoid children learning to manipulate the apparatus without being able to transfer their understanding to the number system.

Figure 3.1 Place-value or arrow cards

Figure 3.2 Spike abacus and base-10 apparatus

The spike abacus in Figure 3.2 shows the number 831 and the base-10 apparatus shows the number 111.

Both the abacus and base 10 apparatus model *column value* rather than quantity value, showing that 831 is made up of eight hundreds, three tens and one unit, and that 111 is made up of one hundred, one ten and one unit. Ian Thompson (2003a) explains the difference between column and quantity value, and concludes that column value is not a necessary prerequisite for early calculation, whereas an understanding of quantity value is important.

Base-10 apparatus was developed to help children develop their understanding of abstract concepts through enactive manipulation. However, this idea has been a focus of debate and underlies the caution given in curriculum guidance about the use of place-value apparatus mentioned earlier. Threlfall (1996) questioned the use of base-10 apparatus in helping children to carry out written calculations. He argued that children may learn how to obtain the correct answer to a calculation by manipulating base-10 apparatus, but they can do this without any understanding of what the apparatus represents. The use of such apparatus does not automatically lead to any understanding of the relationship between a base-10 place-value system and the way in which written algorithms perform the calculation. It is now unusual to see such apparatus being used as a step towards the mastery of calculation strategies in most English primary classrooms.

Though not mentioned in the 1999 guidance, teaching of place value is also supported in many classrooms by the use of a place-value or Gattegno chart (see Figure 3.3). Such charts are used to help children build and recite numbers. This is often used alongside arrow cards which are used to help children recognise how to write numbers in the contracted form. The teacher might point to '300' then '50' then '6'. Children would say 'three hundred and fifty and six' and also put together the matching arrow cards to make the contracted written form '356'. Finally, they will say it correctly – 'three hundred and fifty-six'.

100	100	100	100	100	100	100	100	100
10	20	30	40	50	60	70	80	90
1	2	3	4	5	6	7	8	9
0.1	0.2	0.3	0.4	0.5	0.6	0.7	0.8	0.9

Figure 3.3   Place-value or Gattegno chart

For a discussion of Gattegno charts see the article 'Gattegno charts' in the journal *Mathematics Teaching* (Faux, 1998). A number of other articles in the same journal issue also discuss the use of Gattegno charts, demonstrating the move by mathematics educators towards helping children build ideas about larger numbers through focusing on quantity value rather than column value. Alan Wigley (1997) discusses the difficulties presented by the irregular way in which numbers are spoken – for example, 17 as 'seventeen' rather than 'onetyseven' – and suggests ways in which arrow cards and place-value charts may be used to overcome these difficulties.

Thompson (2003a) suggested that arrow cards and place-value charts provide better representations, to help children recognise the relationship between spoken and written numbers and to understand quantity value. It is important that decisions about using arrow cards, spiked abaci, base-10 apparatus or a combination should not be based on aesthetic or pragmatic considerations alone. The use of such charts and cards reflects the move away from developing understanding through the physical manipulation of materials and towards a concentration on the relationship between the spoken and written forms of numbers.

A resource found in almost all classrooms in some form is the number line. Curriculum guidance stated that 'Beside a board, each classroom should have a large, long number line for teaching purposes, perhaps below the board, and at a level at which you and the children can touch it' (DfEE, 1999: 29). It is one of the central ideas of the 1999 curriculum guidance for England that children should be helped to build visual images of our number system, and the use of number lines is one way in which teachers are expected to do this. For Reception (age 4–5) and Year 1 (age 5–6) classes it was recommended that number tracks rather than number lines are used. In the former it is the spaces which are numbered, whereas in the latter the numbers appear on the lines. For a detailed discussion of number tracks and number lines see Iannone (2006). In early years classes there will usually be number tracks displayed around the walls showing numerals, often illustrated by pictures of a related number of objects.

Throughout a primary school 'washing lines' are to be found, like that shown in Figure 3.4, with a variety of different numerals pegged on them in some sort of sequence. In Reception (age 4–5) these might be 0–10, in Year 2 (age 6–7) 10, 20, 30, ..., 100, in Year 4 (age 8–9) –3, –2, –1, 0, 1, 2, 3, 4, and in Year 6 (age 10–11) the washing line may be used to show equivalence between fractions, decimals and percentages. Some classrooms will have number lines displayed on the walls, possibly below the whiteboard. There are also desk-top number lines in many classrooms,

Figure 3.4   Birthday card number line

with marked or unmarked intervals from 0 to 10, 20 or 100. All of these number tracks and lines are intended to help children develop a visual representation of the number system and can be used to aid calculation.

Empty number lines

Empty number lines have also been promoted in curriculum guidance and are often used by teachers to demonstrate a way of representing calculations, including addition. The empty number line originated in the Dutch Realistic Mathematics Education movement (RME). This movement has been so influential that it is worth saying something about it here. The development of RME in the Netherlands began in the 1970s and has been supported by a constant stream of research in Utrecht and elsewhere. The fundamental RME philosophy is largely due to Hans Freudenthal (1905–1990), who believed that mathematics should be connected to children's real and imagined worlds. Rather than viewing mathematics as a subject to be passively received by pupils, Freudenthal believed that mathematics lessons should offer them guided opportunities to 'reinvent' mathematics by doing it. For further details, see van den Heuvel-Panhuizen (2001).

The empty number line representation consists of a line on which can be written any numbers helpful in arriving at the solution to a calculation. It facilitates the use of counting strategies, providing a means of recording intermediate steps in the process. For example in the calculation 36 + 27, the 36 is written towards the left of the line. The 20 is then counted on in tens, recording 46 then 56 on the line, or in one jump going straight from 36 to 56. The remaining 7 may be counted on one at a time, 57, 58, ..., 63, or seen as 4 + 3 and counted 60, 63 (see Figure 3.5). The empty number line representation allows children to count on in jumps with which they are comfortable. A different, possibly more sophisticated, strategy for this calculation might be to count on 30, arriving at 66 on the line, and then to compensate by counting back 3 to arrive at 63 (see Figure 3.6). The empty number line has the flexibility to support any of these strategies.

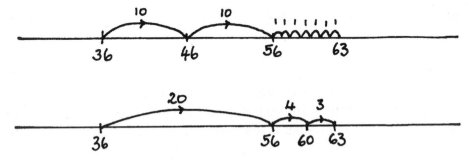

Figure 3.5   Empty number line representation of 36 + 27

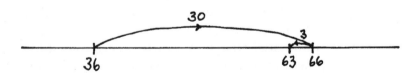

Figure 3.6   Empty number line representation of 36 + 27 using a compensation strategy

Empty number lines are also often used to record counting methods in subtraction. There are two different models of subtraction, which we discuss in some depth in Chapter 7. The model of subtraction being used will determine the form of the representation on an empty number line. To represent a 'take away' or 'change' model of subtraction, the number from which something is to be taken away (the minuend) would be written to the right of the line. Counts or jumps to the value of the number to be taken away (the subtrahend) would be recorded on the line, eventually arriving at the answer. For example, in the calculation 62 – 43, the 62 would be written to the right of the line. The 40 may then be counted backwards in tens recording 52, 42, 32, 22 written from right to left on the line. The

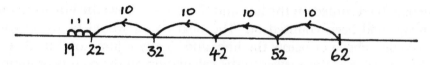

Figure 3.7   Empty number line representation of '62 take away 43'

remaining 3 to be taken away would then be counted back 21, 20, 19 to arrive at 19 as the answer to the calculation (see Figure 3.7).

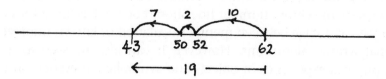

Figure 3.8   Empty number line representation of 'the difference between 62 and 43' – counting backwards

To represent a 'difference' or 'comparison' model of subtraction, the two numbers between which the difference is to be found would both be written on the line with the smaller to the left of the larger. The difference is found by recording how many it is necessary to count from one to the other. This may be done by counting backwards from the larger to the smaller, as in Figure 3.8, or forwards from the smaller to the larger as in Figure 3.9. Since people generally find it easier to count forwards than backwards the latter is usually the preferred strategy. As the counting takes place it is recorded by writing the number counted forwards or backwards above the line. Children are encouraged to count forwards or backwards to 'friendly numbers' – those numbers ending in zero.

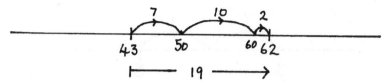

Figure 3.9   Empty number line representation of 'the difference between 62 and 43' – counting forwards

For example, in the calculation 62 – 43 this would be represented by starting at the 43 and counting to the next 'friendly' number of 50, the 50 would be recorded on the line and '7' written above the line to record how many had been counted on. The next count would be to 60 with '10' recorded above or below the line, and finally a jump of 2 made to reach 62. To arrive at the answer to the calculation all the counts or jumps have to be added together to give the total amount counted on: $7 + 10 + 2 = 19$.

Whether representing a 'take away' or a 'difference' conception of the subtraction $62 - 43$ the answer is the same, but the representation is very different. Norfolk County Council (2003) has produced a useful resource for understanding and using the empty number line. Curriculum guidance in the UK suggests the empty number line should be used as an 'informal jotting' and seen as a stage between mental calculation or known number facts and formal written algorithms. However, it can also be seen as a stage between physical experience of objects and symbolic representation in the formal algorithm since it represents counting strategies which can be related to real objects.

As demonstrated above with the two representations of subtraction, the way in which an empty number line is used will reflect particular conceptions of the calculation involved. It may also make some assumptions about children's prior knowledge. The addition $3 + 2$ may be represented on an empty number line as in Figure 3.10. The use of such a representation assumes that the learners are able to use the 'count on' strategy as they start at 3 and count on from there. This representation also suggests an *augmentation* model of addition – in which an amount is increased by a further amount – rather than an *aggregation* model in which two sets are combined. For a fuller discussion of these two models of addition, see Haylock (2006). Neither of these issues need be problematic, but it is important that when choosing to use such a representation the teacher is aware of and considers these issues.

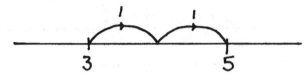

Figure 3.10   Empty number line representation of $3 + 2$

Hundred grids

The 'hundred grid' is another key resource recommended in the 1999 guidance: 'A large 100 square, displayed where children can touch it,

1	2	3	4	5	6	7	8	9	10
11	12	13	14	15	16	17	18	19	20
21	22	23	24	25	26	27	28	29	30
31	32	33	34	35	36	37	38	39	40
41	42	43	44	45	46	47	48	49	50
51	52	53	54	55	56	57	58	59	60
61	62	63	64	65	66	67	68	69	70
71	72	73	74	75	76	77	78	79	80
81	82	83	84	85	86	87	88	89	90
91	92	93	94	95	96	97	98	99	100

Figure 3.11   The 1–100 number grid

is essential in Years 2 to 4 for showing patterns such as 43 + 8, 43 + 18, 43 + 28, 43 + 38 ... or to illustrate addition or subtraction of two-digit numbers' (DfEE, 1999: 30). Though the curriculum guidance refers to Years 2–4 (age 6–9), such a resource may be found in any primary class-room. As well as existing as permanent objects in the classroom, hundred grids may also be produced for the lesson by the teacher on a whiteboard or blackboard or displayed on an interactive whiteboard. These hundred grids may be of two types; the more common 1–100 (see Figure 3.11), or the less common 0–99 (see Figure 3.12). Many mathematics educators would consider the latter to be a more useful representation since it not only includes the zero but also keeps all the tens, twenties, thirties, ... numbers in one row. For the details of this debate, see Pasternack (2003) and Thompson (2003b).

The discussion above described some of the resources that are found in primary classrooms to support the learning of mathematics. We have focused on those recommended in the 1999 curriculum guidance for England since these are commonly used. These resources are representa-tions which may be used in an enactive or an iconic way. We have also

0	1	2	3	4	5	6	7	8	9
10	11	12	13	14	15	16	17	18	19
20	21	22	23	24	25	26	27	28	29
30	31	32	33	34	35	36	37	38	39
40	41	42	43	44	45	46	47	48	49
50	51	52	53	54	55	56	57	58	59
60	61	62	63	64	65	66	67	68	69
70	71	72	73	74	75	76	77	78	79
80	81	82	83	84	85	86	87	88	89
90	91	92	93	94	95	96	97	98	99

Figure 3.12   The 0–99 number grid

introduced some of the debates within the mathematics education community surrounding their use. We hope that knowledge of these debates will aid you in making choices about representations to promote learning in mathematics.

Our observations of beginning teachers' use of representations in their mathematics teaching

In the student teachers' lessons that we videotaped, representations were often used to help form concepts or explain procedures. In many of the lessons we observed, the student teachers had chosen to use one particular representation rather than another to support the children's learning – for example, a hundred grid rather than a number line to demonstrate adding 10, and a pizza divided into 8 slices rather than 16 sweets divided into 8 equal groups to show an eighth. It is clear that some representations more closely reflect the concept or procedure that teachers are trying to convey than others and may help or hinder children's developing understanding of the ideas being taught. In addition, the previous knowledge or understanding required for the learner to make use of the representation must be taken into account. We now consider in some detail the use of representations in one of the mathematics lessons that we observed in our research.

Chloë's lesson

A lesson that we observed in which the choice of representation seemed to be a major issue was taught by Chloë to a Year 1/2 (age 5–7) class. Chloë had gained a good degree in geography and education before going on to the one-year PGCE course to gain qualified teacher status. At school she had gained top grades in biology, geography and history at A level. Chloë had gained a level of mathematics which exceeded the minimum requirement for entry into teacher education and was relatively confident in her own mathematical ability. In the lesson discussed here, Chloë makes much use of the hundred grid suggested in the 1999 curriculum guidance.

In the oral and mental starter Chloë asked a number of questions to test recall of the complements of 10 and 20. The children were asked questions in the form 'How many must I add to 17 to make 20?', 'How many more than 7 is 10?'. The children raised their hands to answer and Chloë chose individuals to respond. In the main activity, Chloë recapped work from the previous day which had been undertaken by the class teacher. This work involved adding 9, 11, 19 and 21 to numbers less than 100. She then asked a child to act as the teacher and explain to the class how this could be done. The child was asked to demonstrate using a 1–100 number grid. The procedure required was that to add 9 you can add 10 and subtract 1, and this was demonstrated by the child moving magnetic counters on the hundred grid (see Figure 3.13).

The child correctly showed that to *add* 9 the counter has to be moved down a row and back one square, to add 11 it must be moved down one row and forward one square, to add 19 the counter must be moved down two rows and back one square, and to add 21 it must be moved down two rows and forward one square.

Chloë went on to explain how to *subtract* 9, 11, 19 and 21 by subtracting 10 or 20 and adding or subtracting 1. She again demonstrated this, using counters on the hundred square. Here is a transcript of part of the lesson:

Chloë: First of all, who can tell me what you were doing yesterday when I wasn't here? What were Circles and Triangles doing? Circles and Triangles, someone from Circles and Triangles tell me what you were doing. Sam?

1	2	3	4	5	6	7	8	9	10
11	12	13	14	15	16	17	18	19	20
21	22	23	24	25	26	27	28	29	30
31	32	33	34	35	36	37	38	39	40
41	42	43	44	45	46	47	48	49	50
51	52	53	54	55	56	57	58	59	60
61	62	63	64	65	66	67	68	69	70
71	72	73	74	75	76	77	78	79	80
81	82	83	84	85	86	87	88	89	90
91	92	93	94	95	96	97	98	99	100

$\downarrow$ +10

$\leftarrow$ −1

Figure 3.13   Using the 1–100 number grid to calculate 38 + 9

Sam:	We were adding nine and adding eleven.
Chloë:	You were adding nine and adding eleven, and what were Squares and Rectangles doing? Rebecca?
Rebecca:	Adding nine and adding twentyone.
Chloë:	Adding nine, Rebecca?
Rebecca:	Nineteen.
Chloë:	Adding nineteen, well done. So I need a teacher from Circles and Triangles. Who thinks they can come up and explain how we add nine and how we add eleven? Uh, Ruth, do you think you can explain how we add nine and add eleven? Up you come, you're going to be the teacher. Now I've put this [1–100 number grid] up so if you need to use it. You stand on that side. Now this is your class. Tell them how you go about adding nine. Don't look at me, look at the class. Big loud voice.
Ruth:	You add ten, and then you, you take away *or* add one.
Chloë:	What do you do if you add nine? Do you take away or add?
Ruth:	Take away.
Chloë:	You take away. Can you show us on the board? Add nine to nine. OK, I'm going to put a red dot here [on 9], and show me how you add ten and take away one. Show the class how you add ten

and take away one on a hundred square. What's the easy way to add nine on a hundred square? Christopher.

Christopher: Go diagonally.

Chloë: Not diagonally. To add ten you just go …

Christopher: Down.

Chloë: Down. Shall we show everybody? Move your red. This is the counter that's going to move [places second counter on nine], so move your red counter down, one of the red counters down. So that adding ten gives us nineteen, and then what do we do Ruth for adding nine?

Ruth: Take away one.

Chloë: We take away one. And what's our answer, class?

Class: Eighteen.

Chloë: Well done, sit down. Right, today, some clever people I have already seen looking at the whiteboard [where the objectives for the lesson were written], we're subtracting nine and eleven and subtracting nineteen and twentyone. So, if we were to have seventy, for example. I've put my counter on seventy.

    [Chloë has a problem persuading the counter to stay in the right place.]

Chloë: Right, to subtract, thank you, Christopher, to subtract nineteen, who thinks, who thinks they know what we might do? Yeah.

Zara: We go up one.

Chloë: Don't tell me what we'd go up, tell me what we'd take away. Yeah.

Zara: You take away twenty …

Chloë: Aha …

Zara: And take away one.

Chloë: You take away twenty, you take away one. Not for nineteen. We take away twenty, which is fifty, and then we add one, because it was only nineteen we wanted to take away, so it actually becomes fiftyone. Let's count back and check that's right. So it's 1, 2, 3, …

Children: 4, 5, 6, 7, 8, 9, 10, 11, 12, 13, 14, 15, 16, 17, 18, 19.

Chloë: There you go, so to take away nineteen, you first of all take away twenty, and then add one. Right, there's seventy. How do you think I'd take away nine, what do you think I'd do to take away nine? What do I take away first of all? From seventy I want to take away nine. What will I do? Rebecca?

Rebecca:	Go up one.
Chloë:	No, don't tell me what I'm going to go up or move, tell me what I actually do, Rebecca.
Rebecca:	Take away one.
Chloë:	Take away one to take away nine? No. Remember when we added nine we added ten first of all, so what do you think we might take away here? Sam.
Sam:	Ten.
Chloë:	Take away ten, take away ten gives us sixty, and then what must we do when we're taking away? We're taking away nine here, so we're taking away ten and?
Sam:	Add one.
Chloë:	Add one. Which brings us to sixtyone. Right, let's write these rules on the whiteboard so we remember.

From the description and transcript above, you should have a good sense of what Chloë was trying to do in this lesson and how she went about it. If possible, discuss the following with a friend who has also read the transcript:

What are your first thoughts about the way Chloë uses the hundred grid to demonstrate a procedure for subtracting 9, 11, 19 and 21?

Why do you think Chloë chose to use the hundred grid?

What, if any, were the difficulties with this choice of representation?

What other representations might she have used? What would be the advantages of such representations?

Our reflections on Chloë's lesson

We would like to offer some ideas of our own about the way in which Chloë used the representation in this lesson. However, these reflections are not intended as answers to the questions above, but rather as ideas that you might consider alongside your own thoughts.

When assessing the effectiveness of a representation two questions that might be considered are:

- Does this representation helpfully illustrate the concepts or procedures being taught?

- Do the children have the prerequisite knowledge and understanding to make use of this representation?

To answer the first question we need to consider Chloë's objective for the lesson. The procedures for subtracting 9, 11, 19 and 21 that Chloë wanted the children to be able to use involved subtracting 10 or 20 and then making the appropriate adjustments for the fact that the subtrahend was one larger or smaller than 10 or 20. At first sight the hundred grid seems to offer a good representation for demonstrating the subtraction of 10 or 20 and adjusting. Because of the way in which the numbers are shown on the hundred grid it is possible to show addition and subtraction of multiples of 10 by vertical movements downwards or upwards and adjustments by horizontal movements to the right or left. To subtract 10 we simply move up one square, to subtract 20 move up two squares, or 30 up three squares, etc. If we have subtracted one too many (for 9 or 19) then we have to 'put one back' and move one space to the right. If we have not subtracted enough (for 11 or 21) we have to subtract a further one by moving one space to the left. The children demonstrated that they had previously learned how to use a hundred grid for adding 9, 11, 19 and 21; however there seemed to be some question about whether they had understood the ideas behind this and understood what was happening as they moved the counters about.

Chloë began the lesson by reviewing the previous lesson on adding 9, 11, 19 and 21. When asked 'how you go about adding 9', Ruth answered 'You add 10 then you take away *or* add 1' (emphasis added). She clearly has a problem in remembering, or working out, which way the adjustment should go. Chloë then rephrased the question to 'What's the easy way to add 9 on a hundred square?' Christopher's correct answer of 'go diagonally' was clearly not what Chloë wanted and she encouraged the children to explain the movement of the counter in two steps, along with explanations of what these steps meant.

When asked how they thought the hundred grid might be used for subtraction, some children showed that they were able to make the connection between addition and subtraction, even if they did not get all the procedures quite right. In order to subtract 19 from 70, Zara initially suggested 'We go up one'. Chloë responded that she did not want to be told 'what we'd go up' but rather 'what we'd take away'. Chloë did not comment that to 'take away 20' it was necessary to 'go up two' rather than one. Zara then offered 'you take away 20' which was greeted with an 'Aha' by Chloë. Zara's next contribution, 'And take away 1', demonstrated the difficulty she was having, knowing which way to move the counter in order to make the necessary compensation. Chloë corrected her on this but it seems likely that Zara, and other children in the class, would continue to have this difficulty.

Chloë seemed to be keen that the children did not simply learn a procedure – to add 9, go down one and one to the left – but were able to verbalise what is happening at each stage – add ten by going down one square then take off 1 by going 1 square to the left. Despite these good intentions, it is possible that this use of the hundred grid encouraged the children to focus on the spatial procedures in order to reach an answer and not think about what happened at each step. In response to being asked what to do in order to take away 9, Rebecca initially suggested 'go up one'. To Chloë's request that Rebecca tell her 'what I am going to go up or move', Rebecca responded 'Take away 1'. It seems she was confusing the number of rows to be moved with the value of what was being taken away.

To successfully use the hundred grid as a tool for addition and subtraction of near-multiples of 10, the children needed to remember four different sequences of procedures. They also needed to remember which procedure goes with which type of calculation. This is clearly difficult, especially if the children lack understanding of why various movements have the required

September						
Sun	Mon	Tues	Wed	Thurs	Fri	Sat
		1	2	3	4	5
6	7	8	9	10	11	12
13	14	15	16	17	18	19
20	21	22	23	24	25	26
27	28	29	30			

Nine days before – 14th	**One row back and one to right – 17th**

Figure 3.14   A calendar: 23rd September and subtract 9

effect. It is not surprising that Chloë felt the need to write out the rules for each type of procedure, with an example for each, as a memory aid.

The procedures for adding and subtracting near-multiples of 10, described above, only work because of the particular way in which the hundred grid is laid out and would not work for other arrangements. A grid with which children might be familiar is the calendar (Figure 3.14). Using the procedure Chloë taught for subtracting 9 – where you move up one row and then one square to the right on the hundred grid – would clearly not work on the calendar!

The second question that we have suggested should be asked when considering the effectiveness of a particular representation relates to the previous knowledge and understanding of the learners. It may be argued that, in order for the children to understand the procedures taught in Chloë's lesson, it was a prerequisite that they understood why the layout of a hundred grid facilitated the addition of tens and near-tens. They might have previously explored what happens when 10 is counted on from any number on the grid and discovered that the number below is reached. Activities which lead children to see the pattern of tens and units digits in each of the columns may have helped them to understand the effects of vertical and horizontal movements around the grid. Pupils might have done 'jigsaw' activities with hundred grids to develop their understanding of how it is made up. We do not know whether these children had had such experiences. If they had, then they would have been more likely to be able to make the most of this representation. Chloë demonstrated that she was keen that the children understood the effects of each move of the counter on the grid. However, the nature of the hundred grid meant that the connection between operations such as adding 10 or 1 and the procedures used to give the correct answer may have been hidden.

Chloë's use of the hundred grid encouraged the children to focus on procedures for answering addition and subtraction calculations rather than on understanding the idea of rounding and adjustment. We suggest that even if the children were able to remember all four procedures addressed, they would have gained only a procedural rather than a conceptual understanding of the idea of rounding and adjustment. In Chapter 2 we introduced the four dimensions of the Knowledge Quartet and suggested that the *foundation* dimension, which is concerned with teachers' theoretical knowledge and beliefs, underpins the other three dimensions. The 'concentration on procedures', seen here in Chloë's teaching, is one of the ways in which student teachers' foundation knowledge was seen to be demonstrated through their teaching. It suggests an underlying belief about mathematics as being largely a series of facts and procedures to be learned. Though Chloë did want the children to know what happened at each step in the procedures, she seemed to concentrate on the children being able to carry out these procedures rather than on building an understanding of rounding and adjusting as a helpful way of carrying out some calculations.

The hundred grid therefore is seen to be somewhat problematic as an aid to learning about adding 9, 11, 19 and 21, and we should consider what other representations could have been used. The hundred grid is a number track that has been cut into sections of ten numbers and these sections placed under one another. Would there be any advantage or otherwise, for the purpose of teaching addition and subtraction of 9, 11, 19 and 21, in leaving the number track intact? It would certainly need to stretch over a greater distance, and it may not be possible for all the numbers from 1 to 100 to be visible to the whole class at once. However, when demonstrating addition of 9 it might be helpful to show a movement of ten steps forward

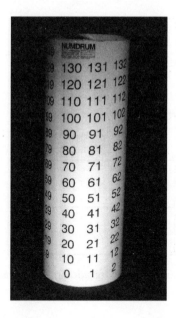

Figure 3.15   Numdrum

then one step back in the opposite direction. When adding 11 it would be clear that a movement of ten steps forward is followed by a further step in the same direction. Similarly, for subtraction of 9 and 11 it could be demonstrated that a jump of ten steps backwards is followed by a step forwards to compensate for having moved too far back, or a further step backwards to account for the eleventh step. Though these may still be thought of as procedures, the connection with rounding and compensation is more 'visible' than in the hundred square where this is hidden by the layout. Another representation that would allow these adjustments to be seen more clearly is J.T. Harrison's 'Numdrum' shown in Figure 3.15. This consists of a number line from 1 to 100 that has been spiralled around a cylinder and so allows continuous counting forwards or backwards but also keeps numbers ending in the same digit in columns, allowing jumps of 10 up and down the grid. For information about the Numdrum, see http://www.numdrum.com.

Chloë's choice of examples, which is discussed further in Chapter 4, did not help when trying to demonstrate using the hundred grid for subtraction. By choosing 70 as a starting number from which to subtract both 19 and then 9, she was unable to easily show the compensation by moving forward one square since the 51 and 61 were on the next rows to the

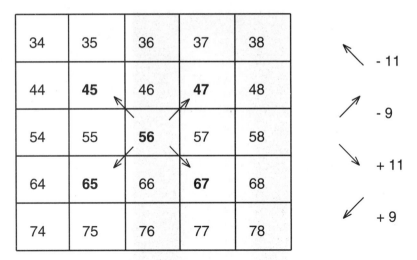

Figure 3.16   Moves on a hundred grid for adding or subtracting 9 or 11 to or from 56

50 and 60. This required movement all the way left across the board. A number track would not have allowed the diagonal move suggested by Christopher, so forcing children to consider each step of the procedure in turn. The hundred grid allows four diagonal moves for the addition or subtraction of 9 or 11 (see Figure 3.16).

However, if these moves are simply learned as procedures the learner would have no way of working out such calculations when the support of the hundred grid is not available. Perhaps after some initial experience with a number track, and after the children had understood the effect of the forwards and backwards movements, it would be helpful to move on to a hundred grid. Provided the children understood the way the hundred grid was formed, diagonal movements could be investigated and explained by connecting them with what happens on a number track.

We have considered the way in which Chloë used the hundred grid in her lesson in some detail. The intention behind this is to provide a way of thinking about your own choices of representations and the way in which you use them when planning your lessons. It is worth asking the two questions we asked about Chloë's choice of representation when planning and reviewing your own teaching:

- Does the representation I have chosen to use helpfully reflect the concepts and/or procedures I want the children to learn?

- Do the children have the prerequisite knowledge and understanding needed to make use of this representation?

Summary

In this chapter we have focused on the use of representations in teaching primary mathematics. We began by introducing Bruner's ideas of enactive, iconic and symbolic modes of learning in relation to the use of representations in mathematics teaching. When planning your teaching, consider how different representations act as 'scaffolds' between concrete (enactive) experience and the abstract (symbolic) recording used in mathematics. Will the children you are teaching benefit from could further concrete experience before or in conjunction with the representations? Could they use abstract symbolic representation and, if so, how can you help them make the connections with supporting pictorial or iconic representations? We have considered a number of objects that are used as representations in primary mathematics and suggested that their use should be evaluated critically. We introduced some of the debates surrounding the use of common teaching resources and suggested that considerable thought should go into the choice of these representations. We focused on a number of iconic representations that are commonly used in English primary classrooms, and finally we discussed in detail how we had seen one of these forms being used.

In order for you to make good choices about representations, you will need to know what is available and how these might be used. It is not our intention to try to give a definitive list of such representations here. That would not be possible. You will become familiar with different ways of representing mathematical procedures and understandings through your taught courses and through your experience in classrooms. You may even develop some original ones of your own! We hope that this chapter will help you recognise the role of certain resources in mathematics teaching and learning, and give you a framework for evaluating their effectiveness as representations in your teaching. When evaluating your lessons you might think about how well the representations you used reflected the ideas that you were trying to teach and whether the children had the prerequisite knowledge and understanding to make use of these representations.

(Continued)

(Continued)

In Chapter 8 we cite a number of examples of lessons that we observed during our research. We suggest that you use these to think about the ideas we developed in the Knowledge Quartet framework and have put forward in this book. One aspect of this would be to think about the teacher's use of representation in these lessons.

Further reading

Jerome Bruner (1974) 'Representation in childhood', in *Beyond the Information Given*. London: George Allen & Unwin.

> Though not always 'easy', it is a good idea where possible, to read original work that is often quoted in the educational literature. In this essay, Bruner explains his three forms of representation and discusses how they relate to cognitive development. As well as the theoretical perspective, a number of experiments are described indicating how forms of representation affect children's ability to carry out tasks. Reading this section of Bruner's book will give you further insight into the role of representations used in mathematics teaching.

Marja van den Heuvel-Panhuizen (2001) 'Realistic mathematics education in the Netherlands', in J. Anghileri (ed.), *Principles and Practices in Arithmetic Teaching: Innovative Approaches for the Primary Classroom* (pp. 49–63). Buckingham: Open University Press.

> The empty number line representation is widely used in the UK and elsewhere to aid calculation. It originated in the RME movement in the Netherlands. In this chapter, a leading Dutch educator explains the principles behind RME and how these have determined the Dutch mathematics curriculum. The rest of this book contains other valuable insights into 'innovative approaches' to teaching primary mathematics. These insights include not only descriptions of the approaches but also, importantly, the rationale behind them. The ways in which the mathematics is represented are an important consideration in the approaches discussed.

Doreen Drews and Alice Hansen (eds) (2007) *Using Resources to Support Mathematical Thinking: Primary and Early Years*. Exeter: Learning Matters.

> This is one of a series of 'practical handbooks' for teachers published by Learning Matters. In this book, a wider range of resources are considered than is possible in our chapter on the use of representations. Case studies are used to consider the way different resources facilitate learning. You might think about the use of resources discussed in these case studies in the light of ideas we have suggested in our chapter.

Transformation: Using Examples in Mathematics Teaching

> **In this chapter you will read about:**
>
> - the role of examples in the learning of mathematics;
> - ways of using examples in mathematics teaching;
> - how teachers sometimes choose unhelpful examples, and why;
> - considerations to guide your choice of mathematical examples.

In Chapter 3 we focused on one aspect of the transformation dimension of the Knowledge Quartet – the ways in which teachers use various resources to *represent* mathematical ideas in order to make them accessible to children. In this chapter we will consider in depth another key aspect of the same transformation dimension: the ways in which teachers *choose and use examples* in mathematics teaching.

If you were going to introduce line symmetry (sometimes called 'reflective' symmetry) to a Year 3 (age 7–8) class, how would you begin? Most likely, you would have some pictures of things with line symmetry (such as those in Figure 4.1 – a butterfly, a house, a bridge reflected in a river) to show the class. They might be posters, or computer images, or something you have drawn.

Of course, when you stop and apply your mathematics subject-matter knowledge, you would realise that these examples are all two-dimensional

Figure 4.1   Examples of line symmetry in the environment

representations of three-dimensional objects. As such, the pictures in Figure 4.1 have line symmetry, although the things they represent do not. The corresponding three-dimensional analogue of a line of symmetry is a plane of symmetry (like a wall running through the middle of a house, from front to back). That need not stop you using these pictures, but it might alert you to the questions (and even misconceptions) that could arise from them.

If you were going to teach the strategy of adding 9 by 'compensation' – as we saw Chloë doing in Chapter 3 – how would you begin? The strategy being taught was 'add 10 and then subtract 1'. Most likely you would begin by talking with the children about adding 9 to … well, 16, for example. Why did we choose 16? What would you choose? What would be a good choice, what numbers would be best avoided? Would 1 be a good starting number, or 20, or 97? In each of these cases, there are reasons for suggesting that they would not be good choices. With 97, for example, there would be a complication in using the 'add 10, subtract 1' strategy, because of the shift from two-digit to three-digit numbers. Rather, it might develop the child's number sense to suggest instead adding 3, then adding 6. This more flexible approach – 'bridging' through the next multiple of 10 into the hundreds – brings out the proximity of 97 to 100.

In any case, you have to choose *something* – what will it be? And the next, and the next?

When teachers teach mathematics, they use examples like this all the time to 'make their point'. Surprisingly, perhaps, some beginning teachers do not always see the value of this. Quite a few lesson plans begin by introducing the focus of the lesson with 'Ask the class: what is a …?'. Thus 'What is a rectangle?', 'What is multiplication?', 'What is a fraction?', 'What is symmetry?', and even 'What is time?'. A reasonable answer to the last of these would be 'I don't know, but Stephen Hawking is working on it!'.

The 'What is …?' question essentially asks for a *definition* of the concept in question. Definitions are typically the starting points for the development of topics in university mathematics, and some people even doubt whether that is a good idea. But, as a rule, definitions are not where learners begin in school mathematics. We return to this issue in Chapter 5, and a beginning teacher who *did* ask his class 'What is a fraction?'.

Rather than ask for the definition of a rectangle, it is more helpful to show a variety of shapes to pupils, and to ask which ones are examples of rectangles, and which are not. Eventually that might well lead to discussions about *why* some are and others are not – the square is the classic pivotal case – and so lead us to the defining qualities of a rectangle. Another very fruitful approach is to invite pupils to sketch an example of a rectangle, and another, and another … and one that is, in some way different from your last one, and so on. Some possibilities are shown in Figure 4.2. This teases out the range of things that children would count as rectangles, and what they feel that they can allow to vary while retaining a rectangle. Does anyone draw a square? You can read more about this approach to 'learner-generated' examples in Watson and Mason (2005).

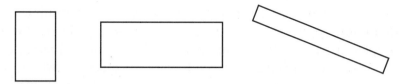

Figure 4.2   An example of a rectangle, and another, and another …

The fact that a square is a rectangle presents a problem when we want to refer to a rectangle that is not a square. One way is to use the word 'oblong'. Although this is not strictly a mathematical word, its use emphasises the fact that 'rectangle' includes squares and oblongs.

Ways of using examples

In order to teach something, we often provide pupils (or ask them to provide) examples of the thing to be learnt. The 'thing' is *general* in character (e.g. the notion of line symmetry, or some strategy or procedure for subtraction); the examples are *particular* instances of the generality. Teachers frequently use examples in mathematics teaching in two ways. The first is to do with teaching mathematical concepts and procedures. The second is the provision of exercises for children. We will say more about these uses in this section.

There are two additional uses of examples, as counterexamples and generic examples, which we will explain towards the end of this chapter. These are important, but our data suggests that they are less evident in primary classroom practice.

Teaching concepts and procedures

The rectangle example was an example (we can't avoid it! – our writing, in its own way, is a form of teaching) of *teaching a concept*. The notion 'rectangle' is an abstract one, captured by a definition such as 'a shape with four sides and four right angles'. You might think about the adequacy of this definition, and about alternative definitions. For example, it is sufficient to say that there are three right angles, but you might think that rather strange and artificial. Should we have said that the shape was 'planar' (two-dimensional) or that the sides were straight lines?

In any case, as we remarked earlier, it is better to begin from examples rather than a definition. So, if the target concept were 'factor', you would want to find examples of pairs of whole numbers such that one is a factor of the other, like 7 and 21. You would do well to vary the quotient (which is 3 in this instance): for example, it would not be good if, in every example, one number were double the other, because that would imply a restricted notion of 'factor'. Nor would it be helpful to include the pair 7 and 133 as an introductory example, because the effort to determine whether 7 divides into 133 'exactly' might get in the way. On the other hand, the same example might be ideal as an assessment or practice exercise.

Similarly, we *teach a general procedure* by a particular demonstration of that procedure. For example, as we said earlier, if we were going to teach the compensation strategy for adding 9, we would choose a starting number and then add 9 to it, using the 'add 10 and subtract 1' strategy. If we set out to teach the 'grid method' for multiplication (see Chapter 5 for details) for, say, a two-digit by two-digit product, we would choose two two-digit numbers, and multiply them using the grid method. Typically, if we want pupils to see *why* it works, we build in a kind of commentary with the demonstration, to explain what is going on, and draw attention to potential difficulties and pitfalls. Presumably you wouldn't choose, for example, 10×20. Maybe some other 'bad' demonstration examples come to mind.

In recent times, Eddie Gray and David Tall (1994) have pointed out that the learning of concepts and the learning of procedures are not completely different dimensions of mathematics learning. Many concepts grow out of familiarity with a procedure. They capture this duality in the word *procept*: a procept is both an abstract mathematical 'thing', or concept, and also a procedure intimately associated with the concept. Gray and Tall's examples include 'addition' as a procept, which is both doing addition – associated with the verb 'to add' – and addition as a 'thing', and therefore a noun. So if someone says 'I'm good at addition', they refer to a concept, a particular operation on numbers. At the same time, their understanding of what addition is, and their belief that they are good at it, will almost certainly be conditioned by their experience of adding numbers.

In the same spirit, we offer 'mean' as an exemplary procept. The word 'mean' (informally, the average) captures the concept of a number somewhere in the middle of a set of numbers, and therefore often used to represent the whole set. It is difficult to separate that concept from the process of adding the numbers in the set and dividing by the size of the set.

Our point here is that exemplifying a procedure frequently paves the way for the acquisition of a concept, and that the distinction between procedure and concept is not clear-cut. You can read more about procepts in Gray (1997).

The provision of exercises

The second use of examples in teaching is usually directed towards familiarisation and practice, *after* a new idea or method has been introduced. Examples in this instance are often called 'exercises'. Exercises *are* examples, usually selected from a wide range of possible such examples. Suppose you had taught the two-digit grid multiplication procedure (see above) to a class. After your introduction, you might well want them to do ten or so exercises in their group work, and maybe a few more for homework – to assist retention of the procedure by repetition, then to develop fluency with it. Such exercises are also, often, a means of assessment, from the teacher's perspective. Practice does not need to be drudgery: sometimes it can lead to different kinds of awareness and understanding. Again, the selection of such examples by teachers is neither trivial nor arbitrary. In the case of the grid multiplication, it may come as a surprise to realise that there are about 4000 possible examples from which to choose. Why choose some of them in preference to others?

The use of introductory or 'demonstration' examples, and the subsequent provision of exercises for practice, relate to the teaching of both concepts and procedures. These concepts and procedures are aspects of the 'content' of mathematics, or what Shulman calls the 'substantive' dimension of subject-matter knowledge. There are two further uses of examples in teaching – counterexamples and generic examples – that have more to do with general patterns of mathematical reasoning. They relate to the 'process' of mathematics more than to content. Shulman calls this the 'syntactic' dimension of subject-matter knowledge, a term coined earlier by Joseph Schwab. Later in this chapter, we will have more to say about the nature of counterexamples and generic examples, and how they are used in mathematics teaching.

To sum up, our main point here is that examples are used all the time in mathematics teaching, and for several different reasons. But whatever the purpose for which they are being used, the examples provided by a teacher ought, ideally, to be the outcome of a careful process of *choice*, a *deliberate* and informed selection from the available options, because some are simply 'better' than others. We have already hinted at this and why it is so. We shall move now to some lessons, looking carefully at the teacher's choice of examples.

Examples from student teachers' lessons

Naomi's choice of examples

By way of illustration, we return to Naomi's lesson on subtraction. You were introduced to Naomi and her Year 1 class in Chapter 1. The episode below can be viewed on the companion website (Clip 2).

Naomi's oral and mental starter was about number bonds to 10, such as 7 + 3 and 1 + 9. Recall that Naomi chose individual children to answer questions such as 'If we have 9, how many more to make 10?'. Naomi's sequence of starting numbers was 8, 5, 7, 4, 10, 8, 2, 1, 7, 3.

> Before reading our comments below, look carefully at Naomi's sequence. Do you think she picked the numbers 8, 5, ... at random? If not, can you detect any reason why they might be in that order? What numbers would you choose for this activity, and in what order?

This looks almost random, but we suggest that it is a very well-chosen sequence, for the following reasons. Young children tend to solve these questions by counting up to 10 from the given number – as Owen evidently did for his turn, starting from 2. The first and third numbers (8 and 7) are themselves close to 10, and require little or no counting to arrive at the answer. Therefore the pupils can focus on the strategy without getting bogged down by the count. The 5 brings into play a well-known double – doubling being a strategy for mental calculation that should be emphasised and reinforced in the early years of schooling. The choice of 4 is more puzzling, but, watching the videotape, it seemed to be tailored to one of the more fluent children, who rapidly answered correctly. The case of 10 might be called degenerate – it feels a bit odd, with no counting necessary. Nevertheless, it brings to the surface the fact that 0 is a number, and that it can be added to 10 to make 10. One wonders, at first, why Naomi then returned to 8. The child (Bill) rapidly answers '2'. Naomi's game-plan becomes clearer when she then selects the number for the next child, Owen. Her interaction with the pupils proceeds as follows:

Naomi: Owen. Two.

[12-second pause while Owen counts his fingers]

Naomi: I've got two. How many more to make ten?

Owen: [six seconds later] Eight.

Naomi: Good boy. [addressing the next child] One.

Child: [after 7 seconds of fluent finger counting] Nine.

Naomi: Good. Owen, what did you notice ... what did you say makes ten?

Owen: Um ... four ...

Naomi: You said two add eight. Bill, what did you say? I gave you eight.

Bill: [inaudible]

Naomi: Eight and two, two and eight, it's the same thing.

Naomi's reason for giving the child after Owen the number 1 is not imme-diately clear. It could be justified in terms of 'one less, one more', but Naomi does not draw out this relationship. Instead, Naomi returns to Owen, to ask whether he had noticed the last but one question and Bill's answer, adding '8 and two, two and 8, it's the same thing'. In effect, she is drawing their attention to the fact that if Owen had listened carefully to Bill's answer, he would not have needed to count up from 2 when it came to his turn. She is drawing out a key connection between their two ques-tions and their answers. The mathematical relationship can be stated as: addition is *commutative*. Her example is: if you add 2 to 8 and 8 to 2, you get the same answer. It underpins a key addition strategy involving count-ing – start from the *larger* of the two numbers, and count up. This strategy 'works' *because* addition is commutative. The point she is trying to make when she asks 'Owen, what did you notice?' unfortunately loses some of its punch because Owen has already forgotten his answer.

Nevertheless, we can see some design, some deliberate choices, in the sequence of examples that Naomi gives the children as they pass round the number bond hat. Her choice of examples:

- was at first 'graded', including 8 and 7;

- invoked recall of a double;

- included later the unusual, degenerate case of 10 add 0;

- highlighted a key structural property of addition – commutativity. In fact, she drew attention to this property yet again in her final choice of 7, then 3, and in her comments about this pair of examples.

By contrast with Naomi's deliberate and purposeful choice of examples here, our lesson videotapes show numerous instances of *examples being ran-domly generated*, typically by dice in a number of situations. In fact, Naomi herself uses dice to generate 'difference' examples in her plenary discussion.

At one point, Naomi rolls 3 and 6 on the two dice. Jim appears to have the answer:

Naomi: Who can do this one for me? What's the difference between three and six? [Jim who was sitting quietly] come and tell us.

Jim: Three.

We would say that this randomly generated example, $6 - 3 = 3$, is one that *obscures the role of the variables* inherent in the problem. In this case, 3 is both the subtrahend *and* the difference. (We will explain in more detail what we mean by this expression later in this chapter.) It actually became clear, a little later, that Jim, who seemed to have the answer to Naomi's difference question, was just restating the first of the two numbers with the intention of *adding* the second to it. This will happen when the choice of examples is left to the dice. As the tape runs out, Naomi is asking the class for the difference between 4 and 2. We observed examples that obscured the role of variables in several of the videotaped lessons.

Laura's choice of examples in a lesson about multiplication

Laura was another of the pre-service teacher training (PGCE) students who participated in our research. She chose to specialise in the 'upper primary' years, Key Stage 2 in effect. Her first degree was in political science and international studies. She had last studied mathematics six years before the PGCE. On her school-based placement, she was teaching a Year 5 (age 9–10) class. In keeping with the school policy, her class had been 'setted by ability' with another Year 5 class, and Laura taught the 'middle ability' set, with 18 pupils: 10 boys and 8 girls.

The episode below can be viewed online on the companion website (Clip 3). Looking at the video pictures, we can see a bright classroom, with computers in view and a whiteboard placed on a stand behind the chair where Laura sits as the lesson begins. The main focus of the lesson is on teaching column multiplication of whole numbers, specifically multiplying a two-digit number by a single-digit number. Laura's planning is strongly influenced by the official curriculum guidance (DfEE, 1999). Here is a description of the lesson – an overview of what happened. Later, we shall examine parts of the lesson in some detail.

After Laura has settled the class on the carpet in front of her, the lesson begins with a three-minute oral and mental starter in which they practise recall of multiplication bonds, specifically 9×4, 5×12, 5×9, 8×7, 6×3, 7×4, 4×7. For each one, she targets a pair of children who stand, and have five seconds to answer. The mood is competitive, but relaxed. The pupils' recall is good, if not always rapid.

There follows a 15-minute introduction to the main activity. Laura reminds the class that they have recently been working on multiplication using the 'grid' method. She talks about the tens and units being 'partitioned off'. One pupil, Simon, is invited to the whiteboard to demonstrate the method for 9×37. His recording of the method is shown in Figure 4.3.

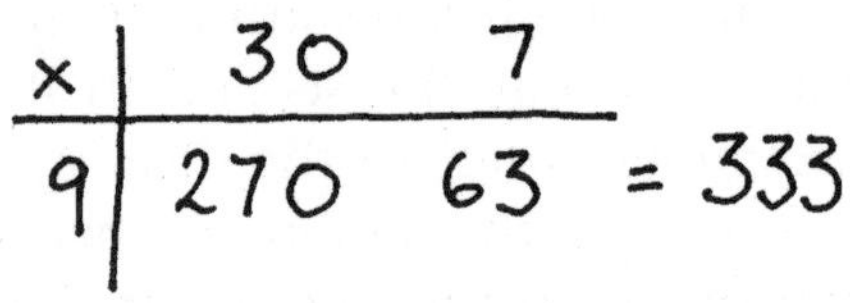

$$
\begin{array}{c|cc}
\times & 30 & 7 \\
\hline
9 & 270 & 63 \\
\end{array} = 333
$$

Figure 4.3   Simon finds 9×37 using the grid method

Simon performs the addition $270 + 63 = 333$ mentally. Laura then says that they are going to 'learn another way'. She proceeds to write the calculation for 9×37 on the whiteboard in a conventional but elaborated column format, shown in Figure 4.4, explaining as she goes along. The sum $270 + 63$ is calculated in the traditional way, adding from the right, 'carrying' the 1 (from $7 + 6 = 13$) into the hundreds column. Laura writes the headings h, t, u above the three columns.

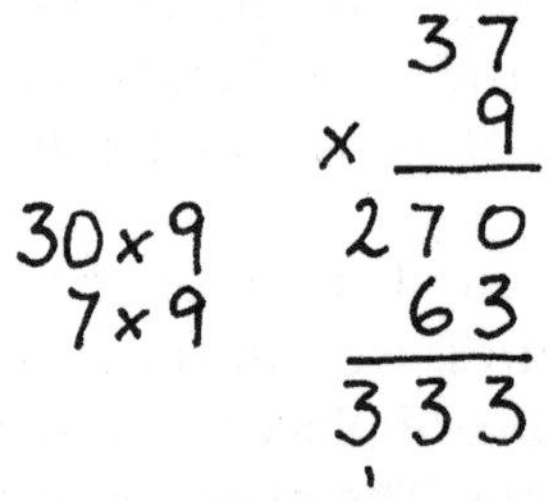

$$
\begin{array}{cr}
 & 37 \\
 & \times \quad 9 \\
\hline
30 \times 9 & 270 \\
7 \times 9 & 63 \\
\hline
 & 333 \\
\end{array}
$$

Figure 4.4   Laura demonstrates the elaborated column multiplication method

One boy, Tom, says that they should have estimated 37×9 before carrying out the calculation. Laura praises him, and picks up the suggestion a few minutes later, when she takes 49×8 as her second example for demonstration. When she asks the children to estimate the answer, one child proposes 400, saying that 8×50 is 400. Laura says that she could make this 'even more accurate' by making an adjustment to this estimate, although her mind goes blank momentarily. Laura proceeds to show how to 'set out' 49×8 in the new format, followed by the first question of the exercises to follow. When demonstrating 19×4 (the first exercise question), she remembers to ask for an estimate first. Bethany says that she would 'Do 10 times 4 is 40, and then 9 times 4 is 36'. Laura replies 'OK, you were right to do it that way, but I'd do 20 times 4'.

For the next 24 minutes, the class works on exercises that Laura has displayed on the wall. The eight exercises that all pupils are expected to complete are:

$$19 \times 4, \ 27 \times 9, \ 42 \times 4, \ 23 \times 6, \ 37 \times 5, \ 54 \times 4, \ 63 \times 7, \ 93 \times 6$$

There are also six more questions displayed, labelled 'extension':

$$99 \times 9, \ 88 \times 3, \ 76 \times 8, \ 62 \times 43, \ 55 \times 92, \ 42 \times 15$$

Within the lesson, none of the children reaches the extension questions. Laura moves from one child to another to see how they are getting on, helping where she judges assistance to be needed. She emphasises the importance of lining up the hundreds, tens and units columns carefully, and reminds them to estimate first.

Eventually, she tells them to stop and calls them together on the carpet for an eight-minute plenary. She begins this by asking them which of the two methods (the grid method and the 'new' method) they found easier. She then asks one boy, Sean, to demonstrate the new method with the example 27×9. Sean gets into difficulty; he writes 27 and $\times 9$ in the first two rows as expected, but then writes 20×7 and 2×9 to the left in the rows below. Sean is corrected by other pupils and by Laura herself. As the lesson concludes, Laura tells the children that they should complete the set of exercises for homework.

Thinking about Laura's choice and use of examples

You should now have a good sense of what Laura was trying to achieve in her lesson, how she intended to go about it, and how things turned out. The lesson might remind you of one that you have observed before, or one that you have taught yourself, in some respects.

Now you are ready to do some thinking about Laura's lesson. We would like you to focus on the examples she chose, and how she used them. As usual, you can do this on your own, but, if possible, discuss the lesson with a friend, colleague, another student or small group of students, according to your circumstances. As before, have something ready to write on.

Think and talk about the examples that Laura chose. These arose as:

- exercises (9×4, 5×12, 5×9, 8×7, 6×3, 7×4, 4×7) to revisit and assess recall of multiplication facts in the *oral and mental starter*;
- an example (9×37) to revisit the grid method and then to demonstrate column multiplication;
- a second example (49×8) to demonstrate column multiplication;
- exercises displayed on the wall for column multiplication (19×4, 27×9, 42×4, 23×6, 37×5, 54×4, 63×7, 93×6, with 99×9, 88×3, 76×8, 62×43, 55×92, 42×15 as 'extension' exercises);
- an example (27×9) for the concluding plenary phase of the lesson.

Look at them carefully. Why did she choose these particular examples, do you think? What 'job' were the examples intended to do? In other words, what did Laura want the pupils to learn, and how would seeing and doing these examples help them to learn it? There might be several answers to those questions. Bearing in mind your answers, ask yourself whether the examples that Laura chose were likely to do the job that she intended.

What might have been alternative examples? How many options (examples of two-digit by one-digit multiplication) are there? Would any be obviously poor examples in this lesson? Which ones would you choose, and why?

Having thought this through, you could imagine that you are Laura's friend, or her mentor, and that she is expecting you to offer her some comments on the lesson. If you wanted to focus discussion on the examples used in the lesson, what would you say? Keep in mind that only Laura knows why she chose those examples. So, in your discussion with her, even if you were Laura's mentor, it would be respectful and very sensible to begin by probing her reasons for choosing what she chose, rather than telling her which examples seemed well chosen, or otherwise, to you.

Make a note of anything that your reflections and discussion have particularly highlighted for you about the choice and use of examples in mathematics teaching. Perhaps something to keep in mind when you prepare a lesson in the future.

Some reflections on Laura's choice of examples

As we did in some of the earlier chapters, we now want to offer some ideas of our own about the examples that Laura chose in her lesson. As we have emphasised before, although we have thought carefully about Laura's lesson, these are not in any sense the answers to our earlier questions. Here are just a few things that struck us.

In her oral and mental starter, Laura is assessing, and the pupils rehearsing, recall of multiplication facts. She finishes with 7×4 and 4×7, both 28 of course. This brings to mind Naomi's reference to commutativity. Both addition and multiplication are commutative, although Laura does not draw attention to the connection between the two questions. The appropriateness of including the second item, 5×12, attracts strong feelings on both sides. Should pupils learn the 11-times and 12-times tables any more? Rapid recall of multiples of 12 was desirable when imperial units were in common use (12 pence in a shilling, 12 inches in a foot). For this reason, presumably, it does not feature in the official curriculum guidance (DfEE, 1999), where the relevant objective – even for Year 6 (age 10–11) – is knowing products to 10×10 'by heart'. However, suppliers continue to manufacture wall-charts with the 11- and 12-times tables, and it takes a thoughtful appeal to *foundation* knowledge to shift this topic from the domain of 'known facts' (known and remembered) to that of 'derived facts' (that can be worked out when they are needed). As it turned out, in the lesson, 5×12 defeats the two chosen contestants, both boys, who gave the answers 50, 51, 54. Laura offered the same question to a girl at the side of the class, who gave the correct answer.

Laura's first example as she demonstrates column multiplication is 37×9. This works well in the sense that there is nothing special or unusual about it, although even that could be questioned – in the pursuit of number sense, it could be remarked that 9 is conveniently close to 10, and so $37 \times 9 = 370 - 37 = 333$, using a 'compensation' strategy. In any case, it is the *same* example that was used a few minutes earlier, when Simon reminded the class about their earlier use of the grid method for multiplication. This gives Laura the opportunity, and the possibility, of showing the children how the two methods are related. Specifically, that 37 is partitioned in the same way in both methods, the same partial products (30×9 and 7×9) are involved, and the same sum ($270 + 63$). We will pick up this point again when we focus on *connection* in the next chapter.

Laura then goes on to work through 49×8 and 19×4. The official curriculum guidance (DfEE, 1999) emphasises the importance of *mental* methods, where possible, and also the importance of choosing the most suitable strategy for any particular calculation. Now 49×8 can be *performed more efficiently by a mental method* – by rounding up the 49 to 50, multiplying by 8, and then compensating (subtracting 8), i.e. $49 \times 8 = (50 \times 8) - 8$. Perhaps Laura even had this in mind in her effort to make the estimate of 400 'even more accurate', although her mind went blank. The video shows that she actually subtracted 100 at that point, instead of subtracting 8.

In the comfort of our own security, we can say that the subtraction that Laura made ($400 - 100$) is not a *logical* one. At the same time, it is important to point out, first, that many – probably most – teachers will tell you that they have had the same uncomfortable experience at some time when teaching mathematics, and that this is not a sign of weakness. It can happen, though mercifully rarely, when we invite and respond to children's mathematical ideas. We call these *contingent* moments, and examine contingency in more detail in Chapter 6. Despite the existence of a little book of the same name, you cannot 'bluff your way' in mathematics! In this sense, mathematics can be likened to performance art such as jazz improvisation or stand-up comedy, in that you have to expect the unexpected. Secondly, we note that Laura recognises that something is wrong, and bravely points it out to the children, which is exactly what such a situation requires.

In fact, a similar comment to that above – about a mental method being the first resort – could be made about 19×4, which is $(20 \times 4) - 4$. The curriculum guidance (DfEE, 1999) also makes much of doubling strategies, and 19×4 could be a double-double: $19 \rightarrow 38 \rightarrow 76$. In any case, to carry out these calculations by column multiplication may give a confused message about selecting 'sensible' strategies. On the other hand, there is an alternative way of looking at Laura's choice of 49×8, which is that the answer to the column multiplication is easily checked mentally, and so it can be verified that the new written method 'works' – for this example, at least.

Her choice of exercises – the practice examples – is also interesting. The sequence is 19×4, 27×9, 42×4, 23×6, 37×5, 54×4, 63×7, 93×6, with 99×9, 88×3, 76×8, 62×43, 55×92, 42×15 as 'extension' exercises. The exercise problems were presented horizontally, as 19×4, as opposed to writing 19 above $\times 4$, followed by a line, as was commonplace in older textbooks. This potentially offers the children some scope for choosing the method they consider most appropriate. However, our earlier remark about the suitability of the column algorithm relative to alternative mental strategies applies to several of these, 99×9 being a notable example.

The pupils probably accepted that they were to use the algorithm for each of the exercises, and not consider a mental strategy. In which case, the *sequence* of exercises might be expected to be designed to present the pupils with increasing challenge as they progress though them. This challenge would be of two kinds. First, the partial products (e.g. 10×4 and 9×4) make demands on their recall of products. There seems to be no obvious consideration of this dimension in the sequence. The first, 19×4, and third, 42×4, are the only ones with a single-digit product anywhere in the calculation (i.e. 4, being 1×4, and 8, being 2×4). Second, and perhaps more subtle, the necessity of 'carrying' when summing the tens digits of the partial products would add to the difficulty of an exercise. This is a factor only in the second of the first eight exercises, 27×9, and in the third of the extension items, 76×8.

Finally, the last three extension exercises are of the form TU × TU which were not part of the teaching in this lesson. It would have been interesting to have had the opportunity to discuss some of these decisions with Laura.

On your own, or with a colleague, imagine that you are preparing a lesson with a Year 5 class. The children have met and used the grid method for TU × U multiplication.

First, consider reasons why you would, or would not, teach the children the column method.

Secondly, if you did decide to teach the column method, or were obliged to do so for some reason, what examples would you use to introduce the method to the class, and what exercises would you give them later?

(Continued)

(Continued)

As soon as possible after reading this chapter, and working on Laura's lesson, take a look at another mathematics lesson. This might be one that you are able to observe, taught by a colleague or perhaps by an experienced teacher, or perhaps a videotape of a lesson. It could well be a lesson that you are about to teach, or one that you taught recently. Look carefully at the examples chosen in the lesson. As before, consider why the teacher chose these particular examples. What 'job' were the examples intended to do? What did the teacher want the children to learn, and how would seeing and doing these examples help them to learn it? What might have been alternative examples? Are there any obviously poor examples in this lesson? Which examples would you choose, and why?

Before going on to think about some general principles behind the choice and use of examples, we give one case involving a choice in the teaching of a different area of the mathematics curriculum – shape and space.

A student teacher, Sonia, taught a lesson with a Year 4 class on symmetry and geometrical transformations. In Chapter 7 we have more to say about these topics, and further analysis of Sonia's lesson. Her learning objective was that pupils will be able to 'make and describe repeating patterns which involve translations and/or reflections'. To prepare them for doing this, she wanted them to understand the particular character of translation and reflection as geometrical transformations. Both translation and reflection transform a geometrical shape to another, 'congruent' shape. One shape is congruent to another when it has the same shape and size, as if a cardboard cut-out of the shape were placed in different positions (Figure 4.5). In the case of translation, the transformation is sliding, without turning over or rotating. In the case of reflection, the geometrical shape is 'flipped over' and there will be a line, or axis, of symmetry.

To help the children 'get a feel' for these two transformations, Sonia needed to have some shapes, and to show what would happen to them under various translations and reflections – what would *change*, and what would *stay the same*. Sonia had not decided in advance what shapes to use for her demonstrations. As she came into the classroom, she saw a pile of shapes on a table. From the pile, she took a circle and a rectangle.

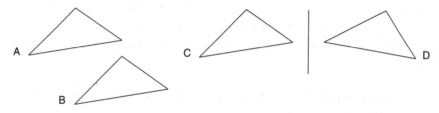

A is translated to B and to C; C is reflected to D in the marked vertical line

Figure 4.5   Translating and reflecting a triangle

Sketch (i) a circle, (ii) a rectangle. Show images of the circle after translation, and after reflection. What might be the advantages and disadvantages of using each of these shapes in order to demonstrate translation and reflection?

As we noted above, we shall have more to say about this in Chapter 7.

The choice of examples: an overview

Now we step back from the classrooms we have just visited to see what general lessons or principles might be learned from them. In an ideal world, perhaps, at this point we would set out some instructions as to how to choose 'good' examples in mathematics teaching. Unfortunately, not enough is known about 'exemplification' to enable us to do that. Surprisingly, this crucial topic has been under-researched, although interest is gathering in the UK and elsewhere (for a good overview, see Bills et al., 2006). What we can do, however, is to describe some rather general principles involved in the development of a repertoire of examples, and to repeat and clarify some 'warnings' that we mentioned earlier in this chapter.

Dimensions of variation

The Swedish educational psychologist, Ference Marton, proposed that humans discern and understand something in the world by experiencing and becoming aware of the different ways in which it can vary (see Watson and Mason, 2005). These differences are captured in Marton's notion of *dimensions of variation*. For example, understanding of the concept of 'square' is marked by growing awareness of the various ways that squares can vary, and the variants that do not qualify as squares. These dimensions include:

- sides – these must have the same length, but the length can vary between different squares;

- angles – these must all be right angles, and there exist rhombuses with equal sides which are not squares;

- orientation – 'diamonds' with equal sides and angles are squares, rotated from the conventional position on the page;

- other, less overtly geometrical dimensions such as colour, texture and so on, can also vary.

Similarly, the concept of fraction entails possible variation in dimensions such as numerator, denominator, proper (i.e. less than 1), mixed or improper, being in lowest terms (or not), positive or negative.

Chloë's lesson

The choice of an example can be approached through a consideration of the dimensions of possible variation. We illustrate this by reference to the lesson (introduced in the previous chapter) in which Chloë was teaching a Year 1/2 class a mental strategy for adding and subtracting near-multiples of 10, such as 9, 11, 19 and 21, to a given number. The strategy for adding 9, for example, involved adding 10, then subtracting 1. In each case, a multiple of 10 would be added or subtracted, and then an adjustment (adding or subtracting 1) carried out.

After introducing the strategy to the class, the children were assigned differentiated worksheet exercises that Chloë had prepared. The worksheet for the 'more able' children involved working with 19 and 21; the other children worked with 9 and 11. A 'dimensions of variation' consideration of the possibilities for these exercises might include:

Dimension 1 – addition or subtraction;

Dimension 2 – near-multiples of 10 (i.e. 9 and 11) or 20 (19 and 21);

Dimension 3 – one more or one less than 10/20, i.e. 11 and 21 as one possibility, 9 and 19 as another.

A teacher makes a judgement, consciously or otherwise, about the relative complexity involved in the different possibilities within each dimension. This judgement might be expected to influence the 'sequencing of instruction' – the order that these different possibilities are introduced in the lessons – and also the examples and exercises presented to the children. What happened for this class was that (a) strategies for addition (Dimension 1) were taught and practised for 9, 11, 19 and 21 (all possibilities in Dimensions 2 and 3) in one lesson, and those for subtraction in the next. It might be inferred that Chloë judged Dimension 1 to constitute the most crucial distinction, and sequenced her teaching accordingly. In the second lesson – the one that we observed – the worksheet for the 'more able' children involved working with 19 and 21, the other children worked with 9 and 11. It is apparent, therefore, that Chloë had taken Dimension 2 into account in this aspect of her planning. Dimension 3 did not seem to have featured in her thinking about the lesson.

First, try the following calculations in turn (either mentally or using a written method):

58 + 21
58 + 19
58 − 21
58 − 19

Reflect on what made some of these more demanding and others less so.

What different kinds of complexity in mental calculation would you think are introduced by Dimension 3?

Our comment would be as follows. Mental addition and subtraction of 11 and 21 entail a sequence of actions in the *same* direction – aggregation or reduction. This is particularly evident if these calculations are represented on a number line. For example, the sequence involved in subtracting 21 from 53 would be 53, 43, 33, 32 (possibly 53, 33, 32), as shown in Figure 4.6.

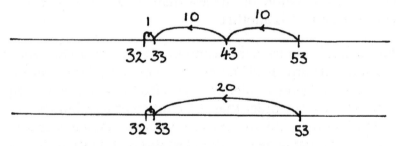

Figure 4.6   Subtracting 21 from 53 on an empty number line

By contrast, addition and subtraction of 9 and 19 (using the strategy that Chloë was teaching) requires a *change* of direction for the final unit, i.e. compensation. So subtracting 19 from 53 involves a sequence like 53, 43, 33, 34, as shown in Figure 4.7. This compensation strategy for adding/subtracting 9 is a kind of 'trick'. So we might predict, on the basis of these reflections, that Dimension 3 is quite significant in terms of what would make the exercises more or less difficult for the children. Deborah Ball (1990a) called this kind of deep reflection on the mathematical content of a lesson *unpacking*. The idea is developed further in Ball and Bass (2000). Our unpacking of Dimension 3 led us to the judgement that working with 11 and 21 would be less challenging than working with 9 and 19. In this instance, research confirms this judgement (e.g. Heirdsfield, 2001), although more often than not we may not be aware of such findings.

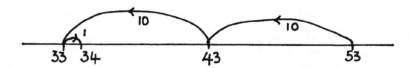

Figure 4.7   Subtracting 19 from 53 by subtracting 20 and adding 1

In the next chapter, we will discuss further this sense of the fact that some mathematical tasks are inherently more challenging than others. We refer to teachers' 'anticipation of complexity' as a factor in their decisions about sequencing their lessons and tasks for pupils. The judgements involved in this kind of anticipation very often derive from thoughtful analysis of the situation (like that in the task above), or from 'experience'. Sometimes, however, there are research findings that help teachers to make such judgements in a more informed way (e.g. Ward, 1979; Hart, 1981; Dickson et al., 1984; Foxman et al., 1986; QCA, 2003).

Examples: the ones to avoid

Our study of beginning teachers has prompted us to think carefully about their choice and use of examples. It has brought to light three types of examples which would be better avoided. That is to say, when you choose examples in your planning, try to keep the following warning signals in mind!

Examples that obscure the role of the variables

Marton's notion of 'dimensions of variation', mentioned earlier in this chapter, embraces the straightforward idea that most mathematical objects, and every example of such an object, consists of two or more components, or variables.

Subtraction   To take a simple example, $12 - 5 = 7$ is an example of a subtraction equation. The values of the variables are 12, 5 and 7. The names given to these variables are, respectively, *minuend* (12), *subtrahend* (5) and *difference* (7). The terms 'minuend' and 'subtrahend' are somewhat archaic and obscure, but 'difference' is more common and is useful as a way of referring to the outcome of a subtraction. These three variables are not entirely independent, since the choice of any two of the variables determines the third. In Chapter 1, and elsewhere, we saw that Naomi chose (or invited the children to choose) minuends and subtrahends so that she could illustrate and help her children to understand the concept of 'subtraction as difference'.

Especially when children meet a new mathematical object, concept or procedure for the first time, it is helpful if the examples used help them to distinguish between the different variables, and to discern the roles of the different variables. Thus, in the above example $12 - 5 = 7$, the three variables minuend, subtrahend and difference are easily distinguishable because they take different values. In her very first example of 'subtraction as difference', Naomi did not separate out the variables in this way,

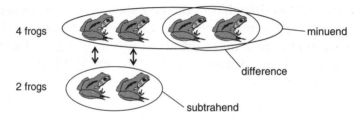

Figure 4.8 Naomi's representation of the comparison subtraction

because – as we noted earlier in this chapter – her example was the difference between 4 and 2, that is, 4 – 2 = 2. In this case, both the subtrahend and the difference take the same value. As we noted in Chapter 1, when Naomi represents this concept of subtraction (as comparison) she makes a neat row of four magnetic 'frogs', with two frogs placed below in a second row, as shown in Figure 4.8. The idea is that when the first two frogs (from the minuend set, the row of four) are matched with the two below (the subtrahend set), two frogs in the minuend set will remain *un*matched. It is this unmatched pair that now represents the difference. But the distinction between the matched frogs on the bottom left of Figure 4.8, representing the subtrahend (2), and the unmatched frogs in the top right, representing the difference (also 2) is obscure, because the two sets are the same size. We call this an *example of obscuring the role of variables*. In effect, one value (2 here) is being made to do the work of two variables in the situation. Our point is that a very small adjustment to the example, to 5 – 2 = 3, say, would immediately resolve the dilemma and clarify the roles of the three variables in the representation.

Coordinates   An even more striking case of *obscuring the role of variables* occurred in a Year 6 lesson on coordinates. This episode (Clip 4) below can be viewed on the companion website. Kirsty began by asking the children for a definition of coordinates. (As we remarked earlier in this chapter, this is a common gambit, but a questionable one.) One child volunteered that 'the horizontal line is first and then the vertical line'. Kirsty reinforced this, and then assessed their understanding of this convention by asking the children to identify the coordinates of a number of points as she marked them on a coordinate grid, projected onto a screen at the front of the classroom. She reminded them that 'the *x*-axis goes first'.

> Kirsty is reviewing integer coordinates in all four quadrants (positive and negative coordinates). If you had to suggest five points for Kirsty to mark on her coordinate grid, what would they be, and in what order?

Kirsty's first example was in fact the point (1, 1). Subsequent examples were (–2, 1), (1, –2), (–2, –3), (3, 4), (–2, 4), (3, –3)

> Compare Kirsty's sequence with your own. Discuss your ideas with a colleague. Consider the issue of obscuring the role of variables, and also what sequence order of your examples (and/or Kirsty's) might be helpful, and why.

Telling the time   In Michael's lesson with a Year 4 class, the main activity was about telling the time with analogue and digital clocks. One group was having difficulty with analogue quarter past, half past and quarter to. Michael intervened with this group, showing them first an analogue clock set at six o'clock. He then moved the minute hand to show them a quarter past six and half past six. When asked to show half past seven on their clocks, one child put both hands on the seven.

> What would you infer from this? Why might the example of half past six be problematic as a way of conveying the general concept of 'half past' on analogue displays? In what sense it a case of obscuring the role of variables? What are the alternatives, and which might work better in this respect?

We mention in passing that there is also an issue here in terms of the *representations* that we considered in Chapter 3. Some analogue clocks designed for classroom use, and 'telling the time', have the hour hand and minute hands linked by 'gears', so that the hour hand rotates once for every 12 rotations of the minute hand, like pedals and wheels on a bicycle. With such a resource, or representation, the two hands would always be correctly coordinated.

Daniel, aged four, pointed to the clock on the wall at home. He said 'The little hand is on 12 and the big hand is on 10. What time is it?'

> In what ways is this example potentially problematic in terms of Daniel's learning to say times after the half hour, that is, so many minutes *to* the relevant hour?

Adding 9   We visited Chloë's lesson with a Year 1/2 class in Chapter 3 and earlier in this chapter. Chloë asked one of the children, Ruth, to demonstrate adding 9. Recall this passage from the lesson:

Chloë: Ruth, do you think you can explain how we add nine and add eleven? Up you come, you're going to be the teacher. Now I've put this [1–100 number grid] up so if you need to use it. You stand on that side. Now this is your class. Tell them how you go about adding nine. Don't look at me, look at the class. Big loud voice.

Ruth: You add ten, and then you, you take away *or* add one.

Chloë: What do you do if you add nine? Do you take away or add?

Ruth: Take away.

Chloë: You take away. Can you show us on the board? Add nine to nine. OK, I'm going to put a red dot here [on 9] and show me how you add ten and take away one.

The dimensions of variation of this $a + b = c$ addition situation – the variables – are the two addends a and b, and the sum c. The second addend (b) has been fixed at 9 because Ruth has been asked to demonstrate adding 9. Clearly Chloë has considerable scope in her choice of the first addend (a). In fact, she chooses 9. This is clearly another potential instance of confusing the role of variables.

It is interesting to speculate why teachers are so often drawn to use the same value for two variables in this way. One suggestion is that humans seem to be attracted to the symmetry inherent in doubling and halving: this is one reason why these mental strategies are recognised and exploited in the Dutch RME curriculum (Anghileri et al., 2002) and in the English official curriculum guidance (DfEE, 1999).

Examples intended to illustrate a particular procedure, for which another procedure would be more sensible

One use of examples in mathematics teaching, to which we referred earlier in this chapter, is to teach a general procedure by a particular demonstration of that procedure. In primary mathematics, such procedures are usually mental calculation strategies or written calculation algorithms. A number of options exist in both categories. Our suggestion here is that an example chosen to demonstrate one procedure ought not to cry out for another procedure to be used instead, otherwise children will, quite reasonably, wonder what is the point of learning a method for which there seems to be no need. We mentioned this earlier in this chapter, in connection with Laura's demonstrations of a written multiplication algorithm. In two of the examples that she chose for the demonstration it would be more sensible to use a mental strategy.

Another possible example would be the one we have just considered – Chloë's choice of 9 + 9 to demonstrate a procedure for adding 9. These children would previously have been encouraged to memorise 9 + 9 as a 'double', and therefore this was not a good example from which to teach a general strategy for adding 9.

Subtraction   Another instance occurred in Naomi's lesson on 'difference', with the Year 1 class. As we saw in Chapter 1, Naomi was teaching two procedures, or strategies, for solving such subtraction problems. The first was by *matching*; the child puts out two sets of cubes, say – one representing the minuend, the other the subtrahend. The sets are then matched one-to-one; counting the unmatched cubes gives the difference. The second strategy was by *counting on* from the smaller of the two numbers. In either case, some counting is involved. (We discuss subtraction structures further in Chapter 7.)

One of the exercise questions on the worksheet that she gave the children asked for the difference between 11 and 10. Now it is very evident, without any deliberate act of counting, that 11 is one more than 10, that is, the difference is 1. Therefore it would not make sense to deploy either of the intended procedures to solve this problem. On the other hand, a typical Year 1 child really would need to use one of them to find the difference between 12 and 5, say.

This is akin to giving, for example, 302 – 299 in a set of exercises on subtraction by decomposition. Decomposition executes the 'take-away' model of subtraction, whereas 302 – 299 is more sensibly conceived in terms of comparison. This is nicely demonstrated in a training video produced for the English National Numeracy Strategy, in which a 'teacher', Ian Sugarman, presents a Year 5 pupil, Cheryl, with some addition and subtraction problems. One group of subtraction problems is typified by 103 – 98. We see

Ian helping Cheryl to see 100 as a 'landmark' between the two numbers, and Cheryl eventually counts down from 103 to 98 to obtain the answer 5. One of the highlights of the video is Ian's insight when he then asks Cheryl whether she would get the same answer by counting up from 98 to 103. 'I don't know', she says – a brilliant demonstration, on Ian's part, of taking nothing for granted, and a form of 'anticipation of complexity'. In Chapter 5 we associate this kind of anticipation with the connection dimension of the Knowledge Quartet.

Examples being randomly generated, typically by dice

There is something intuitively attractive about generating examples with dice, possibly because the teacher is demonstrating the confidence to 'let go' of some aspect of the lesson, perhaps giving it a more democratic feel. This is speculation, but in any case it is a fact that the beginning teachers whom we observed frequently used dice to generate low-level (for them, if not for the children) mathematical examples.

> Colin was working on number bonds to 10 with his Reception (age 4–5) class. Rather than having them use sets of objects, or count on their fingers, he *represented* the mathematical situation by setting out 'stepping stones' in the form of large cards labelled from 0 to 10 on the classroom carpet. The children counted as Colin laid out the cards on the floor. He deliberately laid out some of the cards out of sequence – a nice opportunity for the children to correct him, which they enjoyed doing. Colin then explained what they would be doing. One child stands on 10, while a second child randomly generates a number between 1 and 10 with a specially modified large die. The first child then makes that number of jumps along the line of cards. A third child is asked to record this as a subtraction in the form $10 - a = b$ on the whiteboard.

In the event, the die generated the numbers 5, 3, 8 in that order. This contrasts with Naomi's skilful control of the examples in the episode described in Chapter 1, with a closely-related learning objective (bonds to 10).

Random or controlled?   Earlier in this chapter, we wrote that teachers frequently use examples in mathematics teaching in two ways: to teach concepts and procedures; and as exercises. When it comes to randomly generated examples, a further useful distinction can be made:

- The use of examples to introduce, or demonstrate, some concept or procedure. For example, learning and remembering number bonds to 10. In this case, it is usually better for the teacher to *control* the examples used, to choose and use them with care – as Naomi did. Randomly generated examples may not serve the intended pedagogical purpose well, and may, among other things, confuse the role of variables.

- The use of examples to demonstrate the general application and efficacy of some established procedure. For example, suppose the 'rule' for finding the mean of a set of numbers has been introduced and the teacher judges that it has been understood by one group of children. It would then be quite productive for them to throw, say, three dice, to list the three scores, and to find and record their mean and to repeat this several times. This could be useful for practise in itself, and potentially to think about how the mean itself varies across several trials of this kind.

Our observation from our study of student teachers suggested that there seemed to be some confusion in their minds between the choice of examples to introduce a new procedure or concept on the one hand, and the legitimate random choice of examples to enhance conviction about the truth of some principle or the efficacy of some established procedure on the other. The former is usually best controlled and determined by the teacher, because random selection of examples in this introductory phase is less likely to achieve the intended learning.

Proving and disproving: counterexamples and generic examples

We come now to the two additional uses of examples which we mentioned earlier in this chapter. These support and challenge children's mathematical reasoning in important ways, as we now explain.

Sometimes a mathematical inquiry leads to an unexpected finding. For example, if you add the first few odd numbers like this:

1

$1 + 3 = 4$

$$1 + 3 + 5 = 9$$

$$1 + 3 + 5 + 7 = 16$$

You might notice that the sum in each case – 1, 4, 9, 16 here – is a *square* number, that is, a number multiplied by itself. It would be natural, and very mathematical, to wonder if this is *always* the case: is $1 + 3 + 5 + \ldots + 39 + 41$ a square number? You could check a few more examples, but you still would not know whether it was true in *every* case. There are an infinite number of cases, so it would be impossible to check them all. On the other hand, you are likely to believe that it is true in every case, or strongly suspect that it is. Such a belief, suspicion or 'hunch', based on incomplete evidence, is called a *conjecture*. (Try to use the word 'conjecture' yourself, and not alternatives like 'theory' or 'hypothesis', which have slightly different meanings in science and statistics). Some of the richest and most 'mathematical' classroom mathematics activities include the articulation of mathematical conjectures, and the associated debate to decide whether or not they are true. Inquiry like this, including the articulation and testing of conjectures, are typical of the 'syntactic' dimension of mathematics that we mentioned in Chapter 2. To establish whether a conjecture like the one above is true, we need to *prove* it. To show whether it is false, we need a *counterexample* – one case where the conjecture turns out not to be true. We explain these ideas further in the following classroom scenario.

The jailer problem

In 1997, a video titled *Teachers Count* was distributed to all primary schools in England. The video features one teacher, Kate, with a class of 10- and 11-year-olds. It was intended to promote the three-part lesson structure subsequently adopted by the National Numeracy Strategy in England.

> In the middle phase of one lesson, Kate introduces the well-known 'jailer problem'. [A certain prison has 100 prisoners, 100 cells and 100 jailers. One prisoner is assigned to each cell. One night, when the prisoners are all locked away, the first jailer unlocks all the cells. Then the second jailer locks all the cells whose numbers are multiples of 2. Next, the third jailer changes the state of all the cells that are multiples of 3, and so on through to the 100th jailer. The jailers then all fall asleep. Which prisoners were able to escape from their cells?]

The children investigate the problem in small groups. They make various conjectures, such as 'None of the prime numbers will go free'. Kate monitors and comments on their ideas, including examples of numbers who will 'escape', and conjectures about what they have in common.

You might like to try this yourself before reading on.

After a while, Kate calls for attention, and brings the class together for a review of their findings. They make a list of the numbers that will escape: 1, 4, 9, 16, ..., 100. With some prompting from Kate, one girl points out that these are all square numbers. Kate then lists the factors of the first six of these square numbers, notes how many there are in each case – 1, 3, 3, 5, 3, 9 – and asks what these numbers of factors have in common. One child says that the number of factors is a prime number. Kate points out that 9 is not prime. Another says that the number of factors is always odd. Kate points out that this means that an odd number of *jailers* visited those cells, and so they will be left unlocked.

Kate's observation that 9 is not prime disproves, or 'refutes', the first claim that the number of factors is a prime number. This claim is a generalisation – an observation about what *these* numbers – 1, 3, 3, 5, 3, 9 – have in common. It would be a conjecture if it were intended as a claim about the number of factors of *every* square number. Kate's refutation of the claim is by the use of a counterexample: 9 is one of the numbers of factors, but 9 is not prime. Therefore the claim is false.

Kate could have ended the discussion of the jailer problem at the point where they noticed that the escaped numbers are all square. It is interesting, and a nice outcome to the inquiry. It is very much to Kate's credit that she does not leave it at that – instead, she sets about trying to *explain why* the square numbers escape. This kind of explanation is a form of mathematical proof. Without the proof explanation, the class have a *conjecture* – that all the square numbers escape. We nearly wrote 'Without the proof explanation, the class *only* have a conjecture' to emphasise that the ingredient of explanation is missing, but that would devalue the importance of conjecturing in mathematics, and the way that the conjecture came about, by generalising from examples. This is called *inductive* reasoning (Rowland, 1999) whereas the explanation to come will be a case of logical, *deductive* reasoning.

Kate's explanation is in two parts:

1   Cells whose number have an odd number of factors will be left unlocked.

2   Square numbers have an odd number of factors.

The first part is relatively straightforward, with 10- and 11-year-olds at least. The second part is not straightforward at all!

> Spend a few moments thinking about why it is that square numbers have an odd number of factors.

In fact, Kate explains this to the class by reference to 36 – one of the square numbers. She lists the factors of 36 in order:

1   2   3   4   6   9   12   18   36

She then says: 'Let's pair them up. What does 1 pair with to make 36?' Kate draws lines (as shown in Figure 4.9) connecting 1 with 36, 2 with 18 (because $2 \times 18 = 36$), 3 with 12 and 4 with 9, leaving 6 without a distinct pair. 'Six pairs with itself', says Kate (because $6 \times 6 = 36$). So the factors of 36 consist of a number of pairs with product 36, together with 6, which is isolated and unpaired. Therefore the number of factors of 36 is odd – a set of pairs, and one more.

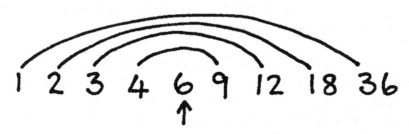

Figure 4.9   Kate pairs the factors of 36, apart from 6

The intention is for the children to see through and beyond the particularities of *this* example to what might happen if they were to pair the factors of any other square number in the same way. Notice that Kate both selects the example (36) and presents it along with a careful narrative about its factors, in which actually counting the number of factors is less important than demonstrating why the number of factors must be odd. This kind of explanation is called a *generic example*. The French mathematics educator Nicolas Balacheff put it like this: 'The generic example involves making explicit the reasons for the truth of an assertion by means of operations or transformations on an object that is not there in its own right, but as a characteristic representative of the class' (Balacheff, 1988: 219).

Kate performed 'operations or transformations' on the number 36. Crucially, she paired up the factors and showed that one of them could only be paired 'with itself'. But the number 36 was not important in its own right. The fact that 36 has nine factors is easily checked, but Kate does a lot more than that. She structures her explanation of why 36 has an odd number of factors in such a way that 36 is intended to be seen as a 'characteristic representative' of square numbers in general.

Her choice of 36 is interesting. It is small enough to be manageable with mental arithmetic, yet it has sufficient factors to demonstrate the pairing process more than once. By contrast, 25, say, has factors 1, 5 and 25. In this case, 1 and 25 can be paired, but the process seems quite limited compared with that for 36, and gives little clue as to what would happen if there were more than three factors. It happens to be the case that 36 is the smallest square with more than one prime factor. How conscious was Kate of this in choosing to work with 36 rather than, say, 25? In any case, it demonstrates that the choice of a generic example is not arbitrary, and a 'good' one is unlikely to be chosen on the spur of the moment. In fact 100 also has nine factors and would probably be just as good as 36. On the other hand, 144 arguably has too many factors; listing them all would distract from the main point of the demonstration, that they can be paired, apart from 12. So, everything considered, 36 takes some beating.

Sums of odd numbers   Earlier, we introduced the conjecture that the sum $1 + 3 + 5 + \ldots$ up to any odd number is always a square number. One possible proof of this, by generic example, is as follows. Focus on one instance of the claim, e.g. $1 + 3 + 5 + 7$ as shown in Figure 4.10. In this representation, we begin with one square at the top left of the figure. The second, third and fourth layers, shown here with different shapes, then add on the odd numbers 3, 5 and 7, resulting in a square array at each stage. This is a *generic* example in so far as it is then clear that the addition of each subsequent odd number preserves the square array.

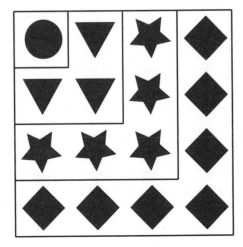

Figure 4.10   Showing that $1 + 3 + 5 + 7 = 4 \times 4$

How might you explain the following statements by reference to a generic example? What kind of 'narrative' would you offer to show how your example is, in some way, a characteristic representative of other possible examples? Which examples would work well in each case, and why? Are there examples that would not work well? One example of each statement is given to clarify its meaning.

1   The sum of two odd numbers is even. [$5 + 9 = 14$]
2   The sum of three consecutive integers is a multiple of 3. [$7 + 8 + 9$ is a multiple of 3]
3   The sum of the integers from 1 to any even number is equal to half the number of numbers multiplied by the sum of the first and last numbers. [$1 + 2 + 3 + \ldots + 8 = 4 \times 9$]
4   The number of ways of 'making' an integer as a sum of two smaller positive integers is one less than the integer itself. [$7 = 2 + 5$, $7 = 6 + 1$, $7 = 5 + 2$, $7 = 3 + 4$, $7 = 1 + 6$, $7 = 4 + 3$, so there are six ways of making 7]

None of the following statements is true. For each statement, suggest a counter example that would refute (disprove) it.

1   All prime numbers are odd.
2   The sum of two even numbers is always a multiple of 4.
3   Multiplying a number by itself always makes it bigger.
4   All rectangles with the same perimeter have the same area.

Summary

In this chapter, we looked in depth at the ways that examples can be used in mathematics teaching. Along with choice of representations, the choice and use of examples is one of the key aspects of the transformation dimension of the Knowledge Quartet. The role of examples is underdeveloped in mathematics teacher education, and this chapter is an original contribution to the growing 'science' of exemplification.

Examples play an essential role in the teaching of concepts, in the teaching of procedures, and as exercises through which children become familiar with new ideas and fluent in the use and application of procedures. Through consideration and careful examination of lessons taught by beginning teachers, we saw that it is not the case that any one example is as good as another. Indeed, the examples used in mathematics teaching should be chosen with care, keeping in mind their intended purpose, and the possible dimensions of variation within a particular example. We singled out three general categories which indicate principles concerning examples that are best avoided. We labelled these categories:

- examples which confuse the role of variables;
- examples intended to illustrate a particular procedure, for which another procedure would be more sensible;
- randomly generated examples.

The chapter concluded with two 'syntactic' uses of examples, in determining the truth or falsehood of some general mathematical claim. Typically such claims will be plausible conjectures, arising from a mathematical investigation of some kind. A suitable *counterexample* can demonstrate that such a claim is false, thereby disproving or refuting it. The normal procedure for establishing mathematical truth is by general proof, but insight into the nature of such a proof can often be achieved by means of a carefully structured argument based on a *generic example*.

Further reading

Anne Watson and John Mason (2005) *Mathematics as a Constructive Activity: The Role of Learner Generated Examples.* Mahwah, NJ: Lawrence Erlbaum.

The importance of exemplification has been largely unrecognised until recently. This is therefore a landmark book, and probably the most comprehensive work to date on the place of examples in the learning of mathematics. The book is research-based and very readable. The authors explain the teaching strategy of asking children to 'construct' their own examples of mathematical objects – as we did in this chapter, in the case of rectangles. This construction of examples is usually thought to be the teacher's job, but Watson and Mason show that learners can beneficially take responsibility for making examples. A great many related activities are provided in the book, many, but not all, relevant to primary mathematics.

Tim Rowland (1999) '"i" is for induction', *Mathematics Teaching*, 167: 23–27.

Tim Rowland (2001) 'Generic proofs: setting a good example', *Mathematics Teaching*, 177: 40–43.

These two articles, published in a professional journal, confirm the importance of proof in mathematics, and explain how convincing proofs can be constructed – as Kate did in the episode in this chapter – through the medium of well-chosen and carefully presented examples.

5

Making Connections in Mathematics Teaching

> **In this chapter you will read about:**
>
> - **different approaches to progression in learning;**
> - **connections in student teachers' lessons;**
> - **strategies for making connections;**
> - **ways of assessing connections.**

In this book we have been developing the practical outcomes of our research into the kinds of knowledge that teachers need in order to teach mathematics well. This research led us to propose four facets, or dimensions, of this knowledge, which together we call the Knowledge Quartet. In Chapter 2 we outlined the Knowledge Quartet framework. In Chapters 3 and 4 we examined aspects of the transformation of knowledge that must be undertaken if it is to be learnt by others. In particular, we saw how abstract features of mathematics are *represented* and *exemplified*. In considering how mathematical knowledge should be *organised* in order that it is learnt, we shall introduce in this chapter another dimension of the Knowledge Quartet, which we call *connection*.

Teaching clearly amounts to more than *telling* pupils what they should learn. No single activity wholly characterises what a teacher does in teaching her class. Some of the time she will be 'telling', at other times she will be demonstrating. There will also be times when she is correcting, advising, listening, explaining, and so on. One especially important aspect of teaching is *questioning* (Wragg and Brown, 2001). The manner in which this questioning takes place gives an insight into this third element of the Knowledge Quartet.

There are various reasons why teachers ask children questions, one of which is to *assess* what children already know, in order to build up their learning in some kind of order or progression. We shall be concerned with the connections that make sense of this 'sequencing' in this chapter. The rationale for this ordering of content has been a matter of debate. Should it lie in some kind of *logical* ordering of the subject matter of mathematics? Or should it be in the *psychological* aspects of the children's learning? Clearly, both logical and psychological factors play a part in the progression of learning. For this reason both factors are central to achieving the necessary connections required to obtain progression in children's learning, and we shall return to a discussion of this issue later. We shall suggest, following various other educationists, that to make such connections is at the heart of *understanding* mathematics. However, in order to do so, teachers must have sufficient foundation knowledge of their own to plan for connection-making with their pupils. So, what we call 'connection' in the Knowledge Quartet will emerge partly from the fundamental knowledge that teachers possess.

An episode from Jason's lesson

We now consider an episode from a lesson taught by one of the student teachers who participated in our research. Jason is asking a question in order to find out what knowledge his class already have about fractions, so that further learning may be achieved. Although Jason genuinely seeks some vital information, he begins, as teachers sometimes do, by feigning ignorance. We join him in the main teaching phase of a lesson with a Year 3 class (age 7–8).

Jason: What's a fraction? I don't know, tell me what a fraction is …

Gary: It's a number, a line and then another number.

Jason: So …

Gary: But the top number has to be smaller that the bottom number.

Jason: Yes, you've described a fraction … but what *is* a fraction?

How would you answer Jason's question?
Was Jason's opening question helpful for either the class or for him?
What can you infer from Gary's response what he has learnt about fractions?
What response might Jason have been hoping for?

Our reflections

In Chapter 4 we raised the difficulty that novice teachers often experience when they adopt the opening gambit of asking the kind of head-on questions which request a definition for a term or concept, rather than by asking for examples. In this respect Jason's question was not very helpful. To 'have' a concept of a fraction, one might expect that at some stage a child can give some sort of general account. Precisely what a concept of fraction is like will be discussed later.

However, the acquisition of any concept is more than simply a matter of providing a definition. To have a concept is, as Dearden (1968: 108) put it, 'to be in possession of a principle of unity according to which a number of things may all be regarded as being the same, or of being of one kind'. Such a unifying principle collects a number of objects, ideas or situations under one name, such as 'triangle', 'dog' or 'happiness'. So to have *acquired* a concept is also to have the capacity to pick out *instances* that fall under it, as we elaborated in Chapter 4. In this way, it is often more straightforward to approach the task of conceptual development by a consideration of these instances, that is, to provide some examples. This might have been what Jason had hoped Gary would do. If so, you may think that he should have posed his question slightly differently. A more helpful question for the class might have been to request some examples of fractions before asking the children what the similarities are among them. In assessing children's understanding of fractions a teacher will, at the very least, expect them to be able to refer to examples – as we suggested in Chapter 4.

It does seem to us, however, that Gary knows something that is important. He has associated the word 'fraction' with one form of *notation* for recording a fraction. Mathematics is a network of related ideas, and learners make sense of mathematics by understanding how different ideas are related and linked to each other, and how some concepts build upon others. Every concept is associated with several interconnected notions, including its name and, sometimes, a symbolic form. Of course, the connection between word ('fraction') and symbol ($\frac{number}{number}$) that Gary made is apparently not the one that Jason had intended him to make. His reply to Gary – 'but what *is* a fraction?' – suggests this, and Jason continues his lesson in another direction, as we shall soon see.

Interestingly, in an earlier part of the lesson, Jason had been using fractional language. He had been playing a team game in which points were scored by carrying out the procedure of finding tenths, quarters, halves and fifths of numbers that Jason provided, such as 'a fifth of 25'. Although one child did query the meaning of 'quarter' at one point, the question ('a quarter of 4') was still answered correctly. Furthermore, since all of the responses provided were correct and Jason had given no direct instructions on how the class should carry out these operations, it seems that the children came to the lesson with some understanding of fractions.

The questions set in this simple game provided Jason with some opportunities for assessing the children's ability to find a fraction of a number. It is therefore surprising that Jason's next step, as we have seen above, was to ask what a fraction is, without any hint that a definition of sorts could have been obtained by thinking about the game that the children had played successfully only a few moments earlier. As it was, Jason began an explanation of fractions based on regions of shapes. So are these two ways of thinking about fractions totally different, or was there some way that Jason might have brought them together in his lesson?

An important aspect of a teacher's knowledge is that some key mathematical concepts have several interpretations or models by which they may be exemplified (Haylock, 2006). Without this knowledge teachers are limited in terms of the ways they are able to *represent* such concepts. (We discuss models, or structures, of subtraction and division in Chapter 7.) This is certainly true of the fraction concept. In terms of the Knowledge Quartet, this means that teachers need a certain kind of foundation knowledge of fractions on which they base a transformation for teaching purposes. Without this knowledge, it is difficult to help children to make connections between the various ways that fractions can be represented.

The typical remark that fractions are 'parts of a whole' can be thought of in two different, but related, ways. The first is in terms of regions of space, as in Figure 5.1, where a geometrical shape has been separated into four equal-area regions, each of which is a quarter of the whole figure. Secondly, a fraction can be represented as a subset of a set of discrete objects. Figure 5.2 shows two fifths, and also three fifths, of a set of five pens.

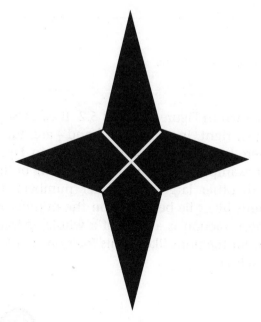

Figure 5.1   A shape divided into quarters

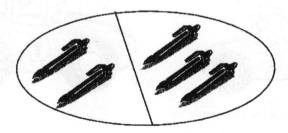

Figure 5.2   A collection of objects divided into two fifths and three fifths

So, we *can* think of a fraction as, say, a portion of a rectangular figure, as Jason did. But equally, we can think of it as a part of a number. The part – like a fifth of 25 – is found by division, and this was precisely the task that constituted the game that Jason had set up earlier. In Jason's game, the set of discrete objects was represented only by its size. For example, a fifth of 25 nuts becomes 'a fifth of 25'.

In fact, there are at least three more models of the fraction concept. A fraction can be regarded not simply as the description of a part of a region, or

Figure 5.3 Fractions on a number line

part of a set, as shown in Figures 5.1 and 5.2. It can also be thought of as a *number* in its own right. In this sense, $\frac{3}{4}$ and $\frac{5}{4}$ are numbers that can be located somewhere in a number line, as shown in Figure 5.3. The idea here is that $\frac{3}{4}$, for example, has a life and a meaning of its own, as a number in relation to other larger or smaller numbers. Indeed, so-called 'improper' fractions like $\frac{5}{4}$ lie beyond 1 on the number line. For this reason the idea that a fraction is a 'part of a whole' is inadequate, since it does not account for fractions like $\frac{5}{4}$. This fraction is not 'part' of 1, in the usual sense of a subset.

Figure 5.4 Comparing two cars in size

The fourth model for a fraction arises when two quantities are *compared*. Then a fraction is thought of in its *ratio* sense, so that one object (or quantity) is a fraction of the size of another (see Figure 5.4). Once again, it is clear that the idea that a fraction is 'part of a whole' is no longer an adequate explanation. In Figure 5.4, neither car is a 'part' of the other. There is, incidentally, a potential ambiguity about exactly what is being compared in the case of these two cars (and similar examples). If it were intended that the *length* of the smaller car is, say, $\frac{4}{5}$ times the length the larger car then the *heights* of the cars would also be in the same ratio, and the *area* of the small car would then be $\frac{16}{25}$ (or about $\frac{2}{3}$) times that of the larger. Furthermore, since – by convention – these particular illustrations represent three-dimensional objects, the *width* of the smaller car would also be $\frac{4}{5}$ of the larger car, and the *volume* of the smaller car a mere $\frac{64}{125}$ (about a half) that of the larger. When this situation appears – intentionally or unintentionally – in the presentation of statistics, the effect can be highly misleading. Suppose that a company represents a 25% growth in profits by illustrations of, say, two bags of gold, one being $\frac{4}{5}$ the size of the other. If the illustrations actually show all *lengths* in this relationship, then, as with the cars, the reader is likely to perceive the volumes to be in a ratio close to a half. In other words, the impression is given that the profits have doubled!

A final model of a fraction is as the *result of a division*: for example, $\frac{2}{3}$ is 2 divided by 3. Once again the idea of 'part of a whole' only makes sense if we regard the 2 as 'the whole', and this is perhaps stretching the meaning of the notion of 'a whole'.

There is a suggestion in the research (Dickson et al., 1984) that Jason's region model of a fraction – in his case, part of a rectangle – is the most fundamental, basic idea of a fraction. This is a plausible view to take because very young children may be more familiar with dividing up single items of food (like cakes, apples and bananas) than countable collections of objects, although some sharing out of objects also takes place quite early in many children's lives. Jason's class do seem to have grasped the idea of fractions as subsets of discrete sets – found by division of numbers – and so he could have taken that as a point of departure for the definition that he sought. Of course, in this particular case, it may not have been made explicit to the children, during the game, that they were finding *fractions* of 4, 25, etc. by dividing. Nevertheless, it seems that Jason missed an opportunity for making a connection between his question ('What's a fraction? I don't know') and the earlier game.

Progression in learning

The idea of making mathematical connections by building upon what is already *familiar* to the class is clearly vital. By analogy, if you were trying to find your way around a town you did not know very well, then it would be useful to establish what was already familiar. A junction, the supermarket, or the railway station, which you had left behind, would help you to make sense of where you are. In other words, we learn to find our way around a new town by making connections between that of which we have some knowledge and that which is new. Similarly, connections in our learning of mathematics are made when we link new ideas to points of familiarity. These connections between different aspects of what we know are captured in Piaget's notion of a 'schema'. The ways in which we adjoin new knowledge to old are forms of 'assimilation' and 'accommodation', whereby new experiences enhance or challenge concepts that have already been formed (Skemp, 1986).

The contrast between the *psychological* aspects of learning and understanding and the *logical* structure of the content of a subject like mathematics is illustrated by consideration of what it means to *count*. Counting is perhaps the most basic skill in arithmetic for young children, because they start to learn it from a very early age, and often at home. Yet what are most typically counted are *kinds of things*, such as coins, cards or toys. The task of ensuring that these kinds of things are explored and established is, from *a logical point of view*, even more basic than the process of counting. So, since (logically), before we can count, we need to establish what it is we wish to count, the ability to *classify* appears to precede counting in the order in which it is taught. For this reason, until the 1990s, work in the early years classroom was characterised by sustained work on sorting tasks. Counting was usually delayed until these so-called 'fundamental principles' were acquired.

Thompson (1997) gives a detailed account of critiques of this approach, as Hamlyn (1967) had much earlier. We note that in a child's life, an emphasis upon the logical precedence of sorting tasks can hinder the opportunity to connect a child's more formal school work with his or her informal pre-school experiences. These experiences of reciting the counting words 'one, two, three, …', which are essentially linguistic, have become familiar and meaningful for the child. So, it makes good psychological sense to build upon them, rather than to set them aside.

Another area of learning, where the order in which young children are taught certain ideas has been the subject of debate, is shape and space. Again, there are experiences that many young children will have had at home that will have a bearing on the sequence of the curriculum in school.

In teaching shape to young children, would you begin with two-dimensional or three-dimensional shapes?

With a friend or colleague, list some activities that young children might carry out with both two-dimensional and three-dimensional shapes, and think about their relative complexities. Are they likely to build on things with which the children are familiar?

Whilst 2D shapes are logically simpler, since they have (one) fewer dimensions than 3D shapes, 3D shapes are arguably more familiar to children as they are surrounded by them every day. With this in mind, the connections that young children might make with play activities and more structured games should not be ignored in favour of something that appears to be more *logically* basic. Nevertheless, there are good reasons – in the case of shape and many other topics – for finding tasks that connect with previous experience whilst making *additional* connections within mathematics. In the case of shape and space with young children, for example, this might be building and talking about 'junk models' alongside exploration of the faces of such models by printing with their faces, or drawing round their edges, to achieve a 2D image. Work with nets of 3D shapes also makes a connection between 2D and 3D. The net itself is 2D, but the shape it folds into is 3D.

Supporting progression, then, requires some knowledge of the logical structure of mathematical content, but also a good deal of knowledge about the particular children whom we teach, and about how children learn in general. It is valuable to make connections with what children already know before they come to the mathematics lesson, and to ensure that this prior knowledge is connected to the learning that we intend in our lesson planning.

Caroline's lesson

One of the student teachers in our research project, Caroline, demonstrated the foundation knowledge required for making connections in her planning for a lesson with her Year 2 class (age 6–7). From the outset it was clear that she had set out to make a connection between two models of the fraction concept – relating regions of shapes to subsets of discrete sets of objects – which we mentioned earlier. Although Caroline does not quite succeed in making the connection that she intended, this is because the resource – the *representation* – that she used needed a little modification. The (conceptual) connection that she had in mind is clear and profound. Indeed, Caroline displays an impressive mark of ingenuity in her teaching as she attempts to make a crucial link between fractions of regions and fractions of numbers.

In her introduction to the main activity phase, having carried out some divisions of regular shapes into congruent regions, she placed on the board a circular card with four smaller circles attached at equal distances round the circumference which was supposed to represent a flower (see Figure 5.5). She encouraged the children to see how halving the whole of this *spatial* configuration also determined half the *number* of the petals.

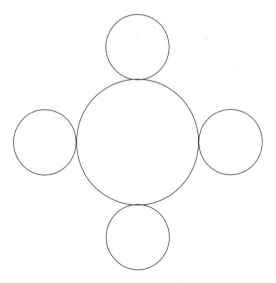

Figure 5.5   Caroline's flower representation

Of course, if this quotient (two petals) is to be displayed in whole petals, it will depend upon where the 'halving' line is placed. If the line passes through a petal then the petals themselves would be partitioned, making the model less helpful. However, Caroline was careful to ensure that the way that she positioned the line each time did not allow this complication to arise, as illustrated in Figure 5.6.

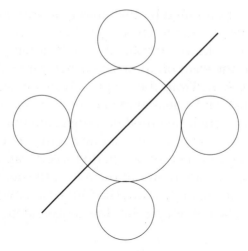

Figure 5.6   Halving the flower representation

For her next example, Caroline produced an eight-legged 'spider' diagram (Figure 5.7). Again, she used a halving 'line', in this case a piece of card, to split the spider in two, showing four legs in each half. Unfortunately, any two legs of the spider were thin enough to be completely hidden by the strip of card that she was using to separate the two parts. This did not go unnoticed by one child, who demonstrated that when the cardboard strip was strategically positioned through a pair of opposite legs, only three legs remained in each half! Caroline was not sympathetic to this response. She simply placed the dividing line elsewhere, without acknowledging the loophole in her model that the child had uncovered.

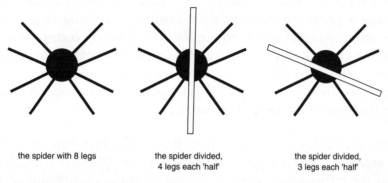

the spider with 8 legs   the spider divided,   the spider divided,
                            4 legs each 'half'   3 legs each 'half'

Figure 5.7   Halving the spider

The tricky complication raised by the child is an instance of *contingency*, which we discuss in Chapter 6. We suggest that, despite this hiccup, this episode of Caroline's lesson remained a bold attempt at connection-making; moreover, she went on to make further impressive mathematical connections *interactively*. From the spatial model she went on to explore ways of finding a half and a quarter of various numbers, and was surprised and delighted by one child's method of recognising that a half is one part of a 'double' that she already knew. Caroline connected this idea to addition, multiplication and division-as-sharing (see Chapter 7 for different division structures) and also drew out the role of the denominator in finding fractions of numbers. In this way, she formed a network of approaches to finding fractions before setting the class independent tasks to work on.

Understanding

Making connections between ideas, as Caroline set out to do, is part of what it means to *understand* something. There are various accounts of what it means to understand mathematics. For the British psychologist, Richard Skemp (1976), authentic, or what he called 'relational', understanding is demonstrated by a child's ability to give an explanation for mathematical procedures or results which would otherwise remain as mere 'instrumental' understanding. (Incidentally, Skemp's very readable article is one of the most frequently cited in the whole literature of mathematics education. One recent source is O'Sullivan et al., 2005.) A child who has only instrumental understanding can carry out a mathematical task, but is unable to provide an adequate rationale for the steps involved. Part of what is involved in Skemp's account is the idea of justifying or explaining a particular mathematical result by showing that it follows from a more general set of principles. The idea of connection *within* aspects of a concept, and also *between* related concepts, ideas, objects or contexts, is the central focus of this chapter. So, 'understanding', in the terms that we are now considering, is situated within concepts and a *network* of those to which they are related.

Mathematics differs to some extent from, say, literature and history, which arguably make use of fewer technical interlocking concepts. This explains the rather linear form of the mathematics curriculum, at school and beyond. It is not possible to learn most mathematical topics without already having studied others. Moreover, the understanding of mathematical concepts is to a large extent attained and assessed by the extent to which children can see how they are related. It is at this point that the notion of connectivity runs deep.

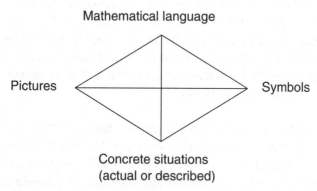

Figure 5.8 A representation of Haylock's model

Haylock (1982) has suggested a simple model, illustrated in Figure 5.8, for assessing the extent of children's understanding, on which the routes between different aspects of a concept (the labelled vertices on the diagram) indicate a variety of possible connections between those aspects. Haylock's suggested labels are *mathematical language, symbols, concrete situations* (actual or described) and *pictures*. Haylock uses this diagram to point out that understanding is not an all-or-nothing state. His model admits different degrees, or kinds, of understanding, each of which may occur in the making of any connections – single or multiple – on his diagram. As he puts it, 'to recognise understanding … we must look for behaviour in mathematics which indicates that the pupil has made connections' (Haylock, 1982: 54). We would add, incidentally, that the diagram can never be said to be complete. It follows that 'understanding' is a lifelong process and is never complete. Therefore it is inappropriate to say that a child, or an adult for that matter, 'fully understands' something. One of the pleasures of learning is constantly having new insights into, and new ways of thinking about, things that we thought we 'fully' understood.

The discussion of different modes of representation in Chapter 3 is directly related to Haylock's model of understanding, since the labels on his diagram – language, symbols, concrete situations and pictures – are various representations of mathematical ideas. There are clear echoes of Bruner's modes of representation, as outlined at the beginning of Chapter 3. A picture of a mathematical situation, for example, would be – in Bruner's terms – an iconic representation. A familiar example of this is a wall display in a classroom showing an ordered collection of objects, accompanied in each case by the numeral that indicates their size. Again, the symbol '+' can be associated with the words 'plus', 'add', 'total', 'and' and 'sum', and similar connections can be made with the subtraction sign and the words 'subtract', 'minus', 'difference' and 'take away'. Part of the unavoidable complexity of mathematics is the lack of a simple correspondence between words and symbols.

In the short exchange (above) on fractions initiated by Jason, the pupil Gary had already made a connection between the word 'fraction' and the symbolic representation of fractions. We have also suggested that another possible connection, related to what Haylock calls 'concrete situations' – that of dividing numbers – was already available in the lesson, but not picked up by Jason. Furthermore, since Caroline connected the *mathematical language* of fractions to two different *pictures* we can say that she made more connections for her pupils, and thereby created the conditions for richer understanding.

Haylock's diagrammatic model of understanding is reminiscent of 'concept maps', or the related 'mind maps'. Concept maps were devised by Joseph Novak in the 1970s in the context of science education, to show diagrammatically the concepts related to a given topic, and how these are interrelated. Novak built on the ideas of the psychologist David Ausubel who famously wrote: 'The most important single factor influencing learning is what the learner already knows. Ascertain this and teach accordingly' (Ausubel, 1968: 337). A concept map can be thought of as a set of nodes, or junctions, each representing a concept, or some aspect of the topic being considered, with a set of lines (usually directed, with arrows) joining some of the nodes to other nodes. Each of the concepts at the nodes can be represented in various ways – as pictures, words, symbols and so on. Indeed, different representations of the same concept might appear at different nodes. Brinkmann (2005) gives an interesting account of these 'knowledge maps' in mathematics education.

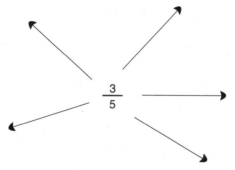

Figure 5.9 How can you represent $\frac{3}{5}$?

Copy the diagram in Figure 5.9 and write, or draw, different things at the ends of the arrowheads that capture, for you, different aspects of the mathematical symbol $\frac{3}{5}$.

This is a useful exercise in assessing how profound a concept one has of the symbol $\frac{3}{5}$. Indeed, if we had omitted the arrows and had asked you to draw as many pictures as you can, connected by arrows to the symbol, then the degree of understanding of your concept of $\frac{3}{5}$ could, in a sense, be 'measured' by the number of successful and distinct connections that you made. We say 'distinct' connections because it may be possible to draw, say, shaded pictures of a pizza, cake, or chocolate bar, all of which show essentially the same picture of $\frac{3}{5}$. This is what we earlier called the region, or area, model. Pictures of shaded pizza, cake and chocolate bar may simply be different *tokens* of the same *type*. In general, the strength of assessment of this kind would ideally be measured by the number of different *types* of connection that relate to the mathematical symbol in question.

More specific concept maps can be devised that require the child to fill in the particular kind of relationship that holds between items on a map. The completed map in Figure 5.10 is based on a helpful discussion of concept maps by Baroody and Bartels (2001). Several more examples are given on a website which supports the 5–14 curriculum in Scotland (see http://www.ltscotland.org.uk/5to14/specialfocus/mathematics/mindmapping/conceptmaps.asp).

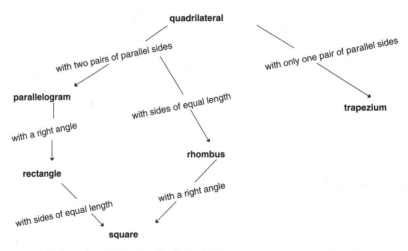

Figure 5.10   A concept map about quadrilaterals

In our discussion so far we have been concerned with the connections within and between ideas or concepts. In some respects, learning mathematics is a matter of acquiring concepts and making connections between them. Indeed, as we have remarked, such connection-making is at the heart of understanding mathematics. Nevertheless, whilst 'relational understanding' (Skemp, 1976) is a high priority in learning mathematics, 'instrumental understanding' has its place as children must learn and acquire fluency with various routines and procedures.

Returning to a student teacher from our study

As we mentioned earlier in this chapter, one of the most basic procedures or routines is that of counting. In Chapter 7 we will discuss some important aspects of counting that need to be known by a teacher. Among these is an understanding of the *kinds* of things that are to be counted. In the following example, this understanding of the early stages of learning about money provides a subtle example of connection-making. The subtlety lies in *anticipating the complexity* entailed in teaching and learning a particular topic. The student teacher, Colin, is teaching a Reception class (4–5 years).

During the introductory activity of his lesson, Colin asks one child, Andrew, to demonstrate publicly the number of elephants shown on a card by counting. Colin commends Andrew on his counting procedure, which he drew to the attention of the class by asking them the question 'How did he [Andrew] count … so that he didn't count any of them twice?'

Some children respond that Andrew went, as they put it, 'down and down' the column of elephants on the card. Colin repeats this to the class, to emphasise Andrew's systematic approach.

Having used Andrew as the focus for the class assessment, Colin can reasonably suppose that, since their counting procedures are secure, he can move on to applying these to the more complex context of money.

Colin had stuck large magnetic coins onto a whiteboard and had produced a toy dog bearing a 5p label. The children were asked to discuss, in pairs, the combination of coins that could be used to buy this toy. It was Andrew, again, who selected a 2p and three 1p coins. However, Colin verified this combination to the class by saying 'one, two' whilst pointing to the 2p coin and then 'three', 'four', 'five' with the three 1p coins.

Of course, in order to reach the required price of 5p he had to count the 2p coin *twice* since he was now counting the *value* of this coin. But this important shift – one which many young children often find difficult – was passed over by Colin without comment. Given his earlier praise of Andrew for counting in such a way that one object was not counted twice, his counting here would appear to be in need of justification.

He repeated this way of counting – which involved linking two words with each of the 2p coins – in his public checking of Samantha's choice of coins, which was two 2p coins and one 1p coin.

However, there is a clear distinction between counting *natural* objects and *conventional* values on such things as coins. In the counting of the elephant illustrations that Andrew carried out earlier, each picture is 'individuated', and a one-to-one correspondence between number words and pictures is visually straightforward. With a single 2p coin there is no visual individuation of 1p values to show this correspondence, so it has to be imagined as we, perhaps, tap the coin twice. In moving from visually individuated objects to non-visibly individuated values without comment, it appears that Colin has not *anticipated the complexity* of the matter. It is a mark of a teacher's pedagogical content knowledge when this kind of complexity is anticipated, and somehow built into the development of the connections between ideas as the lesson progresses. More often than not, a failure to anticipate complexity in elementary mathematics – finding 5p as a combination of coins is trivial for most adults – arises because the teacher simply cannot see what could be complex about something so familiar to them. But awareness of this kind of complexity can be learnt: once again, it is part of the teacher's *specialised* knowledge of mathematics.

That a single coin may be worth, say, two, five or ten pence *in value* is a difficult idea, but without it the process of counting the value of coins is impossible and progression in this aspect of counting cannot take place. The point to note, therefore, is that although the teaching and learning of certain mathematical procedures is a matter of demonstration and practice, such procedures are nevertheless built on particular kinds of prior knowledge.

Multiplication algorithms

Learning mathematics at all levels involves developing competence with various calculation algorithms. These are step-by-step procedures designed to solve a specific problem. The most familiar algorithms are those used for addition, subtraction, multiplication and division. An important progression in children's learning of mathematics occurs when they are expected to make connections between two or more alternative algorithms, both of which achieve the same result.

In recent years the learning of so-called 'standard written algorithms' for calculation has been delayed in favour of mental strategies that are often developed (or rediscovered) by children themselves. But even when written algorithms are introduced around the middle of Key Stage 2, the official curriculum guidance (DfEE, 1999) recommends the introduction of a range of 'expanded methods' before the more traditional 'compact' methods are tackled. Some of the expanded methods, though making use of the same mathematics as the standard algorithm, are more transparent in their presentation, and therefore more likely to be understood. They do look different from the standard algorithms on the page, or on the whiteboard, and have been, until recently, less familiar to many teachers. This is particularly true of the so-called 'grid method' for multiplication. So, if and when 'progression' to the traditional counterpart of some expanded method is attempted, the teacher needs to try to make a connection between two superficially different procedures. In the excerpt below, we return to the student teacher Laura's lesson introduced in Chapter 4, where we were interested in the choice of examples that she had made. Here we will focus on her attempt to make the connection between an expanded ('grid') form and the traditional compact ('column') form. A description and explanation of the grid multiplication is given below, and an extended account is given in Haylock (2006: 98).

Laura is teaching a Year 5 class: you can see extracts from this lesson on the companion website (Clip 5).

> Laura's lesson begins with a three-minute oral and mental starter, in which the children rehearse recall of multiplication bonds. There follows a 15-minute introduction to the main activity. Laura reminds the class that they have recently been working on multiplication using the 'grid' method. She talks about the tens and units being 'partitioned off'. Simon is invited to the white-board to demonstrate the method for a one-digit by two-digit calculation, 9 × 37. His recording is shown in Figure 5.11. Laura then says that they are going to 'learn another way'. She proceeds to write the calculation for 9 × 37 on the whiteboard in a conventional but elaborate column format (as shown in Figure 5.12), explaining as she goes along.

$$\begin{array}{c|cc} \times & 30 & 7 \\ \hline 9 & 270 & 63 \end{array} = 333$$

Figure 5.11   Simon finds 9 × 37 using the grid method

$$\begin{array}{r} 37 \\ \times\ \ 9 \\ \hline 270 \\ 63 \\ \hline 333 \end{array}$$

30 × 9
7 × 9

Figure 5.12   Laura demonstrates the elaborated column multiplication method

When Laura says that she is going to show the class 'another way', we might think that she will make a connection between the 'way' by which the same product is calculated in the two versions of the algorithm.

> Discuss with a friend of colleague to what extent you think that these two 'ways' are different *methods* or simply different forms of *recording* the calculation?

Essentially, the grid method for, say, a two-digit number multiplied by another two-digit number is carried out by splitting the two numbers into their tens and units components and arranging these along the outermost squares in a grid, so that the multiplications are carried out piecemeal inside the grid. Take the example of 56×24. The 50, 6, 20 and 4 are arranged round the boundary squares of the grid. Inside the grid we have the calculations 50×20, 20×6, 4×50 and 4×6. These four partial products when summed become the solution to the required product of 56×24, as shown in Figure 5.13.

$\times$	50	6	
20	1000	120	1120
4	200	24	224
			1344

Figure 5.13   The grid method for 56×24

One advantage of this method lies in its connection with the 'rectangular array' model of displaying any product of two whole numbers as a rectangular arrangement of objects. This arrangement is so common in the everyday world that its pedagogical value can be overlooked. A milk crate with five 'rows' and four 'columns' holds 5×4 milk bottles. In the classroom, the formation of trays in which children keep their books and pencils is another helpful example. The trays may be arranged in, say, six rows of four and thus provide a visual example of 6×4. If we extend this model to a slightly larger array of, say, 13×7 objects, this can be 'partitioned' into smaller adjacent arrays, for example: 10×7 and 3×7, allowing 13×7 to be calculated more easily by summing these two partitioned arrays, $70 + 21 = 91$.

When the array becomes a rectangular grid of squares the product becomes, of course, the *area* of that grid. Finally, when the squares are absent the area is calculated simply from the dimensions of the rectangle. It is perhaps unfortunate that the 'grid method' described above made its appearance in the National Numeracy Strategy (DfEE, 1999) as a stylistic representation of the so-called 'area model' which, as we have described, is an extended version of the rectangular array.

If a child does not understand the area model – and not every primary school child will – then the grid model can lose some of its pedagogical power. One way to avoid this is to develop its use from the rectangular array of objects. Partitioning arrays in various ways is a helpful way of understanding the underlying principles involved in this expanded method for multiplication. Thompson (2008) gives a very helpful commentary on this progression in multiplication.

$$
\begin{array}{r}
56 \\
\times\ 24 \\
\hline
24 \\
200 \\
120 \\
1000 \\
\hline
1344 \\
\hline
\end{array}
$$

Figure 5.14 A 'compact' layout for 56 × 24

One 'compact' way of carrying out the calculation above (56 × 24) is shown in Figure 5.14. At this stage the numbers below the first and penultimate lines in this column arrangement are exactly the same as those in the grid method. A direct *connection* can therefore be made between these two differently recorded calculations. This is no surprise, because exactly the same calculations have been carried out. However, the number of lines in the compact method can be reduced by curtailing the steps undertaken. Thus we can have the 'traditional' and probably more familiar form shown in Figure 5.15. Here the numbers do *not* coincide with the corresponding grid method shown in Figure 5.13. However, they do correspond with a more compressed one, shown in Figure 5.16.

It seems that Laura is aware of this close connection in her own mind as she introduces the main activity to the class. She reminds them that they have used the grid method, and says that she will show them a 'slightly different way of writing it down'. However, after the first example is completed Laura says that they are learning a 'different way to

$$
\begin{array}{r}
56 \\
\times\ 24 \\
\hline
224 \\
1120 \\
\hline
1344
\end{array}
$$

Figure 5.15   A contracted layout for 56 × 24

×	56
20	1120
4	224
	1344

Figure 5.16   The contracted grid method for 56 × 24

work it out'. She says that the answer could be the same whichever way they did it 'because it's the same sum'. Of course that presupposes that both methods are valid multiplication algorithms, but she does not clarify the *connection* between them, that is, that the same processes and principles – partition, distributivity and addition – are present in both methods. The fact that Laura includes demonstration of 37 × 9 by both methods does help to establish the connection, but the effort to sustain the connection is not maintained, and no reference to the grid method is made in her second demonstration example, 49 × 8. Her presentation of this example now relies exclusively on procedural aspects – the need to 'partition the number down', 'adding a zero to 8 × 4', getting the columns 'lined up', adding the partial products from the right. The fact that the connection is tenuous for at least one pupil becomes apparent in the plenary. Sean volunteers to calculate 27 × 9 and writes 27 and 9 in the first two rows as expected but then writes 20 × 7 and 2 × 9 to the left in the rows below.

As we can see, Laura does not quite drive home the connection between the two procedures for multiplication, even though mathematically they are the same. Indeed, we could say that they are only *clerically* different, in keeping with Laura's initial remark about showing the children a different way of *writing it down*, which implies that the deeper structures of the two methods remains the same. However, Laura seems to be influenced by their more superficial differences. This is apparent in her remark that they are learning a *different way to work it out,* which might suggest that the difference is more than a matter of the way in which the calculation is set out. This suggests that the underlying objective of making a connection must be based on a teacher's sound foundation knowledge and their understanding of the mathematical principles entailed in an algorithm. Examples of this kind of understanding, and the lack of it, are given in the first three chapters of the book by Liping Ma that we recommended earlier (Ma, 1999).

> Think about how you might illustrate the connection, visually, between the grid method and the standard algorithm. Describe your ideas to a friend or colleague, and ask whether they see the connections that you are trying to bring out.

Clearly, since precisely the same numbers that are entered into the grid appear in the compact version, Laura could have paired up these numbers in some way. For example, she could have drawn a line from each entry in the grid to the corresponding number in the compact version and pointed out how exactly the same calculation has been made to arrive at each pair. The correspondence between the two methods would be even clearer if she did not insist on adding the partial products (270 and 63) starting with the units digits, as she did. When Simon demonstrated the grid method earlier, he simply added 270 and 63 mentally, and wrote the sum 333 with no intermediate recording.

Before leaving this chapter, it is worth pointing out that the term 'connectionist' has been attached to a particular kind of teacher 'orientation' in some influential research on the teaching of numeracy (Askew et al., 1997). These connectionist teachers held a view of mathematics as a coherent body of knowledge, an ambition for their pupils to learn mathematics as a connected domain, and the belief that they can be enabled to do so. The other two orientations identified by Askew et al. were 'discoverists' and 'transmissionists'. Teachers with these orientations were found, on the whole, to be less effective mathematics teachers than the connectionists.

Summary

In this chapter we have introduced another dimension of the Knowledge Quartet. It concerns the way in which children achieve progress and understanding by making *connections*. In order to support progress and foster understanding, teachers need knowledge of the *logical* structure of mathematics itself, and also the *psychological* aspects of a child's learning. To miss opportunities to link new mathematical ideas with those that are already familiar to children is to miss a rich opportunity for such connection-making. To enlarge the range of connections that children can make with a particular concept, on the one hand, or among related concepts, on the other, is to enhance their understanding, because *mathematics is at heart a network of ideas*. Connections may be found not only within concepts but also among various ways in which different procedures can be presented or 'set out'. Connection-making also involves *anticipating the complexity* involved in learning a topic, especially within familiar and apparently elementary school mathematics topics.

Further reading

Mike Askew (1999) 'It ain't (just) what you do: effective teachers of numeracy', in I. Thompson (ed.), *Issues in Teaching Numeracy in Primary Schools* (pp. 91–102). Buckingham: Open University Press.

This provides a very clear and arresting prelude to a short synopsis of the *Effective Teachers of Numeracy* study (Askew et al., 1997), mentioned above, where teachers with a 'connectionist' orientation were found to be more effective than those described as either 'discoverists' or 'transmissionists'.

D.W. Hamlyn (1967) 'The logical and psychological aspects of learning', in R.S. Peters (ed.), *The Concept of Education* (pp. 24–43). London: Routledge & Kegan Paul.

Not an easy read – written by a former professor of philosophy – but this is a classic article, renowned for the way that it gets to the heart of issues central to progression in learning.

Richard Skemp (1986) *The Psychology of Learning Mathematics*. London: Penguin.

Another classic, written by one of the pioneers of modern mathematics education. Skemp was a mathematician and a psychologist, and this book has the rare distinction of treating both with lucidity and conviction.

Contingency: Tales of the Unexpected!

In this chapter you will read about:

- the final dimension of the Knowledge Quartet – contingency – characterised by
  - the unplanned-for or unexpected responses that a child may give in a lesson;
  - how teachers may respond to them;
- examples from student teachers' lessons.

In earlier chapters you were encouraged to consider a range of aspects of teaching mathematics – the use of resources in the classroom to *represent* ideas or concepts, the choice of *examples* that teachers make to use with the children, and the ways in which a teacher elicits what a child may know in order to develop the child's network of *connections*. In this chapter we come to the final dimension of the Knowledge Quartet – *contingency*. We shall start by asking you to think about the times when you have observed another teacher, an experienced colleague or someone at the start of their career, perhaps a fellow student teacher or a recently qualified teacher. One focus of this observation may be the way in which the teacher talks with a child, or a group of children, and the decisions that they make as a consequence of this discussion.

Many of the conversations that happen within a classroom may be related to organisational matters, such as ensuring that children have the necessary resources, or managerial ones related to the smooth running of the classroom. In Chapter 1 we outlined the difference between these generic issues and others which are content-specific. However, some of these exchanges will be linked to the content of the lesson – the aspect of mathematics being taught. The teacher may be assessing whether the child has grasped a new idea or skill, and whether their understanding is being extended beyond the particular example that they are working on. In Chapter 1 we met Naomi as she taught her Year 1 class. In this lesson there is a point where she is organising children and seeking to discover more about an individual child's thinking all in the same breath, typical of the multi-tasking that teachers, including student teachers, are able to achieve:

> Naomi: Excellent. Can you tell us how you worked it out? Come to the front. Owen, stand up. Sit in your rows please. Right, Stuart just worked out the difference between three and five and said it was two. How did you work it out, Stuart?

So in this very short interchange, she has praised a child, Stuart, asked him about his way of working, given him directions to come to the front of the class, indicated that she was not happy with another child, Owen, reminded the whole class how they should be sitting and then returned to Stuart to ask him about his working. Naomi refers to six different aspects within about 20 seconds. Typically a teacher will be juggling several aspects in this way and often will have anticipated them.

However, there are times when the teacher is faced with an unexpected response to a question or an unexpected point within a discussion and so has to make a decision whether or not to explore the idea with the child. Laura, whom we met in Chapter 4, was working with a Year 5 class. In the second videotaped lesson she was building symmetrical shapes with them, using two copies of a given starting shape. As she was collecting diagrams of the symmetrical shapes on a large sheet of squared paper, one child suggested that they looked like capital letters. The manner in which the student teacher was direct in her acknowledgement of the child's observation is laudable.

> Laura: Tom, you'd noticed a pattern there which I hadn't. You said that they looked like letters.

This was not part of the planned lesson, and so Laura could have chosen to deviate from her planned agenda. It is these moments of decision, about which avenue to pursue, that will be the focus of this chapter, and we will come back to this incident with Laura later.

Often these moments of decision for the teacher are characterised by a pause as the teacher thinks about the implications of a response, suggestion or question before responding to the child's idea. There may be a moment of managing for time – 'That's an interesting thought', 'Could you explain that a little more?' – while the teacher is weighing up the possibilities. There may be a moment when the teacher really cannot see the connection of a response to what has been happening in the lesson. Sometimes it may be that there is simply not enough time to consider every response in depth. But there may also be those 'aha' moments when a child has an insight that is unexpected and worth developing with the rest of the class. In any of these situations, teachers have to decide whether they are going to deviate from the agenda or 'script' that they set out when they planned the lesson.

Caroline (whom we met in Chapter 5) was teaching a Year 2 class about fractions of shapes – in particular, about quarters. Before we get to the point of considering the unexpected contribution in this lesson, we want you to think about the mathematics that is involved.

> In her introduction to the main activity, Caroline asked the children to 'split a shape in half'. First, they considered a paper square which children folded along the various lines of symmetry. Fixing the square on the whiteboard, Caroline then placed paper strips on the two lines of symmetry parallel to the sides, thus dividing the square first into halves, then into quarters.

To get a feel for what was happening, make a paper square and fold it to show the four lines of symmetry. Then draw in the two lines of symmetry, as described above, so that the square is split into quarters. Cut the square up and check that the four pieces are all identical in size and shape. Now repeat this, but this time draw in the two diagonal lines of symmetry; again cut the square up and compare the quarters.

Now use two paper rectangles (we should say 'oblongs', as a square is a special type of rectangle and we do not want a square again). With the first one, fold along the lines of symmetry and again cut it into quarters. With the second one, mark in the two diagonals and fold along these. Cut along these fold lines to get four pieces. Has the oblong been split into quarters? How can you convince yourself and others? Discuss it with a colleague.

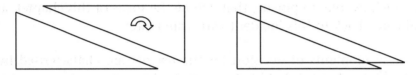

Figure 6.1 The congruence of the two halves of a rectangle

The difficulty here arises because a diagonal of the oblong is not a line of symmetry. A diagonal does indeed divide the oblong into two halves. The fact that they are identical can be seen by rotating one half about the centre of the oblong rather than folding it (see Figure 6.1). Because the two halves are identical in shape and size, they are said to be *congruent*.

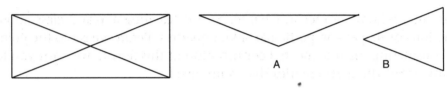

Figure 6.2 Quarters of a rectangle?

But once we get the two different shapes from using both diagonals to divide the oblong into four pieces, things are rather different. It is not obvious on first sight whether these different shapes (A and B in Figure 6.2) do have the same area and hence are quarters. Indeed, if you want to convince yourself then it may well be that dividing one of the triangles and rearranging the pieces is helpful. Have a look at the diagram in Figure 6.3 and see if it helps.

So what happened when Caroline introduced an oblong?

> Caroline fixed an oblong to the board, intending that it be split similarly into halves and then quarters. She asked: 'How would you split that in half?' One child, Simon, wanted to mark in the diagonal in order to split the oblong in half.

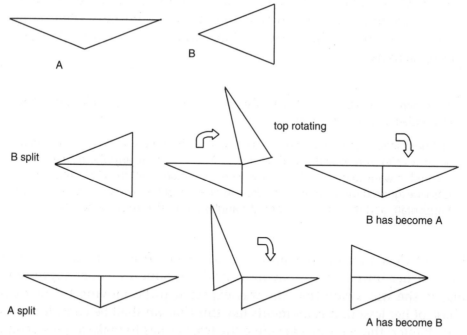

Figure 6.3   Parts of a rectangle – do they have the same area?

How would you respond to this unexpected response? In discussion with a colleague, decide whether you would:

- ignore his suggestion, saying that the diagonal is not what you meant;

- acknowledge but sideline, perhaps saying that this is a good suggestion for halves;

- respond to the suggestion, incorporating it in the lesson to see what it gives;

- do something else.

The way in which Caroline had posed the question, 'How would you split that in half?', had elicited a broader range of possibilities than she had anticipated. Although Caroline did not want to explore halving this way, she asked the class whether such a line would split the shape in half. She suggested that the children 'imagine we turn this round the other way'. In saying this she showed her ability to respond well to the child's idea and also realised that the matter could be settled by performing a rotation, whereas reflection had been implicit in the earlier folding activity.

> A moment or two later Caroline had another unexpected response and this time responded in a very different way.
>
> The next shape she considered was a circle, and this time she did not respond at all to a child who called out three times 'You can do it anywhere'. The child seemed to want to point out that any diameter would 'split' the circle into halves. Caroline ignored this response and drew in one line of her own choice (which was horizontal), and then a second at right angles (vertically) to show quarters.

It is not clear why she was unwilling to deviate from her agenda at this stage of her introduction, having considered Simon's earlier suggestion; maybe she was aware that she was expected to be moving to the next phase of her lesson. It is moments like this that we shall be considering in this chapter; those moments where the teacher has to make a split-second decision about which avenue to go down. We shall see a variety of ways in which these moments can arise as well as thinking about the possibilities that are then available to the teacher.

Why are we interested in contingency?

We call the fourth dimension of the Knowledge Quartet 'contingency'. This dimension of the Knowledge Quartet is all about in-the-moment actions and interactions in the classroom and the unpredictability of some of these actions. Teachers are continually responding to the interests and understandings of children as part of their engagement with the children's learning. However, because it is impossible to know how each individual will react and respond to any situation, teachers have to be ready to make decisions 'on their feet' during the course of a lesson.

In the following section we will consider some of the work of a number of people who have influenced our thinking about this aspect of teaching and learning. Where possible, we will illustrate the ideas with examples from the writing of these authors or from our own videotaped lessons.

We return here to Alan Bishop's anecdote which we mentioned in Chapter 2 (Bishop, 2001: 244). He recounts the occasion when a class of 9- and 10-year-olds were asked to give a fraction between $\frac{1}{2}$ and $\frac{3}{4}$. One girl answered $\frac{2}{3}$, 'because 2 is between the 1 and the 3, and on the bottom the 3 lies between the 2 and the 4'. Here a child has given a correct answer ($\frac{2}{3}$) but will her reasoning be true in all cases? What is the teacher (we shall call her Cathy) to do? Quite probably she was not expecting this response and so she has to make a split-second decision. Will Cathy follow up on this reasoning, possibly teasing out its limitations? Does she herself know if it can be used in all cases? This is quite a challenging idea within mathematics and we have the luxury of being able to think this through at our own pace, unlike Cathy in the immediacy of the classroom. There are a number of factors which will determine her choice, and among these will be the mathematical specialised content knowledge that Cathy possesses, both substantive and syntactic. We shall think about some of these possibilities.

One option for Cathy is simply to tell the child that she thinks that her reasoning does not hold true in all cases. If Cathy knew that a counterexample would disprove the child's reasoning, this would be an example of her own syntactic knowledge. In the classroom, an interactive relationship typically exists between the teacher and the learner, and this interactivity appears to be a key contributory factor in the child's learning. The process is two-way, so that the teacher can use the ideas that a child offers within the lesson to enhance their learning of the subject-matter – using the teacher's syntactic knowledge.

So, could Cathy have asked the child further questions? These might have revealed if there are limitations in the child's approach. Thinking of such possibilities during the ongoing lesson would be quite a challenge, but it might be worth returning to in another lesson; this could give Cathy time to think through the child's suggestion. In Chapter 3 we discussed the important role that the choice of examples plays in mathematics teaching. Here is a case where the use of relevant examples, and particularly counterexamples, could help to investigate if the child's reasoning holds or not. There are many pairs where all is well. One is $\frac{1}{3}$ and $\frac{3}{5}$, where $\frac{2}{4}$ is in-between: $\frac{2}{4}$ is larger than $\frac{1}{3}$ but smaller than $\frac{3}{5}$, with the numerator, 2, lying between 1 and 3 and the denominator, 4 lying between 3 and 5. Other pairs include $\frac{1}{5}$ and $\frac{3}{7}$, with $\frac{2}{6}$; or even $\frac{1}{4}$ and $\frac{5}{6}$ where there are three possible 'in-between' fractions, $\frac{2}{5}$, $\frac{3}{5}$ and $\frac{4}{5}$.

How would you check that the 'in-between' fraction(s) with these three pairs are indeed valid? Try diagrams – perhaps sectors of a circle or a number line with decimal equivalents, or equivalent fractions. Are any of these more convincing than others?

Perhaps, then, Cathy could suggest two fractions where there is no possibility of using the process that the child has suggested, say $\frac{1}{2}$ and $\frac{2}{3}$, where there is no 'between number' possible since the numerators (1 and 2) and denominators (2 and 3) are consecutive. Another example could be $\frac{1}{4}$ and $\frac{2}{3}$ – again no 'between number' but additionally the denominator of the second fraction is smaller than the first. So here we have examples where the rule, as it stands, does not work. Another possibility would be two fractions such as $\frac{1}{2}$ and $\frac{3}{5}$, where the process is possible, $\frac{2}{4}$ would be the result, but $\frac{2}{4}$ is equivalent to the first fraction ($\frac{1}{2}$) and so again the process is not giving us a new fraction whose value is between the two given fractions.

Within our fourth dimension of the Knowledge Quartet, it is the link between the teacher and the child that we see as central. It is the teacher's skilful intervention that can enable the child to make new connections in their own knowledge. So another alternative for Cathy might be to ask the children to concentrate on equivalent fractions in order to help them find these 'in-between' fractions.

Deviating from the agenda

As we remarked in Chapter 2, planning often begins from some form of agenda – a textbook, a syllabus, a web-based lesson plan, ultimately a sequence of planned, intended actions to be carried out by the teacher and/or the children within a lesson or unit of some kind. Shulman (1986) called these the 'text' for the lesson. However, while the stimulus – the teacher's intended actions – can be planned, the children' responses can only be predicted. Interactive teaching generates classroom events that are almost impossible to plan for, and the teacher's reaction to them is necessarily contingent. Such contingent action can be informed by the teacher's subject matter and pedagogical content knowledge.

In Chapter 5 we met another of the student teachers in our study, Colin, who was teaching a Reception class. He was using coins, of value 1p and

2p, within an activity. The children needed to recognise that each coin had a *value* and that the amount of money that a collection of coins represents was dependent upon their value and not simply the number of coins (the cardinality) in the collection. This is illustrated in Figure 6.4 with two different collections of coins having a value of 5p.

3 coins, value 5p   4 coins, value 5p

Figure 6.4   Different sets of coins to represent 5p in value

In the introduction to the main activity, Colin had stuck large magnetic coins onto a whiteboard and had produced a toy dog bearing a 5p label. The children were asked to discuss, in pairs, the combination of coins that could be used to buy this toy. As the activity was a vehicle for understanding the notion of value, as opposed to simple cardinality, Colin was expecting addition of different values. After two children had given anticipated answers, involving 1p and 2p coins (such as those above), Niall suggested 10p minus 5p.

Here is one of those moments where the unexpected has happened. Colin was not anticipating subtraction and so he had to decide rapidly what to do. From our videotaped lessons, there are three strategies that are used to respond to this type of situation. The teacher may choose to:

- ignore the suggestion;
- acknowledge the suggestion but sideline it;
- respond to the suggestion and incorporate it.

For ease of reference, we shall refer to these choices as type I (ignore), type AS (acknowledge but sideline) and type RI (respond and incorporate).

Ignoring the suggestion may be the course of action if the teacher is uncertain what the child means, or feels that there is insufficient time to explore it. However, the child may then feel that the contribution was not welcomed and may be less inclined to offer contributions in the future. Acknowledging the suggestion, but sidelining it, can alleviate the difficulty of rebuffing the child by welcoming the suggestion and deflecting discussion to another time, perhaps on an individual basis with the child. Responding to the suggestion needs confidence on the teacher's part that there may be some gain in following up the suggestion and incorporating it into the lesson. That confidence may well arise from the teacher's own knowledge, enabling them to see the potential from the suggestion.

> Rather than ignoring (I) or acknowledging but sidelining (AS) Niall's idea, Colin welcomed it, and responded and incorporated (RI) the notion of subtraction with the class. In doing so, he deviated, for a few moments, from his lesson plan.

Here it seems that the child had seen the situation in a way that Colin had not anticipated. But he listened to Niall and responded to the idea of incorporating subtraction as well as addition, moving away from his 'text'. He was allowing the interactivity of the lesson to change the flow of the lesson. Perhaps most importantly, in responding to the child, he was allowing the child to make the types of connections that have been discussed in Chapter 5.

Some theoretical perspectives

A constructivist view of knowledge provides one fundamental perspective on children's contributions within lessons; we have discussed some aspects of this view within Chapters 1 and 3. When a child articulates an idea, this points to the nature of *their* knowledge construction, which may or may not be quite what the teacher intended or anticipated. The child's indications of their meaning-making may be probed by a teacher's questions, or may be volunteered unsolicited. The ways in which a teacher responds to these indications from the child are at the heart of teaching. To put aside such indications, or simply to ignore them or suggest that the child is wrong, could be construed as a lack of interest in what it is that they (and possibly others) have come to know. This knowledge has come as a consequence, in part, of the teacher's teaching. Arguably, unless a teacher responds appropriately to children's ideas, they cannot be said to be teaching. Harries and Spooner (2000: 28) suggest that 'when the learner appears to deviate from the teacher's expectations it provides an opportunity for exploring the basis on which the learner is making the perceived rational decisions'.

The decision by the teacher to respond or not is often taken in a split-second and with a number of other constraints being in the teacher's mind. Not only is there a need to be thinking about the subject matter in hand, but they may also be juggling with management and time constraints. As a teacher gains experience, some of these other constraints may become less pressing and allow time for thinking on their feet during the course of the lesson. At the very start of this book, we introduced Donald Schön's ideas about the reflective practitioner and in particular his distinction between reflecting *in* action and reflecting in action (Schön, 1983). The expert teacher may be able to reflect in action, during the course of a lesson, whereas the novice teacher may require deliberate reflection on action, often with someone else and after the event. Colin was an example of a trainee teacher successfully making the decision during a lesson to deviate from his planned agenda in order to build on a response from a child. This can be seen as one of the ways in which a trainee or early career teacher is really getting to grips with teaching.

Etienne Wenger actually perceives contingent, what he calls 'emergent', aspects of teaching as underpinning a number of pedagogical issues, and writes:

> Pedagogical debates traditionally focus on such choices as authority versus freedom, instruction versus discovery, individual versus collaborative learning, or lecturing versus hands-on experience. But the real issue underlying all these debates is the interaction of the planned with the emergent. Teaching must be opportunistic because it cannot control its own effects. (Wenger, 1998: 267)

We can gain further insight into the manner in which teachers react to an unexpected response from their students, from the research of Liping Ma (1999). In her well-known study, Ma presented different classroom scenarios to groups of American and Chinese teachers and asked them how they would respond. One scenario involved a child coming to the teacher with a proposed conjecture – that *as the perimeter of a closed figure increases, the area also increases*. The child had a diagram to support the theory, as shown in Figure 6.5. Ma asked the teachers how they would respond to the child.

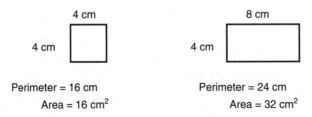

Figure 6.5   Perimeter and area of rectangles: a child's idea

> Investigate this yourself, or preferably with a colleague. Can you find two more rectangles where this relationship is true? Are there any special features of the child's example? If so, does that affect the relationship between the perimeter and the area?

Ma found a range of responses from the teachers in her study. Virtually all the teachers had not met this 'theory' before but many (although not all) were familiar with how to find the perimeter and area of a rectangle. A large number of teachers felt unsure about the claim and believed that they would need to find some more examples. However, the Chinese teachers were much more willing to explore the possibilities themselves and build up an idea of how they would respond than the American teachers. Ma suggests that part of the reason for this is a teacher's confidence which draws on two aspects of their subject knowledge, 'their attitudes towards the possibility of solving mathematics problems on their own and their knowledge of the particular topics related to the proposition' (Ma, 1999: 99). Ma says that these teachers have a 'profound understanding of fundamental mathematics'. They suggested that they would respond either with 'praise with explanation' or 'praise with engagement in further exploration'. However, these responses were significantly more substantial in some cases rather than others. Our 'acknowledge but sideline' (type AS) or 'respond and incorporate' (type RI) approaches to an unexpected offering from a child, outlined earlier in this chapter, are akin to the responses that Ma describes.

All of these writers have emphasised that the teacher needs to hear what a child is saying – the teacher has to be a good listener. Brissenden (1985: 6) emphasises the necessity for the teacher to listen 'carefully to what children actually say and mean' and then to respond to it. But we are very aware that this can be quite difficult to achieve alongside the other pressures on the teacher, particularly a beginning teacher. Brown and Wragg (1993) group together listening and responding in their 'tactics' of effective questioning. They observe that 'our capacity to listen diminishes with anxiety' (p. 20). Uncertainty about the sufficiency of one's subject-matter knowledge may well induce such anxiety, although this is just one of many possible causes. Brown and Wragg add that 'responding' moves are the linchpins of a lesson, important in its sequencing and structuring, and observe that such interventions are some of the most difficult tactics for newly qualified teachers to master. Now we shall look at some more examples from student teachers' lessons of their responses to children – aspects of these 'listening and responding' tactics.

Back to the project lessons

The videotaped lessons gave rise to a number of incidents in this fourth dimension of the Knowledge Quartet, involving a child's contribution, and these can be broken down into three types:

- a child's response to a question from the teacher;

- a child's response to an activity or discussion;

- a child's incorrect answer to a question or in the course of a discussion.

In the first two of these the unexpectedness of the child's answer, comment or observation is critical and the way in which the student teacher deals with it may reflect their own subject knowledge. Importantly, some mistakes or misconceptions may be anticipated and even planned for – as teachers increase their knowledge through experience and research, the teachers may anticipate them, even incorporating them into their planning.

A child's response to a question from the teacher

Sometimes an unexpected response during the ongoing development of a lesson can be quite unsettling to the teacher. The first strategy observed to be adopted by student teachers in such circumstances was to deflect discussion away from the unexpected contribution, thus making space for the student teacher to think about their response to it. So this could be categorised as either an ignore response (I) or an acknowledge and sideline one (AS). An example of this arose during the introduction to the main activity of Laura's second videotaped lesson with her Year 5 class.

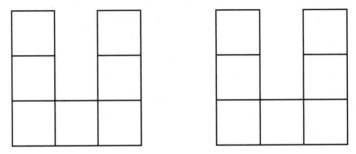

Figure 6.6   Two U-shapes made from squares

She had introduced an investigation into making symmetrical shapes using two identical U-shapes as shown in Figure 6.6. She drew one of them (itself symmetrical, think back to the discussion of choice of examples in Chapter 4 where one property may obscure the role of another) on a whiteboard and explained that this piece was only half of a completed shape; then she drew the other half in one possible position. She asked the children 'What can you say?' about the completed shape. Several suggested that it was symmetrical and the children showed the lines of symmetry. Then she drew another shape. Laura returned to Tom, who had offered an idea earlier, commenting that both of the completed shapes formed a letter of the alphabet. Laura admitted that he had found a 'pattern' that she had not seen.

Laura: Tom, you'd noticed a pattern there which I hadn't. You said that they looked like letters.

Tom: Yes.

Laura: They do, what letters?

Tom: They look like an H and an I.

Laura: OK, a capital H and a capital I. That's good. It's always good to be reasoning and thinking beyond what we're doing, but that's not actually why we're, I didn't realise that they were going to make letters, so you noticed a pattern that I hadn't even thought about. OK, but that doesn't have to be the way it is. You don't have to confine yourself to that.

Laura used the word 'pattern' to describe what Tom has noticed. She seemed to be using 'pattern' to group the shapes that have a common characteristic – in this case making a capital letter.

> What is the full set of possible symmetrical shapes that can be made? Tom spotted an H and I – are there other letters that may arise? If you were using this activity, what are the advantages and disadvantages of finding all the shapes as part of your planning?

During this part of the lesson Tom saw a very different feature of the shapes they were drawing than that which Laura had anticipated. Even if she had found all the shapes prior to the lesson, she may not have 'seen' the letter connection. She appeared to use a hesitant, somewhat defensive strategy although not completely dismissing the idea or ignoring it – she acknowledged it but did not embrace it (AS). This type of totally unexpected response can cause real difficulties for the teacher if she cannot make sense of the reasoning or ideas that the child is suggesting. Sometimes there may be limitations in the verbal communication of ideas by the child which will exacerbate these difficulties. The teacher may be anxious about losing control of the flow of ideas, even that her intended curricular objectives may be completely subverted. Willingness to explore such unexpected contributions is supported by secure specialised content knowledge; possibly in this case, there was a connection with work that the children had done earlier (prior to her working with them) in considering the symmetry of capital letters.

Over six minutes later, the following interchange occurred after another two examples had been drawn on the large sheet of squared paper:

Laura: What are all these hands up for? Is it another letter?

Children:	Yes.
Laura:	OK, what letter is it?
Children:	W.
Laura:	It's a W. This is an amazing little discovery we've got going on here this morning. OK, hands down please.

Here Laura is really embracing the idea in a much more positive way and indeed celebrating the way in which they have been ready to run with it (RI). She has acknowledged the link that Tom, and subsequently others, have made to a different part of the curriculum. Capitalising on such opportunities can develop the connections that a child makes between different areas. In this case the link is not of fundamental mathematical importance but shows an awareness of ideas that the children have learnt about. This readiness to build connections is one that we have discussed in depth in Chapter 5.

A child's response to an activity or discussion

An example of a child's response to an activity having a major impact on the course of part of the lesson comes from Chantal's first videotaped lesson with a Year 1 class.

At one point during the oral and mental starter to the lesson, the class was split into two groups and proceeded to count in ones, with the two groups alternating.

Group A	Group B
1	2
3	4
5	6 and so on

A child noticed that the class would be counting in odds and evens, as they had done the previous day, although this was not a deliberate outcome that Chantal had incorporated in her planning.

So what could Chantal do? The child had highlighted an important connection and it would be an ideal opportunity to review the idea of odds and evens and their properties – key ideas at this age. However, this was not in her plan and could result in her needing to adapt other parts of her lesson. But the gains for the children could be considerable.

> Chantal took up the opportunity and developed it further with the class. She discussed which numbers are odd and which are even, concentrating on the final digits. She followed this through by looking at the 1–100 number square, and then wrote the odd and even end-digits on the board. Chantal gave some two-digit examples and children had to say whether they were odd or even. Having told the children to begin counting at 1 (odd), a child asked if they can start at zero. Chantal then suggested they start at zero, which she told them is even. When they had finished counting, Chantal asked each group what sort of numbers their counting ended in.

The whole of this part of the lesson was totally changed because of the response of one child to the counting activity. Chantal made the split-second decision to respond to the child's suggestion and was able to incorporate it into the lesson (RI). Not only did she develop the activity to build on the idea of odd and even within the counting activity, she related it to resources that they were using within the class – the hundred grid. There has been much discussion of the use of this resource in Chapter 3; in this instance it is ideal, with the odds and evens falling into distinct columns. The suggestion of another child to start the counting at zero was another opportunity to develop the children's understanding and make further connections. Most 100 squares start at 1 and so to count from zero further builds the concept of the continuity of whole numbers – ultimately including negative numbers. Chantal told the children that zero was even – this is a convention, in order that it fits with the numbers on either side of zero, although, of course, it has no size. Chantal built connections to earlier work and actively involved the children in their own learning. Her readiness to make the most of this moment indicated both her own *knowledge* of the importance of some of these fundamental ideas and her *confidence* in altering her planned agenda.

These two examples give a clear picture of the essential relationship between teacher, child and subject matter. The nature of that relationship can change as a consequence of the contribution of the child to the lesson. We have argued that one determinant of a teacher's response to a child's ideas is the teacher's content knowledge for teaching, both subject-matter knowledge and pedagogical content knowledge (see Chapter 2).

Responding to an incomplete or incorrect answer from a child

The third type of example that arose in the videotapes was where a child gave an incorrect answer and the teacher responded to this. Brissenden (1985) argued strongly that there was need to reconsider the way in which teachers act upon children's responses during lessons and, in particular, that as a teacher 'you should resolve *never* to evaluate your children's responses' (p. 6). He argued that children should not be 'inhibited by what they feel to be the teacher's judgment of them' (p. 6) but that they should be learning in 'an atmosphere which encourages both the tentative offering and the development of more formal discourse when this becomes important' (p. 6). As we have said earlier, there is a need for the teacher to listen 'carefully to what children actually say and mean' (p. 6) and then to respond to it. In the heat of the moment, this can be a tall order for a teacher. Indeed, there will be many who would feel that Brissenden's urging to be positive at all times is too extreme a view. We have examples where the incorrect answer has been deflected, and hence not evaluated, and the underlying cause of the mistake or misconception has not been investigated.

Several writers, including Koshy (2000), give a helpful overview of how a teacher can use the mistakes and misconceptions of children to improve learning. The sensitivities of the children are an important part of this; the need to build a learning environment where it is safe to take risks and to learn from incorrect answers is clear. Koshy (2000: 175–179) outlines the possible reasons for mistakes and misconceptions as: careless mistakes; reliance on rules; mistakes due to problems with language and mathematical vocabulary; mistakes when special cases present themselves; and mistakes in solving numerical problems. Within these reasons there are other groups and it is not always easy to see where a difficulty has arisen. However, as Koshy (2000: 180) suggests, 'a teaching style which encourages children to discuss their methods with the teacher and other children is likely to be more effective in exposing misconceptions'.

So now we shall revisit one of the classrooms that we have been considering throughout this book to illustrate this final type of contingent action – responding to a mistake or misconception. Mike Askew (1993) suggested that children often make mistakes because of a systematic error, or bug, but that sharing methods with a large group or the whole class can allow these bugs to be detected in a constructive way.

You will remember that Laura was teaching a Year 5 class and had introduced them to the column method of multiplication. In previous lessons they had learnt the grid method. In Chapters 4 and 5 we discussed both the examples that Laura chose and the connections between the two approaches, with diagrams to illustrate. Here we shall be focusing on the final part of the lesson and one child's unexpected contribution. You can see this as Clip 6 on the companion website.

Laura called the children together on the carpet for an eight-minute plenary at the end of the lesson. She gave them the example 27×9 and asked: 'Who thinks they can probably tell us how to do it?' She asked one volunteer, Sean, to demonstrate the new column method. He suggested 180 as an estimate. When Laura asked him how he arrived at 180, he said '20 times 9'. Laura clearly thought that this was a bit surprising and said 'Is that the best way? That's a good start, anyone done anything differently?'

When Sean suggested 180 as the estimate, Laura was surprised. Having asked him how he did it, she asked the other children for their ideas. Discuss with a colleague if there are other responses Laura could have given to Sean.

It is important to recognise the pressure that Laura was under at this point in the lesson. She wanted to review what the children had been doing, needed to set their homework and was keeping her eye on the clock as morning break was approaching fast! We suggest that Laura could:

- accept his suggestion;

- ignore his suggestion and tell him that a better estimate would be 270;

- ask him how he arrived at his estimate;

- ask others in the class what they think.

Here we have four possible avenues. In fact she had used two of these but Laura's surprise seemed to be that Sean suggested 20 rather than 30. Would it have been helpful to ask him *why* he chose 20? Her comment 'Is that the best way?' had an implication that it might not be the best way, in contrast with Brissenden's advice mentioned at the start of this section.

Another child said that they had rounded to 30 and so arrived at an estimate of 270. Does Sean need help in understanding why 30 may be a more appropriate to use than 20 in finding an estimated answer?

> Then Laura asked Sean to lay out the multiplication in the way that they had been practising. As he started to write on the board, Laura was talking to the rest of the class and so did not see his initial partitioning of 27 and recording of the multiplier, as shown in Figure 6.7. She turned to see what he was doing and his faulty attempt appeared to catch Laura unawares.

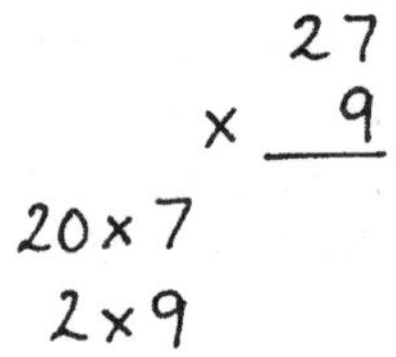

$$
\begin{array}{r}
27 \\
\times\ \underline{9} \\
\end{array}
$$

$$20 \times 7$$
$$2 \times 9$$

Figure 6.7　Sean's attempt at 27×9

It seems that she fully expected him to apply the algorithm faultlessly, and that his actual response really was unanticipated. So now in these closing moments of the lesson, Sean has shown major misunderstandings; there are several 'bugs' in his application of the procedure. The partition of 27 into 20 and 2 is faulty, and the multiplier is first 7, then 9.

> What might be the reason(s) for Sean's error? What would you do at this point, perhaps recognising that morning break is approaching fast? What if you had more time? Discuss this with a colleague.

What is Laura to do? Should she respond to the problems or acknowledge his attempt but reiterate the procedure she had taught them earlier, or ignore the problem by asking another child? Should she say that they will come back to this after playtime? In other circumstances where time was not such an issue, this would seem to be a case where Sean might be encouraged to reconsider what he has written by asking him some well-chosen questions. One such question might be how he would do it by the grid method which they had been learning in earlier lessons. Or Laura might simply ask him why he wrote those particular numbers where he did.

In fact, Laura avoided correcting Sean herself, although her response indirectly suggested that all was not well. She asked the class 'Is that the way to do it? Would everyone do it that way?', a type AS response. Leroy suggested the correct partition and multiplication (20 × 9 and 7 × 9) as shown in Figure 6.8, but there was no diagnosis of where Sean went wrong, or why.

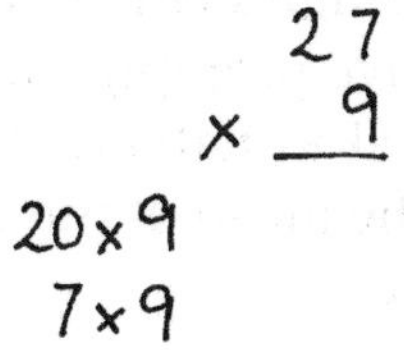

$$
\begin{array}{r}
2\,7 \\
\times\ \underline{9} \\
\end{array}
$$

$$20 \times 9$$
$$7 \times 9$$

Figure 6.8 Leroy's column multiplication

In this short, final part of the lesson, Sean had done two unexpected things – his estimate and then his attempt at the column layout which they had been learning in this lesson. This was an indication of underlying difficulties for Sean and perhaps for a number of other children.

> As the lesson concluded, Laura told the children that they should complete the set of exercises for homework. She finished the lesson in time for break.

Returning to Naomi's lesson

In this lesson, Naomi was teaching the Year 1 class about the 'difference' between two numbers. She had used a comparison of the two numbers by using representations of each number – frogs in two ponds. Naomi had lined up the frogs so that she could pair them up successively, as illustrated in Figure 1.1.

> Early in her introduction to the main activity, Naomi had set up a situation where she had four frogs in her pond and her neighbour had two frogs. Having established that she had two more frogs than her neighbour, Hugh made this interjection.

Hugh: You could both have three, if you give one to your neighbour.

Naomi: I could, that's a very good point, Hugh. I'm not going to do that today though. I'm just going to talk about the difference. Morag, if you had a pond, how many frogs would you like in it?

One can readily sympathise with Naomi's response to Hugh's insight, which seems to deviate too far from the agenda that she had set for the lesson. This is another moment when the lesson is poised to be hijacked. Naomi acknowledges Hugh's observation, but refuses to be diverted from her course – a type AS response. With the benefit of hindsight, one can see that she had the option, if she were brave (or confident, or reckless) enough to choose it, to take Hugh's remark as the starting point of rather a nice inquiry. This might have prompted investigation of the difference between two numbers, as well as halving, the distinction between even and odd numbers and even the mean of the two numbers. We would have classified this as a RI response.

> For the activity part of the lesson, some groups worked with cubes on the pairing approach to finding the difference, and Naomi introduced one group to counting on from the smaller number to the larger one. While working with these children, she used her fingers to tally her counting on (see Figure 6.9). So in finding the difference between 2 and 6, she counted the numbers 3, 4, 5, 6 on her fingers and then tallied how many fingers she had used – 1, 2, 3, 4 – arriving at the difference of 4.

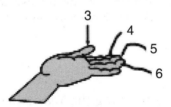

Figure 6.9   Using fingers to count on from 2 to 6

> Later in the lesson, Naomi changed her approach with the children using the cubes when it did not appear to be fruitful. The children were using the cubes to build models of everything but the numbers that Naomi had intended – towers, guns, houses and so on. So she introduced the idea of counting on from the smaller number.

Some tensions may have been present for her. Again we are towards the end of the lesson and Naomi had gathered the children on the carpet for the lesson plenary. The children were being asked to find the difference between two numbers that had been generated by rolling two dice. You can watch this part of the lesson as Clip 7 on the companion website.

The dice showed 3 and 5. Jeffrey added them and answered 'eight'. Stuart then comes to the rescue and gives the answer to the original question saying 'two'.

Naomi: Excellent. Can you tell us how you worked it out? Come to the front. Owen, stand up. Sit in your rows please. Right, Stuart just worked out the difference between three and five and said it was two. How did you work it out, Stuart?

Stuart: I held out three fingers and five, and then there's two left.

> Hold out both your hands and fold down two fingers on one hand. What is Stuart doing? Was Stuart thinking of a 'difference' or 'take away' model of subtraction? How would you find out? (These two models of subtraction are explained fully in Chapter 7.)

Whereas Naomi had used her fingers as a way of tallying when counting on, Stuart used his to model difference in a very direct way. He was using the model that Naomi used at the start of the lesson. He was using his fingers as portable representatives, showing *both* sets simultaneously – as Naomi had with the frogs at the beginning of the lesson. Naomi responded:

Naomi: Ah, OK. That *does* work because you've got five fingers on your hands so if you've got five here and three you've got two left to make five. But I know an even *better* way to work it out. Does anybody know another way to work it out?

It seems that, in her own mind, Naomi had abandoned the difference model in favour of counting on and was unwilling to return to it. There is some profound mathematics underlying these apparently elementary ideas which we will discuss further in Chapter 7. So Naomi was faced with deciding whether it was worth responding to and incorporating Stuart's suggestion (RI response) and whether she felt confident to do that. Or should Naomi have stayed with her own intention (I or AS response)? If we are aiming to build the connections which the children have within their understanding of mathematics, then there is a strong argument in favour of building on Stuart's suggestion.

Later in the plenary, Gavin offered a useful insight after Jim was about to add 6 to 3 rather than subtract 3 from 6.

Naomi: Not adding, it's the difference ... Gavin, do you want to help us out.

Gavin: If you wanted to make six, you could add three there, and make another three, and make six.

Naomi: So three and three makes six. So how can we say that with the difference? What's the difference between three and six? What's the difference between the two numbers? How many more?

Gavin: If you wanted to add on three to make six you'd make six, but if you wanted to take away three to make three, it'll be three.

Naomi: OK, I know what you mean Gavin. Good, so it's, the difference is three. We can say the difference between three and six is three. If we start with three ... Morag?

Morag: It's one.

Naomi: I'm not sure what you mean. The difference between three and six. [counts on her fingers] Three, four, five, six.

Morag :   The answer's one.

Naomi: So it's three.

Gavin seemed to be on to something. He could answer Naomi's difference question not by counting on, but by performing an addition. Naomi claimed to know what Gavin means, but made no capital from the connection that he offered, which relates difference to addition, and then addition to 'taking away'. This small section of the lesson included much of the language associated with subtraction – difference, how many more, take away – each with its different conception of subtraction. Some of the subtleties may be masked by the unfortunate way in which the dice have landed – having 3 as the number to be subtracted and then another 3 as the answer makes some of the conversation quite tricky. In Chapter 4 we highlighted the way in which some examples can hide the role of the variables – this dice-generated example exemplifies the difficulties. Morag, on the other hand, was one of the many children that we see in the video still experiencing significant problems. Naomi was 'not sure' what she meant. *Why* did Morag insist that the answer is 1? How did she 'construct' that answer? If only Naomi could find out, she might have stood a better chance of getting to the bottom of the incomprehension of many of the class. Time was not with her in this lesson.

Teacher's insights

In the work that has developed from this project, we have become aware of a final way in which teachers may need to act contingently. We have seen instances, and indeed have done it ourselves, when there is a moment of realisation on the teacher's part that they themselves may not be on the right track. We call these 'd'oh' moments (after Homer Simpson, of course). It may be that a teacher recognises that the example they have just given is not ideal, that the representation that they have chosen is not helping understanding or that they have not developed a connection that was asking to be made.

In one instance, the teacher had prepared slides for the interactive white-board to demonstrate different methods for carrying out addition and subtraction calculations with her Year 1 class. She had made use of picto-rial representations to help demonstrate these methods. For the subtrac-tion 7 – 2, she had a representation showing seven circles and two circles; so there were nine circles altogether on the slide. It was evident during the lesson, when she reached this slide, that she recognised the potential problem with the representation (suggesting addition rather than subtrac-tion) and skipped quickly to the next slide.

But there are also d'oh moments when a child offers a suggestion which the teacher does not readily grasp. However, with some discussion the teacher may be able to see the potential of this new idea. One such inci-dent occurred in the pilot stages of the project when a student teacher had been asking her Year 5 class a series of multiplication facts. One child said he knew a trick to remember all the multiples of 9 by folding down one of his fingers for each multiple. This was new to the student teacher but she allowed the child to come to the front of the class and demonstrate the technique. Having watched him carefully, she was able to tease out the reason for this technique working, which she explained to the class. Her own understanding of mathematics was very clear, but so also was her readiness to take a risk even though she had no idea what the outcome might be. It might be better to think of this as an 'aha' moment.

Summary

In this chapter we have met the fourth dimension of the knowledge quartet – contingency. We have seen how the unexpected can cause quite dra-matic changes to the course of a part of a lesson. From our videotaped lessons, there are three different causes for these points in a lesson, where the teacher has to think on their feet and make a rapid decision:

(Continued)

(Continued)

- a child's response to a question from the teacher;

- a child's response to an activity or discussion;

- a child's incorrect answer to a question or in the course of a discussion.

In discussing and analysing these decision points, we have seen that the teacher can often be faced with three possible ways to act:

- ignoring what has happened;

- acknowledging but sidelining the response from the child;

- responding to the child and incorporating their response into the lesson.

On some occasions, the subject knowledge that the teacher has may either allow or preclude this incorporating or mean that they may not see the potential for possible development. Indeed, there may be times when it is necessary to go away and think about the suggestion further before returning to it at a later time. It is at times like these that the opportunity to discuss with a colleague (peer or mentor) can be so beneficial, particularly if they have been in the lesson. The readiness to build children's ideas and offerings into a lesson can enable their learning to develop richly.

Now observe a lesson or think about a lesson that you have observed where there was a decision point for the teacher. What happened that caused this point to be reached and what were the possible roads that the teacher could have gone down? Try to think about the nature of this decision point. Was it a response from a child to a question from the teacher, or a spontaneous suggestion from a child as to what to do next, or a question from a child perhaps arising from an activity? What type of response (ignore; acknowledge but sideline; or respond and incorporate) did they give? What would have been the possibilities of pursuing the other responses?

Further reading

Liping Ma (1999) *Knowing and Teaching Elementary Mathematics*. Mahwah, NJ: Lawrence Erlbaum.

Liping Ma's book has already been suggested for further reading in Chapter 2. This indicates the high regard we have for it as a fascinating research study with a very careful analysis of the difference in approach by Chinese and American teachers to a range of scenarios. It puts a very clear spotlight on the specialised content knowledge that some teachers (notably the Chinese) were able to draw on in consideration of their approach to teaching.

Alice Hansen (ed.) (2005) *Children's Errors in Maths: Understanding Common Misconceptions in Primary Schools*. Exeter: Learning Matters.

This book considers the errors and misconceptions that a child may make or encounter in learning across the mathematics curriculum and at ages 4–11. It identifies these errors and makes some suggestions for how they may be remedied. Probably the most helpful aspects are the identification of possible errors and misconceptions – with prior knowledge of these, a student teacher may be able to plan for them or not be too surprised by their occurrence.

7

Foundation Knowledge for Teaching Mathematics

In this chapter you will read about:

- **the foundation knowledge required for counting, subtraction, division, and geometrical transformations;**
- **examples from lessons, in these topics, where a student teacher's foundation knowledge has been a significant factor.**

Introduction

In Chapters 3 and 4, we showed how teachers' ability to transform their own knowledge through appropriate choices of examples or representations affects their teaching. In Chapter 5, the importance of knowing how to make connections between mathematical concepts and processes was emphasised. In Chapter 6, we demonstrated that teachers' ability to use their own knowledge in order to respond to the unexpected, or to act contingently, was another important factor in mathematics teaching. However, in order to transform, connect or act contingently, teachers must have a resource of mathematical knowledge on which to draw. The *foundation* dimension of the Knowledge Quartet is concerned with the knowledge that teachers bring to the teaching situation. It may be seen as the over-arching dimension; it is fundamental because it underpins all the decisions about which examples or representations to use, connections to make, or how to respond to pupils' ideas.

Teachers are better able to help their pupils to carry out a mathematical process or to understand a mathematical concept if they themselves can complete the process or understand the idea. It follows that primary school teachers should have knowledge of the mathematical processes and concepts taught to children at least to age 11. In the UK all teachers are required to have passed the public examination normally taken at age 16. This does not of course mean they retain all the knowledge they had when taking the examination, but they might be expected to know the mathematics that they learned up to 11 years old. Even if this is the case, and our work with beginning teachers suggests it is not always so, there is more to the mathematical content knowledge needed for teaching than understanding the concepts and being able to carry out the processes.

In Chapter 2 we discussed the essential knowledge needed to teach primary mathematics. We saw that the first category in Lee Shulman's typology of knowledge for teaching was *subject-matter knowledge*. This may be described as knowledge of the facts, concepts, processes and connections within the subject (substantive knowledge) as well as the way in which knowledge within that subject is investigated and developed (syntactic knowledge). Both of these aspects of subject-matter knowledge are important facets of foundation knowledge, but they do not make up the whole picture. Theoretical *pedagogical content knowledge* is also seen as a key component within foundation knowledge. Teachers need to understand the ways in which pedagogical strategies relate to the mathematics they are trying to teach in order to make decisions about which strategies to use. These actual decisions would be considered to be part of the transformation dimension; however, the theoretical understanding that underpins them is part of the teacher's foundation knowledge.

In our observations of beginning teachers, as they taught primary mathematics, it was rare to see them making mistakes in the mathematical facts or processes they taught. Conversely, only rarely did we see unusually high levels of understanding of mathematical concepts demonstrated. However, we saw numerous instances when teachers' pedagogical content knowledge appeared to affect their teaching. Our observations suggest that knowledge of *mathematics* and of *mathematical pedagogy* are both important aspects of foundation knowledge. We will demonstrate that the mathematical knowledge needed for effective teaching – *specialised content knowledge* – is different from and wider than the knowledge needed to carry out the mathematics being taught – *common content knowledge*. We will give some pointers towards the type of knowledge that is important for teachers to have. In this chapter we give four key examples of the foundation knowledge held by teachers that we have seen to be significant in influencing their mathematics teaching. These will alert the reader to the types of knowledge needed in order to teach mathematics well, and will help beginning teachers to reflect on their own possession of such knowledge in relation to the mathematics they will be teaching.

We begin by looking at the specialised content knowledge needed to teach *counting* and suggest that teachers need an understanding of the complexities of the process beyond 'common' knowledge of counting. We then consider the specialised knowledge needed for teaching two operations, *subtraction* and *division*. Here we demonstrate that pedagogical content knowledge, in this case knowledge of different structures and methods, is an important factor. We also suggest that children's learning may be adversely affected when teachers do not have the requisite knowledge. Finally, we consider the teaching of one aspect of geometry, the *symmetry transformations*. Reflection, rotation and translation have a place in the primary school curriculum in many countries. However, their position within the wider topic of geometrical transformations is often insufficiently understood by teachers, resulting in connections and commonalities being overlooked. In our discussion of teaching the symmetries, we will exemplify the relationship between understanding the mathematics, knowledge of related pedagogical strategies and effective teaching.

Counting

When we talk about counting, we can mean two quite different things. In one sense we mean recitation of number words in a particular order, something children do and enjoy from an early age. In the other sense we mean finding out, and possibly communicating, the answer to a 'how many?' question. This second meaning of counting is referred to as 'enumeration' or 'quantification' and is of a different order, in terms of conceptual understanding, than 'recitation'. Counting is a key component of the 'core learning in mathematics' for children in the Foundation Stage (age 3–5) and Key Stage 1 (age 5–7) as set out in the non-statutory guidance for England, Wales and Northern Ireland (DfEE, 1999). Counting strategies are also recommended for older children, and used extensively as children progress through the primary school to carry out addition and subtraction calculations. Ian Thompson (1997) gives a detailed discussion of the role of counting in developing effective strategies for calculations.

Most adults have no difficulties with counting, and so it might be supposed that the knowledge needed for teaching this aspect of primary mathematics is common content knowledge and not specific to teaching. Student teachers might well think that their own knowledge of counting, and the resources available to support their teaching of counting, make this an aspect of mathematics content knowledge that is not a concern. This is not the case. There is a body of knowledge concerning the pedagogy of counting that is important for teachers to hold, and this knowledge is different from the 'commonplace' knowledge of the general public.

The practice of teaching in schools has been greatly influenced by learning theorists. In the 1960s and 1970s the constructivist influence of Piaget placed emphasis on young children learning through experience. This led some educationists to believe that counting as reciting strings of number names – 'one, two, three, ...' – was merely an exercise in imitation which masked a fundamental lack of understanding about counting. They contended that young children were not able to count in any meaningful way, in the sense of 'enumeration' or 'quantification', and the recitation of number words was replaced by sorting activities designed to help children understand concepts of quantity within sets of objects. As we remarked in Chapter 5, it was also believed to be more logical to start with sorting. However, the American psychologists Rochelle Gelman and Randy Gallistel (1978) showed that children as young as three and four can count sets of objects, and that they demonstrate some understanding of the process of quantification. Thompson (1997) argued that language plays a major role in developing children's understanding of number concepts, and that the recitation of number strings is an important activity promoting this development. Theoretical understanding of how children learn to count has developed in recent years, and teachers can benefit from knowledge of these theories in order to evaluate and refine their practice.

Penny Munn (1997) drew attention to the need for teachers to understand children's *beliefs* about counting. She found that many children begin school not recognising that we count in order to find out how many things there are in a set. This is different from the idea that young children *cannot understand* the relationship between number names and quantity, but rather that their experiences have focused on the recitation meaning of counting. Munn suggests that it is children's everyday experiences of counting which prohibit understanding of the quantification meaning from developing. Though they were able to count in the sense of reciting number names in relation to sets of objects, Munn found that many children saw counting merely as a playful activity or a way of pleasing others and not as a means of quantification. Knowledge that children might lack an understanding of the purpose of counting is useful to teachers as it might influence the way they organise and discuss counting activities with children.

Gelman and Gallistel's work was cited above as demonstrating that young children can count with understanding. But what does counting with understanding involve? Gelman and Gallistel (1978) found that there are five counting principles that children must be able to accomplish in order to be able to count meaningfully. The first three of Gelman and Gallistel's principles relate to 'how to count' and the other two to 'what can be counted'. The 'how to count' principles are:

- The *one–one principle*. This involves giving each item in a set a different counting word. This is not enough, however, as a child might count three items as 'one, two, three' one time and as 'one, two, four' another.

- The *stable order principle*. This involves knowing that the counting words must always be recited in the same order. A child may still not count 'correctly' if, for instance, they consistently count three objects as 'one, two, four'. This is a case of convention rather than understanding; however, since it is important to be able to communicate meaning to others, the child must learn the 'standard number word sequence' of their language.

- The *cardinal principle*. This refers to the idea that the last number in a count is the answer to the question 'how many?'. When asked 'how many?' after counting a set of objects, young children often begin the count again. This is because they see the answer to the question 'how many?' as the process of counting rather than the number they reach at the end. This principle is fundamental to being able to count, when what we mean by counting is 'quantification' or 'enumeration'.

The 'what can be counted principles' are:

- The *abstraction principle*. This involves recognising that any entities can be counted, whether they are physical or abstract, and that these entities do not have to be similar to be included in a count. This recognition entails being able to apply the abstract idea of number to objects in the same way as physical properties such as colour may be applied to them.

- The *order-irrelevance principle*. This involves knowing that it does not matter in which order items are counted. Children who demonstrate this principle are able to start and finish at any item or make any specified item a given number in the count. They do not see the number names as labels specific to particular items, like the number on the shirt of a footballer in a team, but as a means to reaching the answer to 'how many?'.

It is sometimes possible to perceive the number of objects in a small set, apparently without counting, if the set is small enough. Most people (and some animals and birds!) are able to recognise 'how many' in small sets, particularly if they are arranged in a regular or familiar way, as they are on dice, for example. This direct perception of 'how many' without performing the usual procedures of counting is called 'subitizing'. Pairs, trios and some other small sets can be subitized without requiring children to rehearse strategies which develop or reflect their understanding of the principles of counting.

In our observations of the teaching of counting it has been apparent that having the theoretical knowledge about counting discussed above does influence classroom practice. In Fay Turner's extension of our original study, three teachers in their first year of teaching were observed teaching counting to children aged 4–5. One teacher, Amy, made it clear that she had started from her knowledge of Gelman and Gallistel's prerequisites for counting when planning her lesson, and this was apparent in her teaching. The other two teachers demonstrated more tenuous knowledge of these principles in their teaching and in discussion following their lessons. They were able to recall some of these principles when questioned, but said that they had not drawn on them in their planning, or been explicitly aware of their significance.

> Read the following description of Amy's lesson and identify where she draws on her knowledge of the principles of counting in her teaching.

The lesson began with all the children sitting on the carpet looking at Amy. She reminded the children that they were learning how to count and needed to practise saying the numbers in order. She explained that they would practise their 'rhythm counting'. This consisted of counting to 20 as they all hit their knees and then clapped. On a second count, Amy changed the rhythm to 'knees, clap, knees, knees, knees' as they counted each set of five, from 1 to 20.

Amy then moved all the children into a circle. She produced four coloured cylindrical boxes of different sizes and handed one of the boxes to a child. She asked the child to guess what was inside and how many there were of them. The child guessed there were ten sweets and was asked to open it; she found it contained small plastic snakes. Amy asked her to take them out of the box and count them. The child took out one at a time and put them in a line, counting as she did so, to find the answer of seven. Amy praised the child and drew the attention of the other children to the strategies that had been used – putting the snakes in a line, pointing to each in turn with her fingers, saying the numbers in order and saying that the last number was the answer to 'how many?'.

This was repeated with the other three boxes. The second box contained four frogs, the third 13 'jewels' (glass cubes) and the fourth nine sweets. Amy praised the second child for 'touching each frog just once' as she counted them. She asked the children if there were more frogs or more snakes. The children correctly answered 'snakes' and Amy confirmed this by saying that there were more snakes because there were seven of them. The third child was praised by Amy for moving the 'jewels' from one pile to another as she counted them, and Amy asked whether there were more snakes or more jewels. The children correctly answered 'jewels'. The final child put the sweets into a line as he counted, though like the first child he did not go back and count them once in the line. Amy praised him for putting them in a line and touching each one only once.

Once the contents of all the boxes had been counted Amy revised how many had been in each box and asked the children to put the boxes in a line from the smallest to the largest number of objects they contained. She suggested they might use the number line on the wall to help. This showed the numerals only and did not have pictures of the appropriate number of objects. The children were able to say that the four frogs were the smallest number and to tell Amy which boxes to put next.

Amy then showed the children a transparent jar containing a number of 'bugs'. She asked the children to guess how many, and they responded with numbers from 10 to 100. Amy emptied the bugs on to the floor in a heap. She explained that they were going to count them by putting them in a line and counting. Amy counted the bugs as she moved them from the pile to the line.

At one point she needed to move the line to make room to complete the count. Having done this, she modelled starting at the beginning of the line and counting in order to find the number they had got to. Having reached the final count (20), Amy asked the children 'So how many bugs are there?'. To conclude her teaching Amy posed the questions 'What was good about our counting?' and 'What was helpful when counting?'. After not receiving the desired answers, Amy suggested them herself: 'We said the numbers in the right order, we touched each thing just once and the last number we said was how many there are.'

Our reflections on Amy's use of her theoretical knowledge of counting in her lesson

The lesson began with 'rhythm counting', reciting the number names consistently in the conventional order while keeping to the rhythm of Amy's clapping. This was helping the children to understand the *stable order principle*. Amy used interesting objects in brightly coloured boxes and asked the children to guess what was inside as well as how many there were. Amy's attempt to engage the children in their counting in this way may be interpreted as trying to help them understand the purpose of counting. Amy's praise of the children for touching or pointing to each object just once helped to reinforce the *one–one principle*. She encouraged the children to put the objects in a line or to move them to a new pile as they counted, both strategies for ensuring adherence to the one–one principle. In order to reinforce the *cardinal principle*, Amy asked the children to say how many there were after they had finished their count. She also made this principle explicit by telling the children that the last number they had said was the answer to the question 'how many?'.

When they had completed counting the objects in the different boxes, Amy asked questions about which held more and which held less. She also asked them to put the boxes in line from the smallest to the largest number of objects. To do this the children had to ignore the fact that the objects in each box were different and also to ignore the size and colour of the boxes. This related to Gelman and Gallistel's final two principles of *abstraction* and *order irrelevance*. The children had to understand the idea that the number of the count was an abstract property of the set of objects in the boxes. They needed to understand the type of objects and the colour and size of the boxes were irrelevant.

Though the topic of this lesson appeared to be a very simple one – counting – Amy drew on her bank of specialised theoretical knowledge about what children needed to know and needed to be able to do in order to count meaningfully. In a post-lesson discussion she said that she had planned her lesson around the principles for counting and was able to name the first three, though she did not remember that they had been proposed by Gelman and Gallistel. During a later group discussion with other beginning teachers, Amy claimed that when planning her teaching she thought about an essay on counting she had written during her training year which would have made reference to these principles. This is an example of where we saw a teacher's foundation knowledge having a clear, positive impact on their teaching and the children's learning. It suggests that having specialist knowledge of mathematical topics to be taught beyond that held by the general population is important for effective teaching. It is the kind of knowledge that will be addressed in professional mathematics courses during initial teacher education and continuing professional development, and is to be found in the mathematics education literature.

Subtraction and division

The next two topics that we discuss – subtraction and division – concern numerical operations. Also, the points that we shall make about them are similar. Much of the formal mathematical content that is learnt in school can be used to represent and solve various kinds of everyday problems. A conscious awareness of this is not something that the person in the street needs to have in order to use mathematics satisfactorily, even though it may be known tacitly. We made a similar point about the principles of counting in the previous section. For teachers, however, this sort of pedagogical knowledge does need to be explicit. A lack of pedagogical knowledge of this kind often leads to these topics being taught less well, and even causes some misunderstanding amongst children. We shall, therefore, illustrate this with excerpts from lessons on subtraction and division.

Subtraction

Subtraction structures
One of the ways in which children make sense of mathematical operations, procedures and concepts is by appreciating the range of different

situations to which they apply. The various problems and scenarios relevant to a particular operation (such as subtraction) can be grouped into a small number of categories, each with the same fundamental structure. In the case of subtraction, there are two key problem structures. Consider, for example, the following four problems:

1   Mary had 12 sweets in her pocket. She took out 3 sweets and ate them. How many sweets did she have left?

2   Mrs Jones had 25 children in her classroom. Seven were taken out to change their books in the library. How many children were left in the classroom?

3   Brian has 20 marbles and his brother Michael has 12. How many more marbles does Brian have than his brother?

4   John's family is travelling 35 miles to the seaside. They have travelled 19 miles so far. How many miles do they have to go?

The structure of the first two problems is the same. The structure of the third and fourth problems is also the same, but different from that of the first pair. The four problems therefore exemplify two subtraction structures.

Haylock (2006: 30) writes about the 'range of situations' to which an operation applies, and the four listed above separate into two distinct types. The process whereby a 'real world' problem is translated into an arithmetical calculation is often called 'mathematical modelling' (Haylock, 2006: 23). In the Dutch Realistic Mathematics Education (RME) tradition, the same process is called (horizontal) 'mathematization'. One fundamental principle of RME is that mathematics is a *human* activity and that students learn mathematics 'by developing and applying mathematical concepts and tools in daily-life problem situations that make sense to them' (van den Heuvel-Panhuizen, 2003). Contexts and situations are used which are *meaningful* to students, although these need not be 'real world' scenarios, since fictional and fantasy situations might be very motivating and just as 'meaningful'.

Unfortunately, several names are in use to label these two subtraction structures. There is not much that anyone can do about that, and each name conveys a different insight about the structure. Carpenter and Moser (1983), for example, refer to the subtraction structure exemplified by problems 1 and 2 above as the *change* structure, and they call the structure exemplified by problems 3 and 4 the *compare* structure.

The *change* problem type is exemplified by Carpenter and Moser (1983: 8) by: 'Connie had 13 marbles. She gave 5 marbles to Jim. How many marbles does she have left?' This situation involves an *action* on and transformation of a *single* set – Connie's marbles in this case. The original set of 13 marbles, and the transformed set (the 8 she had left) are of the same kind – here, sets of marbles. Note that this can be thought of in terms of an initial state (Connie had 13 marbles), a change or transformation (Connie gave 5 marbles to Jim), and a final state (Connie had 8 marbles).

In the UK, teachers talk about this 'change' structure as *take away* subtraction (DfEE, 1999: 28), because something is taken away from an initial state set. On the other hand, Haylock (2006) calls it the *partition* structure, because relevant situations all involve 'a situation where a quantity is partitioned off ... and subtraction is required to find out how many or how much remains' (p. 33). Other names given to this structure include separating, pure subtraction, dynamic subtraction, state–transformation–state subtraction (Dickson et al., 1984: 227).

Carpenter and Moser's (1983: 16) example of the *compare* problem type is: 'Connie has 13 marbles and Jim has 5 marbles. How many more marbles does Connie have than Jim?' This subtraction problem type has to do with situations in which two sets (Connie's marbles and Jim's) are considered *simultaneously* – what Carpenter and Moser (1983: 15) describe as 'static relationships', involving 'the comparison of two distinct, disjoint sets'. No change or transformation is involved in these scenarios, and the sets need not even be of the same kind: 'There are 5 cups and 3 saucers: how many more saucers are needed so that every cup has a saucer?' In the UK, the compare subtraction structure is usually called 'subtraction as *difference*'. This is unfortunate because the outcome of a subtraction, whatever the structure, is called the difference of the two numbers. For example, in situation 1 above (Mary and her sweets) the answer to the problem, 9 sweets, is the difference between 12 and 3. For this reason,

Rowland (2006) has argued that it would be better if teachers in the UK adopted the name 'comparison' rather than 'difference' for the second type of subtraction structure.

Other researchers and authors identify subtraction structures additional to the two described above (Dickson et al., 1984: 227). In particular, Haylock suggests two more – the reduction structure and the *inverse-of-addition* structure. These are variants of *partition* and *comparison*, respectively, and we would suggest that a focus on these two fundamental structures is sufficient for most purposes.

Typically, children are first introduced to subtraction as 'take away'. For example, the official guidance (DfEE, 1999) in England recommended the introducing of subtraction, first as take away, in Reception, and then as comparison in Year 1. One consequence of this teaching sequence is the almost universal use of 'take away' as a synonym for 'subtraction' in primary classrooms (Haylock and Cockburn, 1997: 38). This is potentially problematic, and teachers should consider carefully when to use the more neutral 'subtraction' in their own use of language.

To show that it is not simply a matter of splitting hairs to speak of these structures as distinct, it is worth thinking about what is involved in working through problem 3 above (Brian and the marbles), with real objects. The problem is represented symbolically by $20 - 12 = 8$. If this were a change/partition structure it could be represented concretely by setting up 20 marbles and removing 12. However, in the context of the problem above, Michael's collection is *not* removed from Brian's, even though this would lead to the correct answer. Brian's marbles remain intact. In this example what it is important to notice is that there are 32 marbles to which reference is made! So whilst the change/partition structure is demonstrated, in this case, with 20 marbles, the comparison problem requires 32. Awareness of this distinction is another classic example of the special knowledge required for teaching.

Calculate 587 – 164 using the usual written algorithm, writing one above the other. Is this subtraction algorithm based on the partition structure or the comparison structure?

Subtraction strategies

Carpenter and Moser go on to show that the particular problem structure – partition or comparison – by no means determines the actual solution processes adopted by individual children, although the structure might suggest a 'natural', or default, strategy. Some of these strategies involve *actions* on concrete materials. Following Bruner's theory of modes of representation (see Chapter 3), this might be called an 'enactive' approach. Carpenter and Moser call it 'direct modelling'.

The natural enactive strategy in connection with *partition* problems such as problem 1 above (Mary's sweets) is called *separating from* (Carpenter and Moser, 1983). This involves constructing a set corresponding to the initial state (12 sweets), removing an appropriate number of objects corresponding to the change to be effected (3 sweets). Counting the remaining objects (9 sweets) yields the final state – the answer. In this strategy, three sets of objects (state–change–state) need to be *counted*, requiring the particular counting skills described earlier. If one of the sets is small in number, a child may be able to subitize rather than having to count each member.

In the case of *comparison* problems like problem 3 above, the relevant enactive solution strategy involves *matching*: the child puts out *two* sets of objects (cubes, for example), one with 20 objects, and the other 12. The sets are then matched one-to-one; counting the 8 unmatched cubes gives the answer.

A second set of strategies depends on forms of counting, without the necessity to handle actual materials (except, perhaps, fingers). These correspond more to Bruner's symbolic mode of representation, since the child acts on sequences of number-*sounds*, or auditory symbols. The counting strategy corresponding to the enactive *separating from* is called *counting down from*. The child counts backwards, beginning from the initial state (12 sweets). The number of steps in the backward counting sequence is equal to the change (Mary ate 3 sweets, so the count would proceed 'eleven, ten, nine'). The last number uttered ('nine') is the difference.

In the case of *comparison* problems, the counting strategy corresponding to matching (called *counting up to*) involves counting up from the smaller of the numbers to the larger. The child has to keep track – perhaps with their fingers – of the number of counting words uttered in the sequence, since this number is the answer – the difference, in fact. In the case of Brian's marbles, the count would proceed 'thirteen, fourteen, fifteen, sixteen, seventeen, eighteen, nineteen, twenty' – 8 words in all.

The distinction between partition and comparison is made apparent in rather a striking way when we consider calculation strategies based on an *iconic* representation of the numbers sequence – the number line. This would most likely be an empty number line. Remember that while the number line with markings (like a tape measure) is a well-established support for calculation, the novel feature of the empty number line is precisely its emptiness – no decade markings are made initially. The child then takes responsibility for showing on the line those (and only those) numbers that have significance in the mental calculation in question.

Consider, for example, the calculation 85 – 47 and how it might be performed on a number line, first in a partition ('take away') situation, then is a comparison ('difference') situation.

- *Partition.* John has 85p and spends 47p on a drink. How much does he have left? In Figure 7.1, we begin at 85 as a *location* on the number line, and *jump back* 47 to the final state *location*, 38, which is the answer to the problem (in pence, of course). So the difference, 38, is shown as a location on the number line itself.

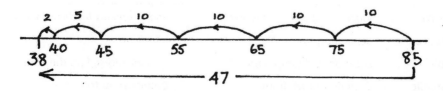

Figure 7.1 Jumping back on an empty number line to show 85 – 47

- *Difference.* John's family is travelling 85 miles to the seaside. They have travelled 47 miles so far. How many miles do they have to go? In this case, it is most natural to represent both 85 and 47 as locations on the number line (as shown in Figure 7.2). To find the difference – how many miles they have to go – it is necessary to find the size of the jump

Figure 7.2   The numbers 85 and 47 as locations on an empty number line

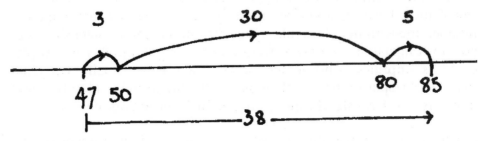

Figure 7.3   Finding the difference between 47 and 85 on number line

needed to get from 47 to 85, shown in Figure 7.3. So in this case, the difference, 38, is a *jump*.

We can summarise these approaches as shown in Table 7.1.

Table 7.1   The different structures of subtraction

	Partition	**Comparison**
Example	*Mary eating some of her sweets*	*Brian's and his brother's marbles*
Enactive	Separating from	Matching
Iconic	Location and jump back	Two locations, find the jump
Symbolic	Counting down from	Counting up to

Back to a student teacher's classroom – Naomi

Back in Chapter 1, we met Naomi, a student teacher, and we asked you to think about aspects of her lesson on subtraction with a Year 1 class. Two episodes from Naomi's lesson are given in the transcript below. You can also see the first one on the companion website at Clip 8. These episodes come from Naomi's introduction to the main activity when she is using magnetic frogs on a board to represent the situations.

It is clear from her lesson plan that Naomi intends to address 'difference' both conceptually and linguistically. That is to say, she wants the pupils (a) to learn to perceive subtraction in terms of comparison, and (b) to be able to answer appropriately questions about the difference between two numbers.

Read the following transcript carefully (you can see the first extract on video). Ideally, read and/or watch it twice. Then think about the following questions. If possible, discuss them with a colleague.

- In what ways is Naomi's foundation knowledge of subtraction reflected in her lesson?

- Which aspects of her knowledge did she draw on in her planning, and which does she put into action in her teaching?

- Are there aspects of Naomi's lesson where she seems to be less clear about the structures of subtraction, and the comparison structure in particular?

- What might Naomi do differently next time she teaches this topic with a Year 1 class?

Naomi: I went to my garden this weekend, and I've got a really nice pond in my garden, and when I looked I saw that [...] I had four frogs, so I was really pleased about that, but then my neighbour came over. She's got some frogs as well, but she's only got two. How many more frogs have I got? Martin?

Martin: Two.

Naomi: Two. So what's the difference between my pond and her pond in the number of frogs? Jeffrey.

Jeffrey: Um, um when he had a frog you only had two frogs.

Naomi: What's the difference in number? [...] this is my pond here, this line – that's what's in my pond, but this is what's in my neighbour's pond, Mr Brown's pond, he's got two. But I've got four, so, Martin said I've got two more than him. But we can say that another way. We can say the difference is two frogs. There's two. You can take these two and count on three, four, and I've got two extra.

A few minutes later, Morag has chosen to have 5 frogs and Leo 4 frogs. There are two lines of frogs on the board.

Leo: Four.

Naomi: Four. One, two, three, four. Right, come and stand here. If we put them underneath each other it's easy to see the difference. How many more does Morag have? …

Right, who can tell me how many more frogs does Morag have than Leo. Jim?

Jim: One.

Naomi: One, so what's the difference? Jim?

Jim: She has more than Leo.

Naomi: Yes, and what do we say the difference is between their ponds? Larry?

Larry: One frog.

Naomi: One. Now can anyone, does anyone know how we can write this as a take away sum? Right, sit down you two. Zara, can you come to the front. How would you write this as a take away sum to show the difference? Nice and big. [Zara writes '5 – 4'] So she's written five take away four *equals* [Zara returns to board, writes '='] and what's the answer, what's the difference? Gavin.

Gavin: One.

Naomi: Equals one. [Zara completes '5 – 4 = 1'] Thank you. Can you see, cos if we had these five frogs in Morag's pond, and took away four of them, there'd be one left over. One extra one. Right, who else would like a pond? Bill. How many frogs would you like in your pond, Bill?

Bill: Six.

Naomi: Six, there we go. One, two, three, four, five and six. Right, can you stand right over there. And Martin, how many frogs would you like?

Martin: Eight.

Naomi: I've only got four left actually, so it'll have to be four or less.

Martin: Four.

Naomi: Four, OK. So, one, two, three. Morag, please don't. And four. OK, come and stand here. OK, who can see, how many more does Bill have? How many more frogs does Bill have than Martin? Can anyone in the Whales see? Bill's got six frogs, and Martin's got four frogs. How many more does Bill have? Ayesha?

[no reply]

Martin's got four frogs, one, two, three, four, but how many more does Bill have? How many more? Leo, can you see? How many more does he have?

Leo:	Um, six.
Naomi:	Right, Bill's got six. [two frogs fall off] Goodness me, the frogs keep jumping off the board. I think they want to go back to their pond. OK, let me explain it this way. Right, looking at me, thank you, Jeffrey, thank you. Martin's got four and I want to know how many more Bill's got. Bill's got four as well, but then he's got the two extra ones. So, what is the difference. What's the difference, Jared?
Jared:	Six.
Naomi:	Right, Bill's got six, but what's the difference between Bill's and Martin's? Stuart.
Stuart:	Two.
Naomi:	Two, good boy. Now, can you stand back? Looking at me and listening. Can you cross your legs, thank you, Morag? Jared. Right, we can do this on our fingers as well. If we start with the small number, four, we can count on the extra two. Right, can everybody show me four fingers? Now, Bill's got six, so you count four, five, six. We've added on two more, and the total is six. The difference is two. Bill, do you think you know how to write that as a take away sum? Does anyone know? Does anyone know? Josie? Do you know how to write that as a take away sum? We've got six here, and four here, and the difference is two. Right, Jared, do you want to come and help Bill?

The video clip stops here. The following transcription comes from later in the introduction when some difficulties have become more apparent.

Naomi:	If I've got fifteen rings, and Moin's got twenty rings, what's the difference? What's the difference between fifteen and twenty? Zara?
Zara:	He's got ten more than you.
Naomi:	Ten more, I'm not sure. Does anyone? How do we work it out? I've got fifteen. We're going to count on with our fingers. Everyone show me your fingers. Martin, stand up. Goodness me. Right I've got twenty, and Martin's got fifteen.
Child:	Moin.
Naomi:	Moin. 15, 16, 17, 18, 19, 20. What's the difference? How many more does he have? Carol, stop making noises.
Child:	Five.
Naomi:	Five more. How could we write that as a take away sum? Lily.
Lily:	Eleven take away one.
Naomi:	No, I've got fifteen and he's got twenty. Right, let's do some more differences first. If I've got ten flowers and Josie's got thirteen flowers, what's the difference? Owen.

Owen: [inaudible]

Naomi: No, if I've got ten, we're going to count on. Show me your hand everyone, show me your hand. Clench your fist, Hugh. Right, I've got ten and Josie's got thirteen. 10, 11, 12, 13. Jared are you doing it? What's the difference? How many have we got extra? Gavin?

Gavin: Five.

Naomi: No, 10, 11, 12, 13. Jim.

Jim: Three.

Naomi: Three. Good. Right, how can we write that as a take away sum? Jim.

Jim: Um, fifteen take away.

Naomi: Thirteen she had.

Jim: Thirteen take away fifteen.

Naomi: Oh, I had ten and Josie had thirteen. Zara. Right, we start with the big number, thirteen, and take away ten, and then we know that the difference. What did we say was the difference? Alex?

Alex: Um, three.

One way that it may be helpful to consider the questions that we asked you about these transcripts is to think about the strategies and structures of subtraction and how Naomi relates these to one another. Try to map the approaches that Naomi is using and discuss with your colleague what the difficulties for the children might be.

Our intention here has been to show that certain persistent difficulties can emerge in teaching subtraction. Even if teachers have a tacit understanding of the various contexts that subtraction may be applied to, many are prone to conveying to children the over-generalisation that subtraction means 'take away'. As we shall see, a similar situation occurs in division.

Division

Now we move on to the second topic concerned with arithmetic operations – division. We suggested earlier that children can be helped to make sense of different operations by relating them to familiar situations 'outside' mathematics. One way is to use, or ask children to invent, word problems to represent 'bare' mathematical statements.

Division structures

In the section on subtraction we started with some situations for you to consider; now we will reverse this procedure, and ask you to suggest a situation, or 'story', for a division 'statement'. Asking children to 'make up a story' about a calculation in this way can be quite revealing. Sometimes children are able to give the answer to a 'bare' calculation, devoid of context, yet have little idea of when that number fact might be relevant. Alistair McIntosh (1979) gives several stories proposed by children aged between 8 and 11, to go with the bare statement $6 \times 3 = 18$. All these children were able to give the answer to 6×3. Their stories included: 'There were 6 cars in the car park 3 more came in so there was 18' and 'At school there were 18 children in a class. 6 were away, but 12 came to school'.

> Write down a word problem that corresponds to the 'bare' mathematical statement $28 \div 4 = 7$.

It is not a trivial task to find authentic examples; we shall suggest some here, and explain why they may provide a helpful context for the division operation.

We could think about 4 people playing a game of dominoes; at the start of the game they share the 28 dominoes equally between them. In the mathematical statement ($28 \div 4 = 7$), the '28' refers to the set to be distributed and the '4' is the number of destinations. Having shared out the dominoes, the '7' tells us the number of dominoes each player receives – their quota. The sharing could be carried out with real objects, so that the distribution is quite apparent, and the equal shares are apparent to all. An analogous example could be sharing 28 sweets between 4 children, each child receiving their quota of 7 sweets. These two situations are examples of the division structure known informally as *sharing*. It is illustrated in Figure 7.4.

However, a different structure for the statement $28 \div 4 = 7$ is illustrated by the following example. There are 28 children in a class and the teacher wants them to practise a task in groups of 4. How many groups will there be? Now '28' is still the number to be distributed but in this example '4' is the quota. The division operation enables us to find the number of groups that will be formed – 7 groups in this case. The earlier situation with the sweets can be changed to illustrate this structure too. Suppose

Figure 7.4   Sharing 28 sweets between 4 children

that we wish to bag up the 28 sweets so that each bag contains 4 sweets. Again the '28' is the number to be distributed but the '4' represents how many sweets there are in each bag. The '7' informs us how many bags of sweets there will be. The action of grouping can be carried out so that the original set of 28 sweets is seen to be successively reduced in size as each group of 4 is removed and bagged up. This structure is often referred to as (equal) *grouping*. It is illustrated in Figure 7.5.

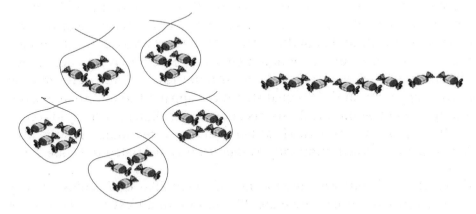

Figure 7.5   Putting 28 sweets into groups of 4

A more formal description of the two structures follows; as with subtraction, there are two or more names for each:

- *The sharing structure* (also referred to as the 'partition' structure). What is known at the outset is the total number of objects (28) to be distributed and the number of destinations to which these objects will be distributed (4). What is *not* known is the number of objects (the quota) that will be at each destination when the distribution has been carried out.

- *The grouping structure* (also referred to as the 'quotition' or 'measurement' structure). What is known at the outset is, again, the total number of objects (28), together with the size of the groups (the quota) that are to be successively removed from this total (4). What is *not* known, until the operation of removing the groups has been carried out, is the number of groups that can be assembled in this way.

> Now look back at your word problem for 28 ÷ 4 = 7 and decide whether it had a sharing or a grouping structure.

We regularly observe, as teacher educators, that a student teacher's first attempt at inventing a word-problem for a statement such as 28 ÷ 4 = 7 is almost always one that embodies the sharing structure. In the United States, Deborah Ball (1990a) found that many beginning teachers – primary and secondary, some with mathematics degrees – lacked sufficient awareness of the grouping structure to be able to explain *why* $1\frac{3}{4} \div \frac{1}{2}$ is $3\frac{1}{2}$, other than just saying 'invert and multiply'. The reason for this can almost certainly to be traced back to the way that division is first introduced in the primary school – as sharing. Thereafter the division symbol, ÷, becomes defined as sharing. This appears to be a reasonable thing to do as it can bring early experiences of sharing at home into a child's mathematics learning. But the grouping/quotition structure brings a very different meaning to the division symbol. In thinking about examples for this section, we were struck by the difficulty in finding ones which could be recast to illustrate the two different structures in a plausible way. Sweets are a good example from a mathematical point of view, if not for our teeth!

> It is impossible to represent $1\frac{3}{4} \div \frac{1}{2}$ as a sharing situation (without being extremely contrived). Devise a grouping situation that would explain why the answer is $3\frac{1}{2}$.

The grouping structure is closely linked to division being the inverse of multiplication. The problem that we outlined above (I have 28 sweets, how many bags with 4 sweets in can I get?) is paralleled by the multiplication question 'I have 7 bags with 4 sweets in each, how many sweets have I altogether?' From this observation, some writers (e.g. Haylock, 2006) identify another aspect of division, namely the 'inverse-of-multiplication' structure. In this structure, a division question such as 28 ÷ 4 = ? is recast into an equivalent question about multiplication, namely, *what number multiplied by 4 is equal to 28?* It should be clear that this relates to the form of the quotative sweet question given earlier: 'I have 28 sweets, how many bags with 4 sweets in can I get?' So, trios of numbers, such as 28, 4 and 7, can be linked by multiplication or division in a number of ways, and the recognition of these conceptual links is one indication of the *connections* that a child is able to make. These are shown in Figure 7.6.

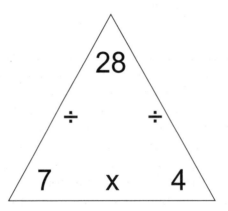

Figure 7.6   Number trio – 28, 7 and 4

In addition, the grouping structure links division with repeated subtraction if, as we did above, we view the formation of groups as taking place successively, one at a time. In the sweets example, we can start with 28 sweets and repeatedly take groups of 4 sweets away. Counting the number of groups gives us the number of bags that can be filled. Again the parallel with multiplication is clear, because whole number multiplication can be modelled as repeated addition.

This repeated subtraction can be represented on a number line as shown in Figure 7.7. We start at 28 and then repeatedly jump back in steps of 4, showing the reduction by 4 at each jump. Finally, we need to count *how many jumps* have been made in order to find the result of 28 ÷ 4.

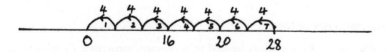

Figure 7.7   Repeated subtraction to calculate 28 ÷ 4 on a number line

So the grouping structure, as well as the sharing structure, has a number of links and interpretations in much the same way as we saw for the two structures for subtraction.

If children learn only that 'division means sharing' then there is every reason to believe that they will be left high and dry when they are expected to tackle situations that have the grouping division structure. This is not to say, of course, that early years teachers should not begin by introducing division through sharing activities. What is important is that children also meet the grouping structure. It is a moot point whether a teacher should avoid saying 'division means sharing' when teaching young children. Certainly, to teach children that *one* of the ways of understanding division is by sharing seems preferable. Teachers should be able to provide experience and explanation of both partition and quotition. To be able to do this, they need knowledge and awareness of both structures.

> Rewrite your word-problem so that it is now has the division structure that was not present in your first attempt.

In order to reinforce our points about these two division structures, we now consider a lesson given by Melanie.

An example from a student teacher's classroom
An example of these two structures at work in a lesson is given below. Melanie is a student teacher in Ireland. She is teaching a lesson with a class of 9–10-year-old girls in which the children have been set questions

where some fantasy 'trading' is to take place using 'galleons' (a Harry Potter currency). Practical apparatus – blocks and beans – is available for the children to support their thinking.

> Read the transcript of Melanie's lesson below.
>
> - Identify where she commits herself to a division structure. Comment on her choice.
> - At what point is this structure abandoned?

Melanie: Could I have a girl to come up front with me? And show us how to do number one? [Samantha volunteers] No you've just got to hand out the sheets. We'll give someone else a chance. How about Megan? I don't think you've been up yet. Róisín could you read out question one for us.

Róisín: Ron has eighteen galleons and a pack of cards costs three galleons. How many packs can he buy?

Melanie: So how many butter beans does Megan need to take out? What do you think, Gemma?

Child: Eighteen.

Melanie: And why does she want to take out eighteen?

Child: Cause Ron has eighteen galleons.

Melanie: That's eighteen galleons; you know that's wizard money. That's like €18 or £18. So … she has her … while Megan is counting out her eighteen galleons, her eighteen beans, and how many groups does she need to break it into and can you tell me why? Hannah, what do you think?

Child: Into three groups.

Melanie: Into three groups. Well done, and why? You can read the question again if you want.

Child: Because there's three packs of cards.

Melanie: It's not that there's three packs of cards. But what is it about the cards?

Child: It costs three galleons.

Melanie: It costs three galleons. So if you share out your three galleons, you see how many packs of cards you're able to buy […] Megan you're already ahead of us. You've got eighteen and what are you doing?

Child:	Splitting them up into three groups ...
Melanie:	Ahh ...? [intending correction?] Into groups of three [she nods]. And how many groups do you have?
Child:	Six.
Melanie:	So how many packs of cards could Ron buy?
Child:	Six.
Melanie:	He could buy six packs of cards. Can everybody follow that? What sentence would you write to explain what we just did?

Melanie starts her questioning with a clear intention concerning the way in which she wanted the children to tackle the question – she asks them *how many groups* Megan needs, implying a sharing division structure. But when a child suggests an incorrect reason for splitting the galleons into three groups (that there are three packs of cards rather than that they cost three galleons), she has a moment of insight, corrects herself and the child, and changes tack. No longer are the children to find three groups but they are to find groups *of* three. Here we have an example of the need on the teacher's part to have a clear understanding of the division structures. We also have an interesting example of one of the components of contingency that we discussed in Chapter 6 – responding to a child's (incorrect) answer to a question.

It is worth reiterating the earlier point (made in connection with Deborah Ball's research) that when we progress beyond the division of whole numbers, it is clear that the sharing structure is out of place in word-problems.

> Explain why the problem $12 \div \frac{1}{2}$ cannot be represented by a sharing situation.

The division algorithm
In fact, we do not need to go to division of fractions to see the limitation of the belief that 'division means sharing'. Despite the apparent conceptual predominance of the sharing structure for most people, much of the division that has traditionally been carried out in written exercises has been the division algorithm, which is underpinned by the *grouping* structure! This can be seen by reflecting upon how one might have been 'trained' to answer such questions as 'How many 7s are there in 469?'.

Spend a moment doing this as a written calculation. If you can, record what you say to yourself as you do it.

With this question in mind we come to an often misunderstood part of the familiar verbal patter for carrying out division calculations by a formal method. In order to carry out a calculation like $469 \div 7$ the tradition has been to tackle 469 digit-by-digit, from the left, beginning with 'How many sevens are there in 4?'. Once the response 'None' has been made, then the task is to consider how many 7s there are in 46, and so on, as illustrated in Figure 7.8.

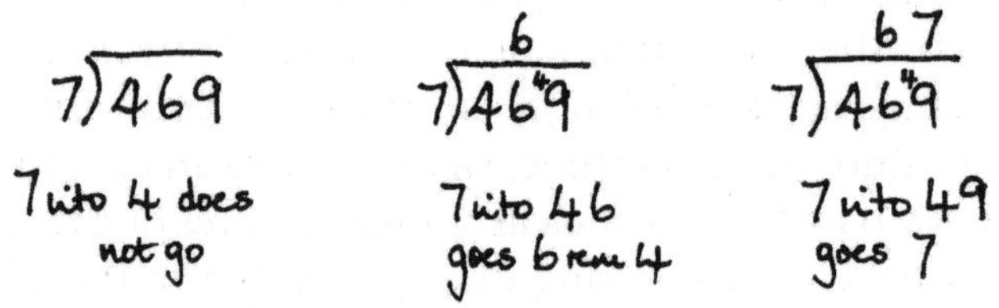

Figure 7.8   Thinking about $469 \div 7$

Although this digit-by-digit approach generally works well enough, there are cases for which it does not. In the case of $235 \div 67$, 67 does not divide into 2, or into 23, so the original question remains! We will return to this point later, but it is worth reflecting upon the apparent incoherence of the typical verbal patter. When we said 'How many 7s are there in 4?', the response 'None' is curious if we think of the 4 as representing, as it does, 4 hundreds. Clearly, 400 *is* divisible by 7, but the patter that is learnt for the method requires us to treat the 400 as 4. It is very rare for one of our student teachers to see why we may treat the 400 as 4 and therefore place no number above it in the solution.

In the example mentioned above ($469 \div 7$), try to explain why it could make sense to say that there are 'no' 7s in 4, although the 4 really stands for 400.

In this example with the standard division algorithm, we are, in the first instance, looking for a digit to place above the 4, as part of the solution. However, any digit placed in that position will represent a certain number of *hundreds*. Clearly, whilst 400 *is* divisible by 7 the quotient (400 ÷ 7) is fifty-something – only a little more than half of a hundred. So, no *whole number* can be recorded above the 4. When we say that there are no '7s in 4', in this context, we are implying that 7 'does not go into 400 a hundred times or more' or, better still, it 'cannot be repeatedly subtracted from 400 a hundred times or more'.

The subtlety of the above account, and the fact that few adults could explain it, is one of the reasons for questioning the teaching of the standard division algorithm. Haylock (2006) emphasises alternative, more comprehensible approaches to written division. Even if the standard division algorithm is taught, the above explanation for the simple patter for the method is not something that every child can, or should, be expected to run through whenever the algorithm is carried out. Actually, to do so would be to lose the purpose of using the algorithm in the first place. But by understanding the explanation, a child (or adult) is able to *recover* one of the underlying principles of the algorithm, especially in those cases when something goes wrong. For this reason a teacher should point it out at various times when the algorithm is being learnt, if it is learnt. We have no hesitation, however, in agreeing with Haylock that there are now more sensible and palatable alternatives. One such alternative is the more transparent or 'holistic' method often called 'chunking' (see, for example, Anghileri, 2006: 101–105).

Suppose that we want to find 319 ÷ 42. The calculation strategy for this, as we have already suggested, has traditionally been one which embodies the grouping structure. That is to say, it is thought of as asking us to group 319 into 'lots' of 42, or to successively subtract 42. As mentioned above, we cannot carry this out by considering the 3, and then the 31, because if we follow the standard patter for this algorithm, 42 will not divide into 3 or 31. The problem, in the standard algorithm, is that we probably don't know, in one 'go', how many lots of 42 can be removed from 319.

In the more recently adopted chunking method, the question is thought of holistically – how many 42s are there in 319? – from the outset. The 319 is not approached digit by digit, but as an entire quantity. We could start by saying that there is at least one 42 in 319. Then when 42 is subtracted from 319 to give 277 we could ask the same question again, and so on and so forth recording how many 42s we could subtract in turn. However, this is very inefficient (and prone to several subtraction errors on the way). It is at this point that much of the mental mathematics learnt by children in the earlier stages comes to play a significant part. Knowing that double 42 is 84, they would be able to curtail the number of steps towards the solution by subtracting increments of 84. Of course there are all kinds of ways in which we could develop this idea beyond the most primitive way of simply subtracting the divisor successively. The idea is that while we do try and get as close as we can to the solution at each step, it does not matter if we need more steps.

Further suggestions often depend upon the ingenuity or 'number sense' of the child. For example, 5×42 is half of 42 multiplied by 10; when we subtract 210 from 319 there is only 109 remaining. A further 2×42 can still be subtracted leaving a remainder of 25, which is less than 42. So there are 7 lots of 42 altogether in 319, with remainder 25. This can be recorded as shown in Figure 7.9.

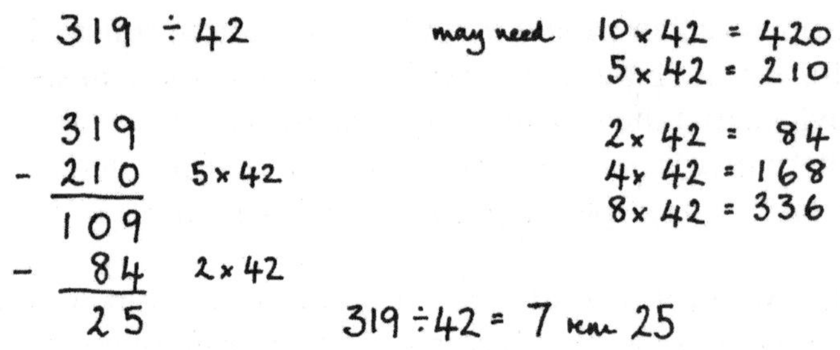

$$319 \div 42$$

may need
$$10 \times 42 = 420$$
$$5 \times 42 = 210$$

$$\begin{array}{r} 319 \\ -\ 210 \\ \hline 109 \\ -\ \ 84 \\ \hline 25 \end{array}$$

5×42

2×42

$$2 \times 42 = 84$$
$$4 \times 42 = 168$$
$$8 \times 42 = 336$$

$$319 \div 42 = 7 \text{ rem } 25$$

Figure 7.9   Using chunking to calculate $319 \div 42$

The value of this method for the child is its transparency of meaning and flexibility. No unexplained moves are made as the whole process is progressive subtraction from a number that gets smaller as each 'chunk' is removed. It may be worthwhile for the child to record some important multiplication facts at the start of their solution; if $1 \times$, $2 \times$, $4 \times$ and $8 \times$ are each recorded then all other multiples can be readily computed. This is standard practice in Dutch schools, where a form of chunking *is* the standard algorithm. See Smith (1999) for an interesting comparison of Dutch and British algorithms. However many steps a child may use, the solution will still be 7×42 with a remainder of 25.

The chunking approach to a division that *could* be performed digit by digit is still holistic. For example, to work out how many 22s there are in 7158, you could say, to start with, that $300 \times 22 = 6600$, leaving 558. How many 22s in 558? Well, $20 \times 22 = 440$, leaving 118. Then $5 \times 22 = 110$, leaving remainder 8. Altogether we have taken $(300 + 20 + 5)$ lots of 22. We did the division in three 'chunks', finding that 7158 is 325 lots of 22, with remainder 8.

In the two preceding sections we have considered two of the arithmetic operations – subtraction and division. In both cases there are different structures for each operation and these, in turn, give rise to different strategies that may be used to perform the operation. For each operation, there are various situations, or 'stories', which link the operation to an 'everyday' scenario in different ways. It is the teacher's own mathematical content knowledge which can ensure that these differences and opportunities are presented to children, and that the narrow, restrictive interpretations of subtraction ('take away') and division ('sharing') are avoided.

Geometrical transformations

Although number and number operations have a substantial place within the primary curriculum, other topics, and especially geometry, or 'shape and space', have a central place in mathematics and in the primary school curriculum. In this final section we will consider three geometrical transformations, the so-called 'symmetries' – reflection, rotation and translation – and the ways in which they might be encountered by young children. These are illustrated in Figure 7.10.

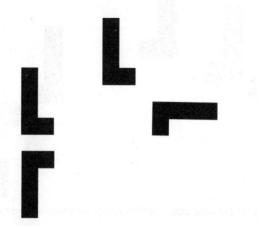

Figure 7.10   Reflection, rotation and translation

These three are amongst the possible geometrical transformations which can change the position of an object, and they have the special property that an object does not change its shape or size when it undergoes one of these transformations. The object and its image are said to be *congruent* to one another.

We shall look at two distinct threads with these transformations – where they act *between* objects and where they show properties *of* an object. Within both of these, there are some ideas for which children seem to have an intuitive feel, but others where the visualisation of a process may be quite hard to achieve.

Objects and images

When one of the transformations acts on an object, it produces an *image*. Often the object and the image are both there to be seen at the same time and indeed the path between the two can be quite clear for a translation or a rotation, as shown in Figure 7.11. A tracing paper overlay, or suitable IT software, can demonstrate the transformation. Both these transformations take place in the plane, with the slide (for translation) or turn (for rotation) producing the new image. Reflection is rather different as it necessitates a flip or fold, with the object ending up in reverse orientation.

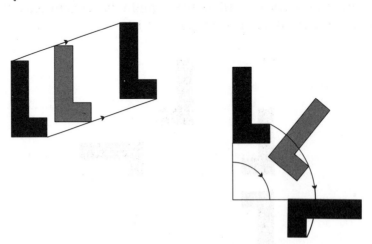

Figure 7.11   The path between object and image for a translation and for a rotation

Some further examples may help – the best thing would be to have some shapes to move around similar to those shown in Figure 7.12. Imagine that the tick is a cardboard shape. As you can see, one side of the tick is black and the reverse side is white, but each shape in Figure 7.12 is the same size and shape: they are congruent.

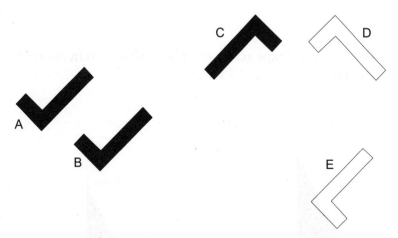

Figure 7.12   A collection of congruent shapes

Each tick can be transformed to one of the others by a translation (a slide in a single direction), rotation (a turn about one point) or reflection (a flip about a line). What transformation (translation, rotation or reflection) would take (i) A to B, (ii) B to C, (iii) C to D and (iv) D to E?

A translation is probably the simplest transformation to recognise (Johnston-Wilder and Mason, 2005: 155) as the orientation of the figure remains the same. So the transformation that takes (or 'maps') A to B is a translation diagonally from left to right. However, reflection is probably the first transformation that children meet, and the reversal of the image is one that some children readily recognise. In this example, C to D is a reflection in a 'vertical' line (whether it is actually vertical depends on how you are holding this page!). Indeed, the change of colour in Figure 7.12 helps to emphasise that physical flipping of the object is required, so that the tick must move outside its two-dimensional plane. It is also worth noticing that the perpendicular distance of equivalent points to the 'mirror line' is the same. Rotations are more difficult to identify and in this case a piece of tracing paper is useful. B moves to C by a rotation of 180°, or a half turn, about a point midway between the 'ends' of the two ticks. D to E is a quarter turn anticlockwise about a point to the right of the two ticks. Can you find this point? We now look at each of these transformations in turn.

Translation

A translation slides a shape across the plane with no reflection or rotation. This is illustrated in Figures 7.13 and 7.14.

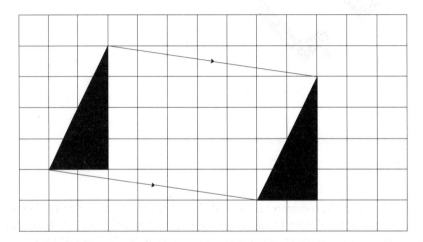

Figure 7.13 Translation of a triangle

In Figure 7.13, the upper triangle has been translated (or slid) 7 squares across and 1 square down. The orientation of the triangle remains exactly the same, so that each side of the triangle is parallel to its image. Now contrast this with Figure 7.14 where the orientations of the two squares *could* be different – there is nothing which makes any corner, say, of the square different from another. The irregularity of the triangle (or the tick in the earlier diagram) helps to focus on the orientation, which does not change.

There are many patterns within art and architecture which are built from an initial block which is translated – the key patterns seen on many ancient Greek artefacts are typical of these (Figure 7.15). Similar patterns

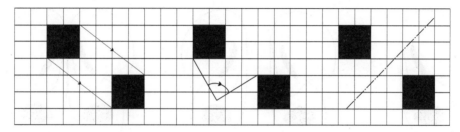

Figure 7.14 Translation of a square?

can be seen on pots held in various museums, including the British Museum in London. On a three-dimensional object, of course, this is not strictly a translation in a plane. There are numerous other patterns of this type – brick bonding in buildings, frieze patterns for wallpapers and so forth. Again the use of computer drawing packages can enhance this work with a visual image of the sliding movement of the shape.

Figure 7.15 A key pattern

Reflection

Children can engage with activities which are based on reflection from an early age, possibly because of their experiences with mirrors. Various researchers have considered young children's understanding of symmetrical patterns and have found that some make these patterns readily. In particular, Garrick (2002) found that 25% of 4½-year-olds were able to construct their own line symmetry pattern. The inclination seems to develop in children to build patterns with reflective symmetry. The delightful book by Marion Walter (2000) invites children to use a mirror, in a playful way, to make pictures which have reflective symmetry.

The process of making a butterfly by paint or ink blots and folding is probably familiar. This production of a symmetrical picture can be achieved using computer painting or drawing packages (such as those that come with an interactive whiteboard) where a shape can be copied and flipped, or reflected, as in Figure 7.16. This use of a variety of ways of doing the same process is helpful in focusing on the essential features of the process.

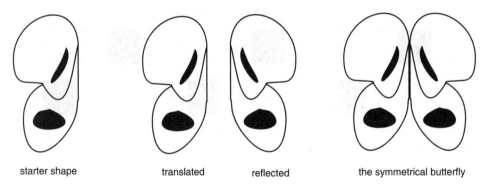

starter shape   translated   reflected   the symmetrical butterfly

Figure 7.16   Producing a butterfly by reflection

As well as these freely-drawn shapes, another activity uses a square grid (akin to a pegboard). A pattern may be started on one side and then it is reflected in a line of symmetry (Figure 7.17). The reflection line may be horizontal or vertical initially but can be at an angle to the grid at a later stage. This added complexity can cause difficulties and it is worth establishing that the perpendicular distances to the line of symmetry are preserved under reflection. Hansen (2005: 96–98) discusses a number of

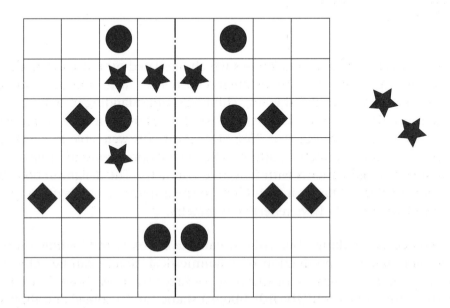

Figure 7.17   Building a reflection pattern on a square grid

errors and misconceptions that children may encounter of this type. Some patterns from Islamic and Hindu culture (particularly Rangoli patterns created for the Diwali festival) are developed from an initial shape which is reflected horizontally and vertically in this sort of way. The Victoria and Albert Museum website has material to support such a study and a visit to the museum (htpp://www.vam.ac.uk). The *Geometric Patterns* books by Robert Field (published by Tarquin Books in the UK) include one about Islamic art and architecture (Field, 1998).

Rotation

Rotation appears to be a more difficult idea to grasp; indeed, 63% of 11-year-olds incorrectly model a rotation as a reflection (Ryan and Williams, 2007: 87). Consider one of the experiences that many children will have had at a young age. A popular toy is the 'letter box' where different shapes can be posted into the relevant hole in the box. Often the shapes have a constant cross-section and many can be rotated into different positions to post them into the correctly shaped hole. So here a child may well be encouraged to turn the shape in order to get it into the hole.

However, it seems that children experience fewer activities which build up a sense of the changing orientation of an object – like the sails of a windmill – as it is rotated. Part of this may arise from the need for some quite high levels of physical dexterity in order to manipulate paper, tracing paper and possibly compasses. It is worth developing these skills so that a child can make a tracing of a shape and then put a pencil at the centre of rotation to see what happens as the paper is turned. The original shape is preserved and the new image can be seen moving around. Initially quarter or half turns may be used where a square grid would help to locate parts of the shape: see Figures 7.18 and 7.19. With a quarter turn it can be helpful to think about horizontal lines becoming vertical and vertical lines horizontal. Once again the choice of the shape to be rotated is important, so that the child can see the essence of the rotation and not be confused by other possible transformations such as reflection. This point is highly significant in Sonia's lesson, which we shall be considering soon. The use of appropriate software can give another experience of some of these processes, although the centre of rotation is often defined.

In Figures 7.18 and 7.19, the centre of rotation was outside the shape but it could be inside it, or on the boundary.

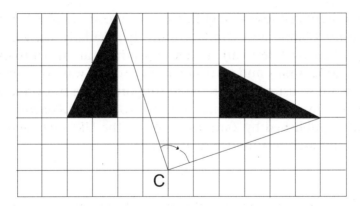

Figure 7.18　Rotation of a triangle, centre C, 90° clockwise

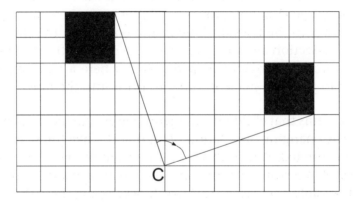

Figure 7.19　Rotation of a square, centre C, 90° clockwise

So far in this section, we have been considering transformations where an object is translated, reflected or rotated in order to produce an image. Then there are two congruent shapes and the transformation could be visualised as a 'movement' between the object and the image. The dynamic nature of these transformations is important. In summary, each transformation is specified by:

- reflection – a line (the axis of symmetry);

- rotation – a point (the centre of rotation), an angle (the amount of rotation) and the 'sense' (clockwise or anticlockwise);

- translation – a length (the distance of the translation) and the direction of the translation; together these are a 'vector' which describe the translation.

Symmetrical objects

The everyday notion of 'symmetry' is tied to mirrors, and to just one transformation: reflection. This is too restrictive from a mathematical point of view: it is important for children to see that there are alternative notions of symmetry, associated with rotation, and with translation. (It is for this reason that these particular transformations are called 'symmetry' transformations.)

We shall consider how some objects are symmetrical within themselves. Here we may reflect or rotate the object itself to demonstrate the symmetry but we are not producing an image in a *different* location. So the emphasis here is on the properties that an object itself possesses. Think about the logos for British Rail and the Isle of Man or the patterns within brickwork and paving (some of these are illustrated in Figure 7.20); there are symmetries present within these patterns and logos.

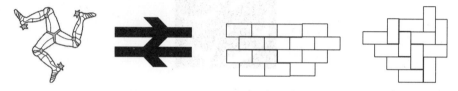

Figure 7.20   Some examples of logos or patterns with symmetry

Reflective symmetry was discussed at the start of Chapter 4 and the use of pictures of objects to show the identical but 'turned-over' nature of the two halves of a shape was discussed. All sorts of objects that we see possess symmetries, and some in rather unexpected places. Car hubcaps come in a vast range of designs and many possess reflective symmetry, or rotational symmetry, or indeed both. There are some examples in Figure 7.21. Would it be possible to fold some of these photographs so that the two

Figure 7.21   Wheel hubcaps

parts of the hubcap were identical? How can you be sure? If you were to use a mirror to check, what are you actually doing with the mirror?

Putting a mirror on the likely line of symmetry reveals an image of part of the shape in the mirror. But there is a need is to check that this reflected part is the same as the actual shape behind the mirror; so lifting the mirror up can allow this simultaneous check on the reflection and the part behind. If they are indeed identical then the mirror is on the line of symmetry.

The first two hubcaps have several lines of symmetry. How many, would you say? Are there more or fewer on the second hubcap?

Figure 7.22   Axes of symmetry on a hubcap

Figure 7.22 shows two of the lines of symmetry on the first hubcap. Add any others and draw them in for the second hubcap.

Now think about rotating these hubcaps. How many times would it be possible to rotate them so that the picture looks exactly the same? Here it may help to have a marker to show where an individual point has moved, as in Figure 7.23.

Figure 7.23   Rotations of a hubcap

Here the hubcap will have rotated five times to get back to its starting point. It has rotated about the centre of the wheel (the centre of rotation) and is said to have rotational symmetry of order 5.

The third hubcap is quite similar to the first one, it has five holes around the edge but these holes do not themselves have line symmetry, and so the whole hubcap does not have reflective symmetry (we cannot fold it onto itself to give two identical halves). However, we can rotate it onto itself and again it has rotational symmetry of order 5.

Karen Hancock (2007) describes a lesson with her Year 7 class in which the children use digital cameras to take photographs of hubcaps in the school car park and then display them on an interactive whiteboard to highlight the various symmetries. This illustrates very well the potential of using everyday objects to bring an extra dimension to the children's learning as well as utilising the power of digital recording and annotation.

We have considered three transformations where the shape and size of an object are preserved – reflection, rotation or translation. Recognising the symmetrical properties of an object will be one dimension of learning about the characteristics of these transformations. Additionally there are activities which children can undertake to develop their understanding of the dynamic nature of the transformations, both recognising and then producing patterns using the transformations.

Back to a student teacher's classroom – Sonia

In a second stage of our study, a student teacher whom we call Sonia was videotaped teaching a Year 4 class by the research team. Soon afterwards we met to view the tape and to identify some key episodes in the lesson, using the Knowledge Quartet as an analytical framework. Later, one team member met with Sonia to view the videotape and to discuss some of the episodes. In the case described here, the whole process occurred within one day. In this 'stimulated recall', Sonia was able to reflect on her lesson and give further insight into the role of her mathematics content knowledge in her teaching.

In her planning, Sonia intended that pupils would be able to 'make and describe repeating patterns which involve translations and/or reflections'.

In introducing this, she uses an overhead projector (OHP) to display the movement of various shapes: she asked some of the children to come up and demonstrate the moves.

Sonia places a rectangle on the OHP and moves it to the left asking the general question, 'How have I moved it?'. She receives a range of non-mathematical replies: 'slowly' and 'with your finger'. However, on pressing the pupils for a mathematical response and requesting them to use the selection of words attached to the wall she receives the response 'horizontally' which she endorses as 'side to side', in this case 'left to right'. However, when she moves the figure downwards and a pupil describes this as a 'vertically, downwards' movement she adds that 'vertically means downwards'. In summing up so far, Sonia says, more than once (in slightly different ways), 'if I'm moving a shape it's called a translation'.

Next she invites pupils to move the figure – which is now a circle – according to her instructions. When Meg is asked to move it vertically she moves it downwards. It is difficult to determine whether Meg is following the restricted definition of 'vertical' as a downwards movement, introduced a few moments ago, as the circle has been placed at the top of the OHT which rather closes Meg's options, although this very placing of the circle by Sonia does suggest that she is cueing the pupil into a downward movement.

Another request for a movement 'horizontally right' is carried out correctly. Asked to move the circle 'horizontally left', Amy rotates the circular disc noticeably as she moves it. Sonia responds with 'oh there's a lot of movement there' but does not use this to indicate that Amy has not simply carried out a translation. However, Sonia presses on with a brief account of rotation and reflection using a star figure and a circle. What she is trying to establish here is that when a shape is transformed a second shape is generated which is 'the same' as the first. Her focus on this probably arises from her intention to generate patterns in the next section. The shapes that she is using are special ones; indeed, one member of the class has some mild reservations about shapes always remaining the same after transformation. Sonia rather sweeps these reservations away, but one child chips in with a suggestion: 'If you reflect it with an L-shape it wouldn't be the same, it would be the other way.' This time, while Sonia acknowledges the pupil's response, she does not develop it.

In thinking about this part of the lesson, what are the aspects that may have caused the children to have difficulties in grasping the ideas that Sonia is introducing to them? How would you adapt her approach in order to help the children?

There is a difficulty with the terminology being used here – movement, transformation and translation. Each has a specific meaning, but at times Sonia is using them interchangeably. There is a further complexity in whether a drawing is being made, so that the original position of a shape and the new one can be compared, or whether an object is being moved, in which case there is only one thing to look at. With the learning objective of pattern-making in place, Sonia tried to establish that when a shape is transformed, a second shape is generated which is 'the same' as the first. This was a sensible strategy but the original position of the shape could have been marked in order to compare it with its new position on the OHP.

The shapes that Sonia chose to transform had an effect too. In particular, she did not appear to realise that the internal symmetry of a transformed figure itself can mask certain effects of a transformation, particularly reflection, where the object 'reversal' is fundamental. This effect would not be evident in a rectangle, for example, which appears 'the same' shape after reflection.

Later the same day, Sonia readily saw the missed opportunity when the astute pupil had suggested the use of an L-shape. Here is part of her conversation with us, having watched the videotape of the lesson.

Interviewer:	… it's about the boy who did the … who asked for the L-shape
Sonia:	Yes
Interviewer:	The shapes that *you* chose were a rectangle …
Sonia:	Yes
Interviewer:	… and a circle, which … have got a certain amount of regularity
Sonia:	Yeah
[…]	
Interviewer:	… if you flip the … the rectangle, the same … but the L-shape … hasn't got any symmetry in it, if you like
Sonia:	Mmm
Interviewer:	Emm, so did you, were you aware of that, or just …
Sonia:	[laughs] I took random shapes off a pile [laughs] um, yes
Interviewer:	Well, you can see the boy's point …
Sonia:	Oh yes, definitely
Interviewer:	It's quite a good reply
Sonia:	If I were to do it again, I would …

Interviewer: It would be striking, what has happened to the shape, if itself
               it didn't have any symmetry
Sonia: It would be much easier for them to see

This reflective discussion helped Sonia develop her understanding of geometrical transformations, and how particular example shapes can demonstrate the essence of a specific transformation while others disguise it. Through the act of teaching, reflection and discussion, it was possible to focus on areas of Sonia's mathematical content knowledge which she can target for further development.

Summary

Within this chapter, we have considered four areas of the primary mathematics curriculum where a teacher's content knowledge needs to extend beyond that of the well-educated citizen. This knowledge can be quite varied – whether it is the unpacking of the underlying processes of counting, understanding the different structures for subtraction and division, or grasping the essential properties of some geometrical transformations. This knowledge can enable a teacher to consider the best ways to introduce mathematical ideas to children, and to enhance their understanding of these topics.

Further reading

Ian Thompson (1997) *Teaching and Learning Early Number.* Buckingham: Open University Press.

> This edited book contains a number of chapters about counting, written by recognised experts in the field, including Penny Munn and Ian Thompson. In these chapters, counting is considered in relation to understanding and beliefs, language and number development. Effie Maclellan's chapter gives a detailed account of Gelman and Gallistel's five principles, and Julia Anghileri discusses how counting is used in the operations of multiplication and division. Whether you teach very young children or those coming to the end of primary school, you will find this book challenging, interesting and relevant.

Julia Anghileri (2006) *Teaching Number Sense,* 2nd edn. London: Continuum.

Derek Haylock (2006) *Mathematics Explained for Primary Teachers,* 3rd edn. London: Sage.

Each of these books gives a clear and thorough account of the different subtraction and division structures discussed in this chapter.

Sue Johnston-Wilder and John Mason (eds) (2005) *Developing Thinking in Geometry*. London: Paul Chapman Publishing.

This book is thought-provoking and challenging but readily accessible. You can engage with activities in the book (and the accompanying CD-ROM) and it enables you to think about both teaching and learning. It has numerous examples from the authors' experiences which help to get to the underlying essence of geometry.

Using the Knowledge Quartet to Reflect on Mathematics Teaching

In this chapter you will find:

- a number of extracts of mathematics lessons;
- our thoughts on these extracts;
- a Knowledge Quartet proforma for use in reflecting on these lessons.

In earlier chapters we introduced you to the four dimensions of the Knowledge Quartet as a framework for reflecting on mathematics lessons. We went on to examine some key aspects of mathematics content knowledge which we have found to be important in the teaching of beginning teachers. We have used lessons which we observed in our Knowledge Quartet research to illustrate discussions about the role of teachers' mathematical content knowledge in their teaching. In this chapter, we offer some further examples of mathematics lessons as contexts to practise reflecting on the content of mathematics lessons using the Knowledge Quartet framework. These lessons have some features that you might want to draw on in your teaching, as well as some that you might not. However, we do not primarily offer them as models of practice, but rather as starting points for discussion and reflection. You could simply read the descriptions of the lessons and then think about them in a general way. However, we think that it might be helpful for you to use the questions we offer as a basis for your reflections in order to help you to focus on content knowledge. We hope that by focusing on content knowledge in these lessons it will help you to ask similar questions about your own mathematics teaching at both the planning and evaluation stages.

We suggest that you write your thoughts about the lessons under the four headings of the Knowledge Quartet. You will find it useful to go back to Chapter 2 in order to remind yourself of the kinds of things that come under each heading. There is a 'Knowledge Quartet reflection proforma' at the back of the book (Table 8.2), if you wish to use it to record your thoughts about the lessons.

Table 8.1   The lessons

Lesson	Teacher	Mathematical topic	Year group
1	Amy	Counting in tens	Reception
2	Sally	Addition and subtraction	Reception
3	Laura	Place value	Year 1
4	Kate	Doubling	Year 1
5	Kim	Capacity	Year 1/2
6	Lucy	Multiplication	Year 2
7	Ellie	'Missing numbers'	Year 2
8	Joyce	Division	Year 3
9	John	Telling the time	Year 3
10	James	Fractions	Year 4
11	Lindsay	Positive and negative numbers	Year 4
12	Nathalie	Probability	Year 6

We have given examples of lessons across the primary age range and selected those which address a wide range of mathematical topics. This will enable you to think about those that are relevant to the age group that you teach, across a wide spectrum of mathematics. If possible, discuss these lessons with a peer or a mentor in order to share your ideas and develop your thinking. Once you have formulated your own thoughts about these lessons, you can compare them with ours, which you will find after all the extracts. Reading about what we saw, when looking through the lens of the Knowledge Quartet, will help you develop your own use of the framework and your ability to reflect on the content of your mathematics teaching. You may have suggestions that we did not think of, which are just as valid as those that we make. Thinking about these lesson extracts, and reading our thoughts, may raise issues of mathematics content knowledge across a wider spectrum than has been addressed elsewhere in this book. Table 8.1 tells you the age group and mathematical topic of each of the lessons.

1 Amy (NQT): Reception lesson on counting in tens

The context of this activity was 'pirates' which fitted in with the general class topic of traditional stories. Amy led the children to sail their pirate ship to an island (table) where they discovered a chest full of gold coins. She explained that, since there were so many coins, they could not count them all at once so she would give each pirate a pile to count. After some discussion, Amy suggested that they could put the coins into groups of ten to make the counting easier.

When all the coins were in groups of ten, Amy tried to explain to the children how to count in tens. She told them to 'put ten in your head then count all the coins in the next ten'. Amy then counted with them, 'ten, eleven, twelve, thirteen, fourteen, fifteen, sixteen, seventeen, eighteen, nineteen, twenty'. She then asked what two groups of ten are, to which a child responded 'twenty'. Amy then demonstrated taking one group of ten coins at a time and counting 'ten, twenty, thirty, forty'. She asked 'what about five groups?'. The children seemed very unsure and did not answer. Amy then showed the children a 1–100 number grid. She demonstrated counting along the top row, 1–10, showing that this made ten, and then continued to count the next ten, 11–20, showing that this made twenty. She then pointed to, and counted down, the tens column '10, 20, 30, …, 100'.

What did you think about this context for developing children's counting skills?

Was the strategy of putting the coins into groups of ten a good one for counting these large collections?

How else might the children have counted the large number of coins?

Was the counting in tens activity appropriate for reception children?

How helpful do you think Amy's use of the hundred grid was in supporting the children's counting in tens?

2 Sally (trainee): Reception lesson on addition and subtraction

In the introduction part of the lesson, a 'Freddie the Frog' puppet was placed on a number line to represent the number of frog friends he had at any time. The number line ran from 0 to 10 and had a picture of a frog at each interval, including the zero. Sally began by asking the children to show her where frog number 3 was, and then to place Freddie above the 3 on the number line to show that Freddie had 3 friends. She asked the children how many 'froggy friends' Freddie had. One child responded 'ten' before Sally received her expected response of 'three'.

Sally went on to use this representation to demonstrate addition and subtraction. She asked: 'What would you have to do if Freddie has two more friends?' A child came out and moved the puppet two jumps to land above the 5. Sally then asked: 'What if one of Freddie's friends has jumped into the pond. Which way are we going to go?'

After Freddie had been taken back to zero to show that, all of his friends had jumped in the pond, a child was asked to move him the appropriate number of jumps to show that he had 7 friends. The child began his count on 0 and finished at 6. He realised that this was not right and immediately moved the puppet to the '7'. Sally did not comment on this.

Why do you think Sally chose this particular number line? Were the pictures of frogs helpful?

How were the *cardinal* and *ordinal* aspects of number represented in this activity? How might this have caused some confusion?

Why do you think that the child finished on the 6 rather than the 7? How might Sally have used this mistake to help the children's understanding?

This lesson was based on the popular song 'Five little speckled frogs'. How else could Sally have introduced addition and subtraction using model frogs?

3 Laura (trainee): Year 1 lesson on place value

Laura told the children that they would be looking at tens and units and she showed them the 'tens and units board' and base-10 materials.

T	U
1	4

Figure 8.1   Tens and units board

Laura held up a 10 stick and asked 'Stick of …?'. A child completed the phrase with 'ten'. Laura showed a unit and asked: 'Who can tell me how much a unit is worth?' A child responded 'one'. Laura emphasised the difference in values between the unit cube and the 10 stick by picking up a 10 stick and asking: 'If I pick up one of these I only have one stick in my hand, but how much is it worth?' A child responded 'ten'. Laura then placed a few units onto a 10 stick and told the children that when they return to their tables they could try placing units onto the 10 stick to confirm that one stick is worth ten units. Laura wrote the number 14 on the tens and units board as in Figure 8.1. She counted out 14 units and placed them all in the 'tens column' asking if this was correct. The children responded 'no' and Laura asked 'If I am going to put the cubes in the right column, what must I do?'. A child replied that she must move them to the units column. Laura did this saying that she had a problem: 'When I wrote fourteen I didn't put the whole number in the units column, so what do I need to do?' A child suggested swapping ten units for a 10 stick and putting it in the tens column. Laura responded that it is 'much easier to have a stick of ten'. She worked with the children through a few more examples like this before explaining what she wanted them to do.

Laura explained that she wanted the children to choose two digit cards from the pots on their tables and combine these to make two-digit numbers. She asked them to write the 'numbers' in the correct columns and then to place '10 sticks' and units in the appropriate columns and to draw around them. They did several examples of this together, first writing the digits of a number into the columns on the board and then finding the corresponding base-10 material to place in the columns. The children went to their tables and carried out the activity modelled in the introduction.

During the activity part of this lesson, Jamie made '18' with his digit cards. He correctly selected one 10 stick and eight units which he placed on the tens and units board under the appropriate headings. He then wrote '8' and '1' indicating how many of each he had placed on the board. However, his board had the tens on the right and the units on the left (as in Figure 8.2), so that he wrote '81'. This happened because he had turned over his paper, on which Laura had drawn the columns, and these showed through to the other side.

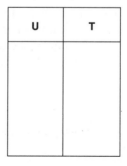

Figure 8.2   Jamie's tens and units board

What understanding do you think Laura was trying to promote through this activity?

What do you think the children learned by doing this activity?

What can you say about the learning of the child who turned over his paper and wrote the digits 'back to front'?

What do you think about the way Laura used the tens and units boards?

4 Kate (trainee): Year 1 lesson on doubling

Clip 9 on the companion website shows this part of Kate's lesson.

Kate used a laminated picture of a cauldron with bubbles coming from it for recording the calculation of doubles throughout the lesson. The 'maths wizard' puppet used this cauldron to make doubles by saying the magic words 'hubble bubble what's the double'. The numbers to be doubled were written in the cauldron in the form '3 + 3' and when the double was found, it was written in the bubble '6'. Kate also wrote the number sentence on the board in the form '3 + 3 = 6'. She modelled doubling all the numbers to 10 in this way before moving on to two-digit numbers.

Kate wrote 13 + 13 in the cauldron and when a child offered the correct answer, she asked how they had worked it out. The response suggested that the child had partitioned the tens and units and Kate demonstrated a way of recording on the cauldron picture that used partitioning. She drew a second bubble on to the laminated picture and demonstrated doubling the tens number and putting the answer in the first bubble, then doubling the units number and putting it in the units bubble. She put a '2' in the tens bubble and a '6' in the units bubble. Kate asked the children to suggest numbers to double and the number 15 was given. Kate started to write this into the cauldron before realising that her form of representation will not work for this example. She told the children that this was 'a hard one' and suggested that they should choose another example, with a smaller number of units.

What did you think of Kate's use of the cauldron picture as a way of representing and recording doubling?

Kate always recorded the procedure of doubling as '$n + n$'. How else might she have recorded this in the cauldron?

Why was Kate unable to record the doubling of '15' using her bubbles?

What was problematic about the way Kate recorded the answer to doubling tens in the second bubble?

5 Kim (NQT): Year 1/2 lesson on capacity

Kim was observed teaching a lesson on capacity to a Year 1 class. She began by looking at relative capacities of containers and estimating how many litre bottles fitted into some larger containers. She also addressed the difficult concept of conservation, by demonstrating that different shaped containers all held a litre of liquid. During the activity part of the lesson, some children were given worksheets with drawings of containers showing various levels of liquid. All of the containers were drawn as being the same size, though their capacities were shown as $\frac{1}{2}$ litre, 1 litre or 2 litres. The units of capacity needed to give the amount of liquid were either litres or half litres.

In the plenary, this teacher used an interactive teaching program in which the whole class could see levels of liquid in a litre jug with a scale on the side. This showed a measuring cylinder with intervals of 10 ml and numbers marked every 100 ml up to 1000 ml. Kim asked a child to come to the board and indicate where the level of water would be if there were 100 ml in the cylinder. The child initially pointed to the 1000 ml mark. Kim asked why this was not 100 and other children responded that it had an extra zero and was in fact a thousand. Kim then asked a child to point to the 1 litre level, which he did appropriately. In order to 'fill the cylinder' on the interactive whiteboard it was necessary to put the number of millilitres into a box; however, this only allowed three digits. Kim was therefore unable to put in 1000 ml. She put in 900 ml and asked how much more was needed to make a litre. A child responded '100 ml' and this was added to bring the level to 1 litre. Kim then asked: 'How many millilitres in one litre?' The children answered 1000.

What difficulties do you see in the way Kim used representations of capacity in this lesson?

What do you think Kim might have done to help the children move from physically using jugs as units for filling a larger container, to the use of scales?

What do you think Kim was trying to do in the plenary?

What were the difficulties encountered by some of the children?

What do you think of the way Kim got over the problem of not being able to 'pour' 1000 ml into the cylinder in one go?

6 Lucy (early career teacher): Year 2 lesson on multiplication

In the introduction to this lesson, Lucy attempted to explain the meaning of multiplication to the children. Lucy was working with a group of children during the activity part of the lesson. She asked the children to solve the problem 6×10. The children were given bead strings and cubes to support their working. One child offered the answer 'sixteen' and Lucy reminded the group that they were not working out $6 + 10$ but rather 6×10. It was apparent from watching the children use the bead strings that several of them continued to calculate $6 + 10$ rather than 6×10. Lucy attempted to address this difficulty by representing the calculation $6 + 10$ on the bead string and reminding the children that they were supposed to be finding 6×10 or 'six lots of ten'. She then demonstrated 6×10 using the bead string and moving six groups of ten beads, while counting 'ten, twenty, …, sixty'. Lucy then used a different representation to demonstrate the same calculation. She made six towers of ten multilink and then counted them in tens with the children. A child then completed the number sentence on the interactive whiteboard as '$6 \times 10 = 60$'.

Why do you think the children persisted in working out '6 + 10' rather than '6 × 10'?

What are the relative merits of using bead strings or towers of multilink to represent '6 × 10'?

What other representations could you use to show the meaning of multiplication?

7 Ellie (trainee): Year 2 lesson on 'missing numbers'

This lesson was about strategies for finding the missing numbers in number sentences. These were of the types 7 + 8 = ?, 7 + ? = 15 and ? + 8 = 15. In the activity part of the lesson the children were working on various examples. Ellie was attempting to help a child with the problem ? + 16 = 49. She suggested using an empty number line to carry out the subtraction 49 – 16. Ellie demonstrated a very complex procedure, in which a jump of 9 backwards from 49 lands on the 'friendly' number 40. There was then a discussion about how many more need to be taken away and the number 7 was arrived at, by counting on from 9 to 16 while keeping a tally with fingers. Ellie demonstrated jumping back 10 and forward 3 to achieve the required backwards jump of 7.

Ellie helped a child who was 'stuck' on 14 + ? = 30, and suggested he used a number line to count back 14 from 30. The child was left to carry out this procedure, while Ellie moved to deal with a difficulty experienced by a different child.

Do you think the empty number line was a helpful representation for solving these problems?

Did Ellie help the children use the empty number line in the way most appropriate to these problems?

How might she have used the empty number line differently to support the children's understanding of how to solve these problems?

What other representations or materials might have been helpful here?

8 Joyce (early career teacher): Year 3 lesson on division

Clip 10 on the companion website shows this part of Joyce's lesson.

At the start of the lesson, Joyce told the children they would be focusing on the word 'share' and would be using sharing to answer some division problems.

Joyce displayed a screen on the interactive whiteboard showing, '16 divided by 2 equals' and 16 small circles as in Figure 8.3. Joyce told the children that 'divided by' or the '÷' symbol means the same as sharing.

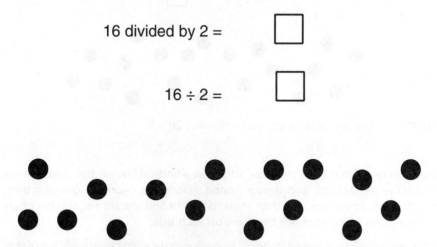

16 divided by 2 =

16 ÷ 2 =

Figure 8.3   Interactive whiteboard screen showing 16 ÷ 2

The children worked in pairs using small whiteboards to find a solution. Joyce asked two children to show their workings on the boards. One child had drawn a vertical line approximately dividing her board in half. She had drawn eight spots on either side of the line. The second child had also divided her board in half and had written numbers on either side of the board so that they alternated as in Figure 8.4.

```
|  1      3  |  2      4       |
|              |              6 |
|  5          |  8             |
|     7       |                |
|        9    |          10    |
| 11          | 12             |
|     13      |          14    |
|    15       |      16        |
```

Figure 8.4   Child's recording of 16 ÷ 2

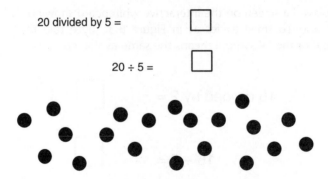

20 divided by 5 = ☐

20 ÷ 5 = ☐

Figure 8.5   Interactive whiteboard screen showing 20 ÷ 5

Joyce congratulated both children. She drew a vertical line on the screen of the interactive whiteboard, and demonstrated sharing the counters, one at a time, to either side of the line. She then showed that to find the answer, it is necessary to count how many counters there are on each side.

After using the interactive whiteboard to demonstrate a similar process, in order to divide 20 by 2, Joyce displayed a screen showing 20 divided by 5 as in Figure 8.5. Joyce suggested that the children drew five circles on their whiteboards and then share the 20 counters into them, one at a time. She drew five large circles at the bottom of the board. Joyce gave the children some time to complete their drawings. She then reminded them that she had drawn five circles, and she redrew them on the board slightly larger. Joyce then put a mark in each circle in turn, counting to 20 as she did so. She asked: 'I have five groups, how many do I have in each circle?' Joyce told the children that the circles show how many groups they are dividing the counters into and the number in each circle is the answer.

Joyce introduced the next example, which was 24 divided by 4, and asked how many circles they needed to draw. One child said 'four'. Joyce repeated her explanation of the process by putting one counter in each circle at a time while counting up to 24.

What were the advantages and disadvantages of Joyce's use of these representations to show the *sharing* aspect of division?

What did the two different ways in which children recorded 'sharing 16 by 2', on their individual whiteboards, suggest about their understanding of the concept?

How else might she have used the interactive whiteboard to demonstrate sharing?

How could you use the interactive whiteboard to demonstrate the *grouping* aspect of division?

9 John (NQT): Year 4 lesson on telling the time

John displayed an analogue clock on an interactive whiteboard. This showed real time and had a moving second hand. He asked the children to write the time on their whiteboards 'in numbers'. One child who had written '10.34' was asked to come to the front and explain why he had written this, using the clock on the interactive whiteboard. By this time, the clock had moved on to show 10.36. The child explained that at the time he had written his answer, the big hand was just before the 7 and the small hand was just before the 11 and after the 10. John reiterated this, focusing on the difference between the roles of the two hands and praised the child for his useful explanation.

John then showed a different analogue clock on the interactive whiteboard, which also had a digital representation, though John had hidden this. This clock showed '2.15'. John asked the children to write the time on their whiteboards. When they had shown their answers, John revealed the digital display which showed '2.16:44'. The seconds were continually changing. John asked the children to explain how they knew the time from the analogue clock, and a child explained that it was 'because the short hand was pointing at the two and the long hand at the three, so it must be 2.15'.

John then changed the time shown on the clock, by pressing the arrows on the display, to show one o'clock. He asked the children to write what the time would be in five minutes' time. John then used the arrow keys, to change the time shown on the clock face to five past one. John asked why this showed *five* minutes past, when the minute hand was pointing to the 1. The children responded that it was the five times table and each number shows the 'lots of five'. John then asked successively what the time would be, when the hand is on the 2, the 4 and the 9, each time resetting the clock on the interactive whiteboard to show these times. The children answered '1.10', '1.20' and '1.45' respectively. After the children had answered '1.45', John said that there was another answer to this, and one child suggested 'quarter to two'.

Why do you think John chose to use the clock face displays on the interactive whiteboard?

In what ways might John's choice of resource have been problematic?

How could he have further exploited the use of the displays on the interactive whiteboard?

What other common classroom resource is available for this task? What would be the advantages using it?

10 James (NQT): Year 4 lesson on fractions

Clip 11 on the companion website shows this part of James's lesson.

This lesson on fractions and decimals was based on a plan, which at that time was available from the internet. James had adapted this plan to make greater use of interactive teaching programs on the interactive whiteboard. This was the third lesson on this topic within a unit of work. In the 'warm-up' part of the lesson, James displayed a screen on the interactive whiteboard, showing a pizza divided into quarters. Next to the picture were the symbols $\frac{?}{?}$ with the words 'numerator' and 'denominator' written next to the appropriate part of the symbol. By touching the screen, James was able to make fractions of the pizza 'disappear'. He began by touching two of the quarters and asked how much pizza was left. The children responded 'half'. He then asked for a different fraction and a child responded with 'two quarters'. The child was then asked to come and check by touching the $\frac{?}{?}$ which gave $\frac{2}{4}$. This process was repeated for different pictures of pizzas, cakes and chocolate bars. Each time, a representation of a whole divided into different fractions was shown. In each case James touched the screen, making sections of the divided picture disappear. The children were asked what fraction of the food was left. Their answers were checked by touching the $\frac{?}{?}$ symbols on the screen. The examples used on the interactive whiteboard were:

- pizzas divided into quarters with two quarters missing, sevenths with one seventh missing and quarters with one quarter missing;

- a chocolate bar divided into sixths with one sixth missing;

- a cake divided into eighths with three eighths missing;

- chocolate bars divided into fifths with one fifth missing and eighths with three eighths missing.

What do you think about the use of pictures, such as pizzas, cakes and chocolate bars, to develop children's understanding of fractional notation?

What may be problematic about using such representations?

In what ways, if any, did the interactive nature of the interactive teaching program help develop children's understanding of fractions?

What other types of representations of fractions could be used to support the development of understanding?

11 Lindsay (student teacher): Year 4 lesson on positive and negative numbers

Lindsay began the lesson with a tables test, and then demonstrated counting forwards and backwards in threes, then in fives, using a 'counting stick' (a metre stick divided into 10 intervals, in contrasting colours). Lindsay then shifted the focus to positive and negative numbers. First, by using the counting stick, she said that zero is at one end, but then she changed her mind, deciding that zero was to be in the middle of the stick. In fact, the middle was the boundary between two coloured intervals, but Lindsay told the class that zero was one of the two central intervals coloured in yellow. She indicated that the negative numbers were to her right (the children's left): and that the positive numbers were to her left. The children counted (to her left) together 'one, two, three, four, five'. Lindsay asked 'What comes after zero in negative numbers?' and Jonathan volunteered 'minus one'. Lindsay then led the counting (to her right) saying 'minus one, minus two, etc'. She then reverted to something that she had identified as a problem in an earlier lesson, saying 'OK. When you want to add on a negative number, you go back toward zero, so negative four add two, where will that take you? Jonathan?' Jonathan answered 'Negative two'. Lindsay then asked: 'If I wanted to take away two from minus two, where would that take me?' Aisha answered 'Minus four'.

Lindsay confirmed this answer, adding, 'OK, so it goes the wrong way. Instead of adding on and going into numbers that are bigger, with a minus sign they get smaller … the larger the number. It's really confusing, but if you remember that, with zero in the middle, that's your positive numbers [indicating] and that's your negative numbers. If you add on you go that way [gestures to her left], just like you would on the positive numbers. If you take away you go this way [gesture right], just like you would on the positive numbers.'

At this point Jonathan asked whether zero should be the middle point on the stick (the boundary between two segments), or the segment that Lindsay had indicated. Lindsay replied: 'That bit here is the middle, isn't it, but we're using this yellow bit as zero.'

The children then set to work on a worksheet on arithmetic sequences of numbers (like 8, 3, −2, −7, …). The sheet indicated, with an arrow pointing right or left, whether each sequence should be increasing or decreasing.

Ten minutes later, seeing that several children were unsure what to do, she drew a number line on the whiteboard. The line extended from −5 to +5. Lindsay marked 11 points on the line, so that each number corresponded to a point on the line. She then wrote 'Top Tips' and drew three arches for forward 'jumps' from 0 to 3, and three arches for backward 'jumps' from 0 to −3 as in Figure 8.6. Lindsay drew the class's attention to these 'Top Tips' on the board, saying that

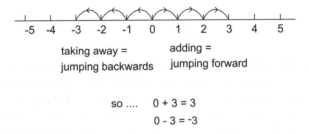

Figure 8.6   Lindsay's 'Top Tips'

this would remind them 'which way you need to go when you are adding and taking away when you go into the minus numbers'. The class continued with the worksheet.

What are the relative merits of the counting stick and number line (drawn on the board) as representations of positive and negative numbers?

Why do you think Lindsay represented the 'integers' (positive and negative whole numbers) as intervals, rather than points, on the counting stick? Was this a well-judged decision? How might she have responded to Jonathan's query about this?

What do you think of Lindsay's 'Top Tips'? Would yours be different, or do you not like the idea of 'Top Tips' anyway?

Is it best to say 'minus one' or 'negative one'? Why?

What exactly did Lindsay think was 'really confusing'? Do you agree with her?

What aspects of negative numbers is it beneficial for Year 4 children to know about? Why? How does this compare with what Lindsay is trying to teach in this episode?

12 Nathalie (student teacher): Year 6 lesson on probability

This lesson was intended to revise probability in preparation for national end-of-primary tests (SATs). Nathalie began by reminding the class that probabilities are about the likelihood of events, and that they can be represented and compared as fractions. She demonstrated this with a box of coloured cubes: 5 red, 3 green and 2 blue. Having established that there were 10 in total, she asked what fraction was red. One child answered 'a half'. She then asked what fraction is blue, attracting an answer 'a quarter'. Nathalie pointed out that there were two blue cubes in ten, and the answer was corrected to a fifth. The first response to her next question, about the fraction of green cubes, was 'a third'. Nathalie asked: 'Are you sure?' She then removed one red cube, and pointed out that now the fraction of green cubes was indeed a third.

For the main activity, most children played two dice games, in pairs. In Game 1, two dice were thrown: one player won a point if the sum of the scores on the dice was 7, the other if the sum was 2 or 3. Similarly, in Game 2, one player threw two dice with the aim of a sum greater than 8, while the other tried to throw a 3 with just one die. The object was to see whether either of these games was fair.

Nathalie concluded the lesson with a ten-minute plenary discussion, in which each game was analysed theoretically. Beginning with Game 1, Nathalie asked what scores were possible with two dice, and listed the ways of scoring each sum in a column on the whiteboard, as the children called them out. Thus $1 + 1 = 2$, $1 + 2 = 3$, $2 + 1 = 3$ (she reminded them that there are two dice, and so 1+2 and 2+1 are different), $1 + 3 = 4$, $2 + 2 = 4$, $3 + 1 = 4$ and so on, as far as the five ways (which she called 'chances') of scoring 6. She then asked them: 'Can you see a pattern emerging here? How many ways are there of making 2, 3, 4, 5 and 6? How many ways do you predict to make 7?' A boy answered 'six'. Nathalie asked 'Why do you say six?', but his answer is inaudible. Nathalie listed the six ways: 1+6, 2+5, and so on. They then listed the five ways of making 8, and Nathalie asked them to predict the number of ways of making 9. Four ways were suggested, and Nathalie said 'Yes, the chances are going down'. They then observed that there are three 'combinations' altogether 'for 2 or 3', and six 'ways I can make 7'.

Without further comment, Nathalie went on to analyse Game 2. With reference to the pattern established earlier, they agreed that the number of ways of making 9, 10, 11 and 12 would be 4, 3, 2, 1 respectively, and therefore $4 + 3 + 2 + 1 = 10$ ways altogether. She then asked 'How many combinations have we got?', and starting from $4 + 3 + 2 + 1 = 10$, counted up the pairs (e.g. $6 + 2$, $5 + 3$) already listed on the board ('eleven, twelve, …'), establishing that there were 36 pairs altogether. She then said, 'There are 36 combinations, to win we need ten of them', writing $\frac{10}{36}$ without comment. Likewise, after brief consideration of Player 2's possible outcomes, she wrote $\frac{1}{6}$ for the probability of throwing a 3 with one dice.

Looking at the two fractions, she asked, 'So which is more likely? How can we work out which of these is more likely?' Larry pointed to $\frac{10}{36}$ and called out 'It's just over a third'. Nathalie responded, 'Good it's just over a third. Is there any other way we could make direct comparison? Remember equivalent fractions. How could we make this [indicates $\frac{1}{6}$] into thirty-sixths? Times by six.' She was writing $\frac{6}{36}$ as the 60-minute tape ran out.

What do you think of Nathalie's use of the red, blue and green cubes in the introduction?

How well equipped do you think Nathalie was to teach probability in this lesson?

What features of her plenary do you think were good, and which do you think she could have handled differently?

Some of our thoughts on these lessons

1 Amy's Reception lesson on counting in tens

The use of the pirate role play and related resources suggests that Amy believes that mathematics should be enjoyable and related to the lives of the children. Putting counting into the context of pirate treasure, which linked to the class theme of traditional stories, was a good way of bringing coherence to the children's learning and engaging them in their work. (Foundation)

Though Amy's strategy, of grouping objects in order to count larger numbers, was appropriate for children at this stage, having such a large number (>100) and using groups of ten, presented difficulties as these children were not yet able to count easily in tens. The group Amy was working with may have needed to be challenged to count beyond 20; however, the jump to counting in tens was too great. In order to introduce the idea of counting in groups, Amy could have given the children fewer coins and suggested that they counted in twos or fives, provided that they knew these counting patterns. (Connection)

The use of the hundred grid, in this instance, was possibly an inappropriate choice of representation since the children were not able to read all of the multiples of 10 and had not had previous experience of working with it. The way in which Amy used the hundred grid was rather *procedural*. She focused on the movement down the tens column, without encouraging the children to explore the layout of the hundred square and understand why this method works. Although Amy did count out the units along the first two rows in the hundred square, the children would have needed significant previous experience of counting whole sets of ten and relating this to the hundred square, in order to make use of this representation. Such experience would involve counting each group of ten in ones along the rows of the hundred square, perhaps with an emphasis on the tens number, for example 21, 22, 23, ... 29, *30*. This would help the children to understand *why* it is possible to simply count down the tens column on the hundred square, when counting in groups of ten. That is not to say they should not practise the rhythm of counting in tens, in much the same way as counting in ones, so that they learn the pattern. (Transformation)

2 Sally's Reception lesson on addition and subtraction

Superficially, the number line with pictures of frogs seems to be ideal for a teaching activity on addition and subtraction, in which the context was frogs jumping in and out of a pond. However, there was confusion between the number of frogs pictured, and the number represented by the place on the number line. The child who responded that there were 'ten' friends when the puppet was above the 3 seems to have been focusing on the total number of pictures of frogs – though there were actually 11, including the frog above the zero. (Transformation)

The activity, in which the frog puppet jumped along the number line to model the additions and subtractions, represented the ordinal relationships between the number of frogs after each jump – 5 is 2 greater than 3. However, these children probably still needed further experiences of counting sets of objects in order to develop their understanding of the cardinal aspect of numbers. As an introduction to addition and subtraction, the children might have worked with frog puppets, counting the set after a number of frogs had been added or subtracted. Such an activity would be a practical or *enactive* representation of the addition/subtraction process. The number line is an *iconic* representation, which can only be helpfully used once children have developed their understanding through enactive activities. (Foundation/transformation)

3 Laura's Year 1 lesson on place value

Laura's intention was to enhance the children's understanding of place value. The activities she chose focused on just one aspect of this – developing ideas of 'column value' (see Chapter 3). In her introduction, she stressed the difference in value between a 10 stick and a unit cube. However, in the activities, the children focused on the number of tens and number of ones rather than on their value. (Foundation/transformation)

Laura emphasised matching the correct number of 10 sticks to the number on the left-hand side of the board and the number of one cubes to the number on the right-hand side of the board. This did not necessarily help the children to understand that the position of a digit designates its value. This was demonstrated clearly by the child who reversed the digits when he turned over his paper. (Transformation)

After the introduction, Laura focused on *procedures* – write a number on a tens and units board then choose the appropriate base-10 materials and draw around them. When monitoring the activities, Laura discussed presentation and correct recording, rather than asking the children to read their answers. The child who turned over his paper and then put his '10 sticks' and 'one cubes' on the reverse side of the tens and units board was correctly following procedures but lacked understanding of place value. (Foundation)

4 Kate's Year 1 lesson on doubling

Kate has used a novel resource (the picture of a cauldron) to present the scenario of the wizard puppet who doubles numbers. This seems a good idea as it will engage the children and we can presume that the children are familiar with the puppet as a means of presenting ideas. This has clear parallels with 'number machines' which may be used at other times. (Foundation)

In her recording of the doubling procedure, as '3 + 3', Kate translated a *doubling* into a *repeated addition*. This is perfectly valid, but not all children would have made this link and it would be important to tease this out. Recording it in words, 'double 3', is a direct representation. This could have been developed during the course of the activity to other recordings such as '3 + 3' or 'two lots of 3' or pictorial representations perhaps with dots. (Transformation, connection)

When Kate moved on to doubling two-digit numbers, she sensibly asked a child how they worked it out. She seems to have chosen her recording as a result of the child's response. In recording the results of the doubling of the partitioned number, Kate focused on the *column value* of each digit rather than its *quantity value*. (We have discussed this distinction in Chapter 3). In the first example (double 13) there are no difficulties. However, when she asks the children to suggest a number, 15 presents problems; it is not a good example for Kate. The double of 5 is no longer a single digit and yet her recording is using the digit in each column rather than its value. She would have had a '2' in the tens bubble and '10' in the ones bubble – potentially confusing in working out the result of doubling 15. She avoids the issue by asking for another suggestion. (Contingency, foundation, transformation)

The idea of the bubbles could have been used for all numbers if Kate had used their quantity values after partition. So 'double 15' might lead to 'double 10 + 5' which would have given rise to '20' in the tens bubble and '10' in the ones bubble. Each bubble represents a quantity which can then be added together to give '30'. (Foundation)

5 Kim's Year 1/2 lesson on capacity

Kim has made an effort to use a range of materials and representations in this lesson. Indeed, having a whole class working on practical activities, with either water or sand, could be a recipe for chaos; she sensibly did not attempt this. So at the start of the lesson, Kim used a litre container to look at the capacity of some large containers. She also had different shaped litre containers; again this is good use of actual objects, in this case demonstrating that the shape is irrelevant. The worksheets introduced the need for children to understand the *iconic* two-dimensional representation of a three-dimensional reality. Indeed, it presented a further difficulty, in that all the containers were the same size although they were marked with different capacities. Finally, the interactive whiteboard litre jug could be 'filled' – again a two-dimensional representation – but the scale was in millilitres rather than fractions of a litre that the children had been using earlier in the lesson. (Transformation, connection)

It might have been worthwhile for Kim to have developed further the idea of half, quarter and perhaps three-quarter litre measures, before moving to millilitres in a later lesson. She could have marked these measures on the sides of some of the litre containers. Then a worksheet with litre containers with markers for these fractional quantities on it (perhaps with different shaped containers) would have been a possible next step. (Connection)

The interactive whiteboard gave a capacity activity where it was possible to see 'liquid' filling up the jug. It seemed that Kim wanted to use this, so that all the children could easily see what was happening, and again she could focus on the capacity of a litre. However, the scale on the jug was not in fractions of a litre but in millilitres. Furthermore, she could not fill the jug in one go. Some children had difficulties with the larger numbers (100 and 1000) which added to the complexity of the activity. Kim made some good decisions when she was faced with some of these difficulties. She suggested that the children fill the jug in stages – 900 ml in the first instance. She could have consolidated some of the earlier work by focusing on half a litre again, but in the pressure of the moment she managed to use the activity to good effect. (Transformation, connection, contingency)

6 Lucy's Year 2 lesson on multiplication

The children will have met addition for some time and may well be very familiar with the '+' sign. The idea of multiplication was new and it seems that Lucy was introducing the multiplication sign '×' as well as the concept. This was probably too much for the children to assimilate in one lesson and so they took this new symbol to represent the operation with which they were familiar. (Foundation, transformation)

When using either of the representations (bead strings or multilink) for 6×10, the fundamental idea is one of repeated addition. For this example, the bead string is ideal as the groups of 10 alternate in colour and so are comparatively easy to count off as they slide along the string. The bead string has the advantage that the beads cannot be lost – they are permanently on the string. When dealing with larger numbers this can be a problem with loose materials such as multilink. If a child has to count out and build the ten high towers, it is an *enactive* process. Once completed, the six towers can be laid end to end or can be kept in a rectangular array. This versatility enables two different models to be seen – repeated addition or the area model. (Foundation, transformation)

The idea of repeated addition can be represented in a number of ways. For example, if pencils (or similar objects) are bundled into tens, then six bundles could be counted out. If base-10 apparatus is used in the classroom, then six rods of length 10 can be used to represent the multiplication. Other structural apparatus – Cuisenaire or Numicon – could also be used. We need to be aware of the difficulties that Thompson, Threlfall and others have highlighted in becoming adept at using the material but not making the link to the operation with the numbers. Another representation could be pegs in a pegboard to give a 6×10 rectangular array. (Transformation)

7 Ellie's Year 2 lesson on 'missing numbers'

It is important to notice that there are three different forms of equations in these missing number tasks, and that they are of varying degrees of difficulty for children. The calculation $7 + 8 = ?$ is fairly straightforward and requires no special skill beyond simple addition. So, if the children have already carried out some addition then there is no reason to suppose that this would require any additional kind of teaching. It is either revision or extension work and can be carried out with objects or on the number line. The remaining two forms, 7 + ? = 15 and ? + 8 = 15, are of a different order and the latter of these two is notoriously difficult. (Connection)

Leaving aside the first equation form, let us look at questions of the form 7 + ? = 15. There is no doubt that Ellie could have carried out examples of this kind by partitioning a set of 15 objects. In this way, the *aggregation* structure of addition is easily illustrated. By partitioning 15 objects into any two parts, those two parts may be *combined* to make 15. The case of the *complement* of 7 in 15 is just a special case of this activity, and it would be well worthwhile for Ellie to allow it to arise from a number of different partitions on 15. (Indeed, the task would lend itself to being presented as an 'open sentence' ? + ? = 15.) However, it would also have been possible for Ellie to solve this equation, with the class, on a number line. In particular, the *augmentation* model of addition would be illustrated in this way. The numbers 7 and 15 could be located on the empty number line and the question would be 'By how much does seven have to be *increased* to make fifteen?', and this could be shown by inviting the child to count up from the 7. Again she could have presented the task initially as an 'open sentence', in which case the 15 would remain fixed and the counting up would take place from various numbers other than, and including, 7. (Transformation)

This leaves the difficult case of equations of the form ? + 8 = 15. If a child understands that this is equivalent to 15 − 8 = ? then a subtraction can be carried out on the number line with relative ease. But Ellie does not seem to have anticipated the complexity of this shift from addition to subtraction. She gives no explanation for converting the task into a subtraction and proceeds to draw out several steps before the number line can be used. So in this respect the number line did not illuminate the problem that she had set. It simply solved a modified version of it! (Transformation/connection)

8 Joyce's Year 3 lesson on division

The representation that Joyce used was a *cardinal* one. That is to say, she used (drawn) objects to represent part of the mathematical statement (16), and instructed the children in an activity on those objects which enacted the mathematical operation of division in terms of sharing. The children, who partitioned the objects (circles in this case) into two lines of eight, appear to have done precisely what she had asked.

For larger numbers, of course, this partitioning of (drawn or physical) objects ceases to be manageable and an *ordinal* representation allows the task to be carried out symbolically by performing it on numbers rather than objects. The children who wrote 1, 3, 5, 7, 9, 11, 13 and 15 on one side of the line and 2, 4, 6, 8, 10, 12, 14 and 16 seem to have anticipated this by *numbering* each of the sixteen circles whilst obediently following the sharing instructions from Joyce. It represents a very interesting compromise between their own inclinations and what the teacher had asked them to do. (Transformation)

Of course, as we pointed out in Chapter 7, the *sharing* structure of division is only one of two important structures, the other being *grouping*. This could easily be carried out using the cardinal model that Joyce is adopting by interpreting 16 ÷ 2 as 'how many 2s are there in 16'. She could demonstrate this by ringing pairs of circles and counting how many rings she has. (Foundation)

9 John's Year 4 lesson on telling the time

John had chosen to use an analogue clock on the interactive whiteboard for the first part of his lesson on telling the time. This showed real time, and though this may seem to be a good way of bringing 'reality' into the classroom, it was problematic in terms of the learning objective of writing the time shown on a clock face. By the time the children had written the times and showed their answers, the time on the clock had moved on. (Transformation)

A further problem with using this analogue clock face, was that John wanted the children to write the time as 10.35 rather than '25 to 11'. The former way of expressing this time is more likely to be used when looking at a digital display and the latter for an analogue clock or watch. John could have capitalised on the combined analogue and digital display, available on the interactive whiteboard, to make links between the two ways of expressing the time. He missed an opportunity to discuss the links between 2.15 and quarter past two. The digital display shown here was confusing, since it included seconds, '2.16:44', which would be impossible to determine from the analogue display. (Connection)

In the final part of this section of the lesson, John addressed the issue of how many minutes are represented by the numbers 1–12 around the analogue clock face. He used some effective questioning to get the children thinking about this; however, the representation he used may not have been the most appropriate. A ratcheted clock would have been a better resource, since he could have used this to demonstrate that as the hands of an analogue clock move between each numbered interval, they have moved through five minutes. The ratcheted clock is a very useful resource for teaching telling the time, since it can be demonstrated that as the minute hand moves, the hour hand also moves, but more slowly. So that, for instance, by the time the minute hand has moved half way around the clock face, the hour hand has moved half way between two of the numbers. (Transformation)

10 James's Year 4 lesson on fractions

The interactive nature of the whiteboard allowed for checking how much of the food was left by touching the '?/?' symbols to reveal the remaining fraction. However, it did not allow for comparing the 'untouched' figure with the 'touched' one. Fractions of sets of objects would be an alternative model where, in place of disappearing parts, a certain number of the objects need not be *removed* but simply partitioned in some way. (Transformation)

As we pointed out in Chapter 5, there are several models of a fraction, one of which is the fraction of a *region*. So, in this respect, the representative images that James presents to the class on the interactive whiteboard do exemplify fractions. Furthermore, since the computer divides the shapes into sub-regions this program does have some scope for teaching notation. (Foundation, transformation)

However, since the (vulgar) fraction notation that he is teaching consists of two numbers – the *numerator* and *denominator* – the ideal model would be one where the regions denoted by *both* of these numbers are visible *simultaneously*. This would allow children to compare the part of the region selected for attention, with the way in which the whole shape had been divided. This is especially true where hesitation or errors are expected to occur, when the shapes are divided into 6, 7 or 8 equal sub-regions. When using this representation, James can attempt to teach fraction notation with these larger denominators by inviting the children to count these sub-regions, but when he touches the pieces they disappear and the children must, in each case, rely on their memory to establish the denominator. The absence of visual continuity in this presentation does, therefore, reveal a lack of anticipation of the complexity of matching model to notation. (Connection)

Indeed, the child who gave a first response of 'one half' before being invited to give an alternative (equivalent) fraction, does not appear to have kept the four parts in mind, but simply recognised the region in its more natural form. Although it is reasonable to suppose that the response of 'two quarters' may be drawn from the pupil by her inspecting the incomplete shape, this would be far from obvious where smaller fractions are involved. If James had asked why the pupil had said 'one half', this might have shown how she had not attended primarily to the fact that the shape had been divided into four parts. (Contingency)

11 Lindsay's Year 4 lesson on positive and negative numbers

Lindsay gives the impression that she is not confident about the way negative numbers 'work', but she has some rules of thumb that have enabled her to get by (her common knowledge). Arguably, giving children 'Top Tips' as a way of getting through an exercise is a sign that the teacher has given up on helping them to make sense of the situation. There was an earlier instance of such 'tips' in Chapter 3, when Chloë was showing her Year 1/2 class strategies to add and subtract near-multiples of 10. She ended up writing a list of rules on the board, such as 'To add 19, add 20 and take away 1'. Many children grow up to believe that mathematics *is* all about learning and applying meaningless rules. (Foundation)

It is very helpful to represent the sequence of positive and negative whole numbers (integers) as *points* on a line, because there are other numbers between them (like $-1\frac{1}{2}$ or +3.2). The line that Lindsay drew on the board, rather late into the lesson, is probably a more helpful representation than the counting stick, and could have been introduced much earlier. (Transformation)

Jonathan certainly had a point! The issues are (a) once again, whether the whole numbers are the points on the line or the intervals between them, and (b) whether zero is, somehow, 'in the middle' when all positive and negative integers are laid out in a line. (Contingency)

At one time, positive and negative numbers were a secondary school topic. In the earliest versions of the National Curriculum for England and Wales they first appeared in the attainment targets at Level 5 – aligned to Year 8 or 9. Perhaps the key issue to think about before teaching this topic another time is what Year 4 children already know about negative numbers, and what they can usefully learn at this point. The suggestions from more recent curriculum guidance (DfEE, 1999) all point to the recognition and use of negative numbers *in context*. The most compelling of such context is temperature, of course. So it would have been really helpful if Lindsay had had (or had drawn) a large thermometer to represent the sequence of positive and negative numbers. Interestingly, this would have presented the children with a *vertical* number line. The guidance for Years 4 and 5 also refers only to *recognising* and *ordering* positive and negative integers. There is no rush to 'do sums' on them – 'adding' and 'taking away'. In Year 6 the guidance targets 'finding the *difference'* between two integers, again 'in a context'. In fact, the notion of subtraction as *difference*, rather than *taking away* (see Chapter 7) comes into its own when a negative number is to be subtracted. In this sense, Lindsay's language of 'take away', for example in her 'Top Tips', was unhelpful. (Connection)

Lindsay says 'When you want to add on a negative number, you go back toward zero'. This seems to be a slip of the tongue, since her gestures suggest 'When you want to add *onto* a negative number, you go back toward zero'. (Foundation)

In counting up (adding 1) in negative numbers, we say, for example, '–5, –4, –3, –2, –1, 0'. Maybe Lindsay believes that this is 'really confusing' because she is attending just to the count as an auditory phenomenon, and to the sounds '5, 4, 3, 2, 1', when the children's previous experience would be of that same sequence of sounds in reverse. It would be much less likely to confuse if presented in a context, as the more recent current curriculum guidance suggests. (Transformation)

12 Nathalie's Year 6 lesson on probability

Probability is one of the least familiar topics for primary school teachers, who may have encountered very little of it in their own study of mathematics at school. Against this background, Nathalie seems remarkably at ease with the topic, and comfortable talking about it. She is noticeably in control when she carries out the extended combinatorial exercise (listing all 36 outcomes when the two dice are thrown) in the plenary. She does not lack the confidence that when she counts the list she has made, the total will be 36. Unfortunately, she seemed to forget to draw out the conclusions regarding Game 1. (Foundation)

At the same time, a key concept in the calculation of the probabilities, in the plenary and in the introduction with the coloured cubes, is that the notion

$$\frac{\text{number of successful outcomes}}{\text{total number of outcomes}}$$

applies only when the outcomes are equiprobable, that is, none is more likely than the other. This is fairly obviously the case with the six outcomes when one die is thrown. It is not, however, when two dice are thrown and the sums 2, 3, 4, …, 12 are taken to be the outcomes. It is important for children to learn this by experiment, by throwing two dice and tallying the total scores. (To be fair to Nathalie, a small low-achieving group were doing exactly that while the others were playing the two 'fairness' games.) Nathalie might have stressed that the reason for listing the individual ways of making each score was that they were equally likely – although even that is not at all obvious. (Foundation)

Nathalie's choice of ten cubes in the introduction is a good one. Ten is a familiar number, with the factors 5 and 2 (red and blue cubes) readily recognised. At the same time, this very familiarity – especially that 5 is half of 10 – might obscure the fact that the fraction is based on enumerating the 5 red cubes as a proportion of the 10 cubes. This is consistent with the suggestion that the 3 green cubes are a third of the whole – the actual numbers are not being considered. Nevertheless, the 10–5–2–3 example was well chosen. Although 12–6–4–2 might have been even better! (Transformation)

Given that these were Year 6 children (age 10–11), Nathalie could have exploited her choice of ten cubes by expressing the fractions – and probabilities subsequently – as decimals. (Connection)

Nathalie's response to the erroneous suggestion, that the 3 green cubes are a third of the total, is very quick-footed and skilful. First, she shows what a third really looks like. Second, she seems to be saying that if it is a third after taking one away, it cannot have been a third before. The pedagogical trick she is using is to provoke *cognitive conflict* in the child's mind: a kind of conundrum that they must think about to make sense of it. At the same time, the earlier suggestion that 2 out of 10 is a quarter was not followed up as it might have been (though Nathalie might simply have wanted to move on). On the face of things, it is indicative of a well-known fraction misconception, in which one part (2) is compared with the other, complementary part (8) rather than the whole (10). (Contingency)

At the end of the plenary, Larry says that $\frac{10}{36}$ is greater than $\frac{1}{6}$ because 'It's just over a third'. Although Larry is incorrect, Nathalie affirms his claim, which she ought not to do. Nevertheless, Larry is so very *nearly* correct: $\frac{10}{36}$ is very nearly $\frac{1}{3}$ and therefore clearly nearly double $\frac{1}{6}$. This very flexible approach to comparison is worth emphasising and commending in its own right. Instead, Nathalie presses on, in rather a blinkered way, with her own intention to compare the fractions by equivalence. (Contingency)

Table 8.2   Knowledge Quartet lesson reflection proforma

Foundation	Transformation
Adheres to textbook, Awareness of purpose Concentration on procedures, Identifying errors Overt subject knowledge, Theoretical underpinning, Use of terminology	*Choice of examples Choice of representation Demonstration*
Connection	**Contingency**
Anticipation of complexity, Decisions about sequencing, Making connections between procedures Making connections between concepts Recognition of conceptual appropriateness	*Deviation from agenda Responding to children's ideas Use of opportunities*

References

Anghileri, J. (2006) *Teaching Number Sense*, 2nd edn. London: Continuum.

Anghileri, J. (2008) *Developing Number Sense*. London: Continuum.

Anghileri, J., Beishuizen, M. and van Putten, K. (2002) 'From informal strategies to structured procedures: mind the gap!', *Educational Studies in Mathematics*, 49(2): 149–170.

Askew, M. (1993) 'Bug detectives', *Junior Education*, 17(5): 20–21.

Askew, M. (1999) 'It ain't (just) what you do: effective teachers of numeracy', in I. Thompson (ed.), *Issues in Teaching Numeracy in Primary Schools* (pp. 91–102). Buckingham: Open University Press.

Askew, M., Brown, M., Rhodes, V., Johnson, D. and Wiliam, D. (1997) *Effective Teachers of Numeracy*. London: King's College.

Aubrey, C. (1997a) 'Re-assessing the role of teachers' subject knowledge in early years mathematics teaching', *Education 3–13*, 25(1): 55–60.

Aubrey, C. (1997b) *Mathematics Teaching in the Early Years: An Investigation of Teachers' Subject Knowledge*. London: Falmer Press.

Ausubel, D. (1968) *Educational Psychology: A Cognitive View*. New York: Holt, Rinehart and Winston.

Balacheff, N. (1988) 'Aspects of proof in pupils' practice of school mathematics', in D. Pimm (ed.), *Mathematics, Teachers and Children* (pp. 216–35). London: Hodder and Stoughton.

Ball, D.L. (1988) 'Unlearning to teach mathematics', *For the Learning of Mathematics*, 8(1): 40–48.

Ball, D.L. (1990a) 'Prospective elementary and secondary teachers' understanding of division', *Journal for Research in Mathematics Education*, 21(2): 132–144.

Ball, D.L. (1990b) 'The mathematical understandings that prospective teachers bring to teacher education', *Elementary School Journal*, 90: 449–466.

Ball, D.L. and Bass, H. (2000) 'Interweaving content and pedagogy in teaching and learning to teach: knowing and using mathematics', in J. Boaler (ed.), *Multiple Perspectives on Mathematics Teaching and Learning* (pp. 83–104). Westport, CT: Ablex Publishing.

Ball, D.L., Hill, H.C. and Bass, H. (2005) 'Who knows mathematics well enough to teach third grade, and how can we decide?', *American Educator*. http://www.aft.org/pubs-reports/american_educator/issues/fall2005/BallF05.pdf (accessed 8 May 2008).

Baroody, A.J. and Bartels, B.H. (2001) 'Assessing understanding in mathematics with concept mapping', *Mathematics in School*, 30(3): 24–27.

Begle, E.G. (1979) *Critical Variables in Mathematics Education: Findings from a Survey of the Empirical Literature*. Washington DC: Mathematical Association of America and National Council of Teachers of Mathematics.

Bills, L., Dreyfus, T., Mason, J., Tsamir, P., Watson, A. and Zaslavsky, O. (2006) 'Exemplification in mathematics education', in J. Novotna, H. Moraova, M. Kratka and N. Stehlikova (eds), *Proceedings of the 30th Conference of the International Group for the Psychology of Mathematics Education* (Vol. 1, pp. 126–54). Prague: Charles University.

Bishop, A.J. (2001) 'Educating student teachers about values in mathematics education', in F.L. Lin and T.J. Cooney (eds), *Making Sense of Mathematics Teacher Education* (pp. 233–246). Dordrecht, The Netherlands: Kluwer Academic Publishers.

Brinkmann, A. (2005) 'Knowledge maps – tools for building structure in mathematics', *International Journal for Mathematics Teaching and Learning*. http://www.cimt.plymouth. ac.uk/journal/brinkmann.pdf (accessed 8 May 2008).

Brissenden, T. (1985) 'Children's language and mathematics: rewriting the lesson script', *Mathematics in School*, 14(4): 2–6.

Brown, G. and Wragg, E.C. (1993) *Questioning*. London: Routledge.

Bruner, J. (1974) 'Representation in childhood', in *Beyond the Information Given*. London: George Allen & Unwin.

Carpenter, T.P. and Moser, J.M. (1983) 'The acquisition of addition and subtraction concepts', in R. Lesh and M. Landau (eds), *The Acquisition of Mathematical Concepts and Processes* (pp. 7–44). New York: Academic Press.

Dearden, R.F. (1968) *The Philosophy of Primary Education*. London: Routledge & Kegan Paul.

DfEE (1999) *The National Numeracy Strategy: Framework for Teaching Mathematics*. Sudbury: Department for Education and Employment Publications.

Dickson, L., Brown, M. and Gibson, O. (1984) *Children Learning Mathematics*. Eastbourne: Holt Education.

Drews, D. and Hansen, A. (eds) (2007) *Using Resources to Support Mathematical Thinking: Primary and Early Years*. Exeter: Learning Matters.

Eisenberg, T.A. (1977) 'Begle revisited: teacher knowledge and student achievement in algebra', *Journal for Research in Mathematics Education*, 8: 216–222.

Faux, G. (1998) 'Gattegno charts', *Mathematics Teaching*, 163 (centre pull-out).

Fennema, E., Carpenter, T.P. and Peterson, P.L. (1989) 'Teachers' decision making and cognitively guided instruction: a new paradigm for curriculum development', in K. Clements and N.F. Ellerton (eds), *Facilitating Change in Mathematics Education* (pp. 174–187). Geelong, Victoria: Deakin University Press.

Field, R. (1998) *Geometric Patterns from Islamic Art and Architecture*. St Albans: Tarquin Publications.

Foxman, D., Joffe, L., Mason, K., Mitchell, P., Ruddock, G. and Sexton, B. (1986) *A Review of Monitoring in Mathematics 1978 to 1982*. London: Assessment of Performance Unit.

Garrick, R. (2002) 'Pattern-making and pattern play in the nursery: special organisation'. Paper presented at the Annual Conference of the British Educational Research Association, University of Exeter, England, 12–14 September.

Gelman, R. and Gallistel, C.R. (1978) *The Child's Understanding of Number*. Cambridge, MA: Harvard University Press.

Glaser, B.G. and Strauss, A.L. (1967) *The Discovery of Grounded Theory: Strategies for Qualitative Research*. New York: Aldine de Gruyter.

Gray, E. (1997) 'Compressing the counting process: developing a flexible interpretation of symbols', in I. Thompson (ed.), *Teaching and Learning Early Number* (pp. 63–72). Buckingham: Open University Press.

Gray, E.M. and Tall, D.O. (1994) 'Duality, ambiguity, and flexibility: a proceptual view of simple arithmetic', *Journal for Research in Mathematics Education*, 25: 116–140.

Hamlyn, D.W. (1967) 'The logical and psychological aspects of learning', in R.S. Peters (ed.), *The Concept of Education* (pp. 24–43). London: Routledge & Kegan Paul.

Hancock, K. (2007) 'Symmetry in the car park', *Mathematics Teaching*, 200: 24–25.

Hansen, A. (ed.) (2005) *Children's Errors in Mathematics: Understanding Common Misconceptions in Primary Schools*. Exeter: Learning Matters.

Harries, T. and Spooner, M. (2000) *Mental Mathematics in the Numeracy Hour*. London: David Fulton.

Hart, K.M. (ed.) (1981) *Children's Understanding of Mathematics: 11–16*. London: John Murray.

Haylock, D. (1982) 'Understanding in mathematics: making connections', *Mathematics Teaching*, 92: 54–58.

Haylock, D. (2006) *Mathematics Explained for Primary Teachers*, 3rd edn. London: Sage.

Haylock, D. and Cockburn, A. (1997) *Understanding Mathematics in the Lower Primary Years*. London: Paul Chapman.

Hegarty, S. (2000) 'Teaching as a knowledge-based activity', *Oxford Review of Education*, 26(3–4): 451–465.

Heirdsfield, A. (2001) 'Integration, compensation and memory in mental addition and subtraction', in M. van del Heuvel-Panhuizen (ed.), *Proceedings of the 25th Annual Conference of the International Group for the Psychology of Mathematics Education* (Vol. 3, pp. 129–136). Utrecht: Freudenthal Institute, Utrecht University.

Hill, H.C., Rowan, B. and Ball, D. (2005) 'Effects of teachers' mathematical knowledge for teaching on student achievement', *American Educational Research Journal*, 42(2): 371–406.

Iannone, P. (2006) 'Number tracks, number lines, number strips … Are they all the same?', *Mathematics Teaching*, 197: 9–12.

Johnston-Wilder, S. and Mason, J. (eds) (2005) *Developing Thinking in Geometry*. London: Paul Chapman Publishing.

Koshy, V. (2000) 'Children's mistakes and misconceptions', in V. Koshy, P. Ernest and R. Casey (eds), *Mathematics for Primary Teachers* (pp. 172–181). London: Routledge.

Ma, L. (1999) *Knowing and Teaching Elementary Mathematics: Teachers' Understanding of Fundamental Mathematics in China and the United States*. Mahwah, NJ: Lawrence Erlbaum.

Maclellan, E. (1997) 'The importance of counting', in I. Thompson (ed.), *Teaching and Learning Early Number* (pp. 33–40). Buckingham: Open University Press.

McIntosh, A. (1979) 'Some children and some multiplications', *Mathematics Teaching*, 87: 14–15.

Munn, P. (1997) 'Children's beliefs about counting', in I. Thompson, (ed.), *Teaching and Learning Early Number* (pp. 9–19). Buckingham: Open University Press.

Nickson, M. (2000) *Teaching and Learning Mathematics: A Teacher's Guide to Recent Research*. London: Cassell.

Norfolk County Council (2003) *The Power of the Number Line*. Norfolk Number Line Project.

O'Sullivan, L., Harris, A., Sangster, M., Wild, J., Donaldson, G. and Bottle, G. (2005) *Reflective Reader: Primary Mathematics*. Exeter: Learning Matters.

Pasternack, M. (2003) '0–99 or 1–100?', *Mathematics Teaching*, 182: 34–35.

QCA (2003) *Standards at Key Stage 2 in English, Mathematics and Science*. Sudbury: QCA Publications.

Rowland, T. (1999) '"i" is for induction', *Mathematics Teaching*, 167: 23–27.

Rowland, T. (2001) 'Generic proofs: setting a good example', *Mathematics Teaching*, 177: 40–43.

Rowland, T. (2006) 'Subtraction – difference or comparison?', *Mathematics in School*, 35(2): 32–35.

Rowland, T., Huckstep, P. and Thwaites, A. (2005) 'Elementary teachers' mathematics subject knowledge: the Knowledge Quartet and the case of Naomi', *Journal of Mathematics Teacher Education*, 8(3): 255–281.

Rowland, T., Martyn, S., Barber, P. and Heal, C. (2001) 'Investigating the mathematics subject matter knowledge of pre-service elementary school teachers', in M. van den Heuvel-Panhuizen (ed.), *Proceedings of the 25th Conference of the International Group for the Psychology of Mathematics Education* (Vol. 4, pp. 121–128). Utrecht: Freudenthal Institute, Utrecht University.

Ryan, J and Williams, J. (2007) *Children's Mathematics 4–15: Learning from Errors and Misconceptions*. Maidenhead: Open University Press.

Sangster, M. (2007) 'Reflecting on pace', *Mathematics Teaching*, 204: 34–36.

Schön, D. (1983) *The Reflective Practitioner. How Professionals Think in Action*. New York: Basic Books.

Shulman, L. (1986) 'Those who understand: knowledge growth in teaching', *Educational Researcher*, 15(2): 4–14.

Shulman, L. (1987) 'Knowledge and teaching: foundations of the new reform', *Harvard Educational Review*, 57(1): 1–22.

Skemp, R.R. (1976) 'Relational understanding and instrumental understanding', *Mathematics Teaching*, 77: 20–26.

Skemp, R.R. (1986) *The Psychology of Learning Mathematics*. London: Penguin.

Skinner, B.F. (1974) *About Behaviourism*. London: Jonathan Cape.

Skott, J. (2006) 'The role of the practice of theorising practice', in M. Bosch (ed.), *Proceedings of the Fourth Congress of the European Society for Research in Mathematics Education* (pp. 1598–1608). FUNDEMI IQS, Universitat Ramon Llull. http://ermeweb.free.fr/CERME4 (accessed 9 May 2008).

Smith, C. (1999) 'Pencil and paper numeracy', *Mathematics in School*, 28(5): 10–13.

Strong, M. and Baron, W. (2004) 'An analysis of mentoring conversations with beginning teachers: suggestions and responses', *Teaching and Teacher Education*, 20: 47–57.

Suggate, J., Davis, A. and Goulding, M. (2006) *Mathematical Knowledge for Primary Teachers*. London: David Fulton.

Thom R. (1973) 'Modern mathematics: does it exist?', in A.G. Howson (ed.), *Developments in Mathematical Education: Proceedings of the Second International Congress on Mathematics Education* (pp. 194–209). Cambridge: Cambridge University Press.

Thompson, A.G. (1992) 'Teachers' beliefs and conceptions: a synthesis of the research', in D. Grouws, (ed.), *A Handbook of Research on Mathematics Teaching and Learning* (pp. 127–146). New York: National Council of Teachers of Mathematics.

Thompson, I. (ed.) (1997) *Teaching and Learning Early Number*. Buckingham: Open University Press.

Thompson, I. (ed.) (1999) *Issues in Teaching Numeracy in Primary Schools*. Buckingham: Open University Press.

Thompson, I. (2003a) 'Place value: the English disease', in I. Thompson (ed.), *Enhancing Primary Mathematics Teaching* (pp. 181–190). Buckingham: Open University Press.

Thompson, I. (2003b) '1–100 rules OK', *Mathematics Teaching*, 185: 14–15.

Thompson, I. (ed.) (2003c) *Enhancing Primary Mathematics*. Buckingham: Open University Press.

Thompson, I. (2008) 'Deconstructing calculation methods, Part 3: Multiplication', *Mathematics Teaching*, 206: 34–36.

Thorndike, E.L. (1922) *The Psychology of Arithmetic*. New York: Macmillan.

Threlfall, J. (1996) 'The role of practical apparatus in the teaching and learning of arithmetic', *Education Review*, 48(1): 3–12.

Turner, F.A. (2007) 'Beginning teachers' use of representations as viewed through the lens of the Knowledge Quartet'. Paper presented at the British Educational Research Association conference held in September 2007 at the University of London Institute of Education. http://www.leeds.ac.uk/educol/documents/165634.htm (accessed 9 May 2008).

van den Heuvel-Panhuizen, M. (2001) 'Realistic mathematics education in the Netherlands', in J. Anghileri (ed.), *Principles and Practices in Arithmetic Teaching: Innovative Approaches for the Primary Classroom* (pp. 49–63). Buckingham: Open University Press.

van den Heuvel-Panhuizen, M. (2003) 'The didactical use of models in realistic mathematics education: an example from a longitudinal trajectory on percentage', *Educational Studies in Mathematics*, 54: 9–35.

Walter, M. (2000) *Make a Bigger Puddle, Make a Smaller Worm*. London: BEAM.

Ward, M. (1979) *Mathematics and the 10-Year-Old*. London: Evans/Methuen Educational.

Watson, A. and Mason, J. (2005) *Mathematics as a Constructive Activity: The Role of Learner Generated Examples*. Mahwah, NJ: Lawrence Erlbaum.

Wenger, E. (1998) *Communities of Practice: Learning, Meaning and Identity*. Cambridge: Cambridge University Press.

Wigley, A. (1997) 'Approaching number through language', in I. Thompson (ed.), *Teaching and Learning Early Number* (pp.113–122). Buckingham: Open University Press.

Wragg, E.C. and Brown, G. (2001) *Questioning in the Primary School*. London: Routledge Falmer.

Index